*James M. Burns, PhD*

*A sp*
*River*
*Dr. Ja*

*Januar,    002*

TECHNOMIC
PUBLISHING CO., INC.

# Child's Play and Play Therapy

**EDITED BY:**

Thomas D. Yawkey, Ph.D.
*Associate Professor of Early Childhood Education; and,*
*Director, Penn State's Project P.I.A.G.E.T.*

Division of Curriculum and Instruction
The Pennsylvania State University
159 Chambers Building
University Park, Pennsylvania 16802

and

Anthony D. Pellegrini, Ph.D.
*Assistant Professor of Early Childhood Education*

Department of Elementary Education
The University of Georgia
Aderhold Hall
Athens, Georgia 30602

*Published in the Western Hemisphere by*
Technomic Publishing Company, Inc.
851 New Holland Avenue
Box 3535
Lancaster, Pennsylvania 17604 U.S.A.

*Distributed in the Rest of the World by*
Technomic Publishing AG

Printed in the United States of America
10  9  8  7  6  5  4  3  2

Main entry under title:
  Child's Play and Play Therapy

A Technomic Publishing Company book
Bibliography: p.
Includes index p. 171

Library of Congress Card No. 83-51730
ISBN No. 87762-339-2

To those who believe in and use the "powers of play" in schools, child service agencies, and medical treatment centers for purposes of developing healthy growth and personalities with and in children.

# CONTENTS

# PREFACE

The idea of and the need for this volume arose in the editors' minds at the 1981 Biennial Meeting of the Society for Research in Child Development, Boston, and at the 1982 Conference of the American Educational Research Association, New York. The apparent lack of and need for narrative and substantive literature on play and play therapy for individuals in the helping professions was and is apparent. With few research studies available, the editors attempted to fill this need, in a small way, by proposing a text that would draw implications from investigative experimentation and to mesh them with the application needs of those in the helping professions. These professional populations include clinical developmental and educational psychologists and those in preparatory programs, medical professionals including physicians, nurses, and medical technicians, and preservice and inservice educators in classroom, centers, and home and residential treatment programs. A majority of these professionals use play and play therapy techniques and routines with children. Therefore, this text is a composite of selected ideas derived from research studies for application to varied settings.

To benefit those in the helping professions, the text focuses on the child, infancy to the beginning of middle childhood—i.e., birth to age eight. In addition, the text is divided into two major, but related, parts. Part 1 focuses on chapters dealing with "Child's Play as Development and Learning." Part 2 deals with chapters on "Child's Play as Therapy." Each of the parts to the text is preceded by introductory narration and comments that highlight the major points and summarize the contributions made to the understanding of play and play therapy in the individual chapters.

Part 1 identifies various perspectives on child's play from developmental and learning orientations that highlight its contributions to physical, socioemotional, personality, and intellectual growth. For members of the helping professions, Part 1 provides a baseline set of understandings on child's play. Overall, it is characterized as a potent source of productive growth rather than a set of aimless and frivolous behaviors and actions. From this perspective, "powers of play" contribute a number of sound developmental and learning actions for young children's present and future living and growth. These contributions include (a) explaining play's relationship with motor growth, (b) identifying appropriate motor experiences for young children, (c) explaining relations between child's play, social and emotional growth, and self-concept, (d) linking child's play with reading and language development, (e) describing hierarchical orders of speech play, (f) explicating sociodramatic play for development of "literate oral language," and (g) pinpointing and discussing five stages in the infant's development of fill and dump play. All of these contributions of child's play developed in these chapters are then applied for adults working with children in varying stages.

Part 2 describes key orientations on child's play as therapy. Drawing heavily from psychoanalytic and neo-psychoanalytic thought, the contributions of child's play for helping professionals in therapy settings are explained. This section of the text prepares helping professionals to understand and use principles of child's play for ameliorating non-social behaviors and actions of young children. From this orientation, the powers of play contribute several learning actions to young children's personality and socio-emotional growth. These contributions include (a) explaining significant play therapy approaches that could be used with young children, (b) detailing the toy materials and their uses by the adult for the child's ego development, (c) providing an understanding of psychoanalytic theory upon which play therapy rests, (d) suggesting ways in which play therapy can be successfully used in hospital, classroom, and home settings to alleviate aggressive behaviors, (e) highlighting relationships that exist between attachment and infant-adult play, (f) describing selected strategies that adults can use in infant-parent play for integrating the ego, (g) understanding the father's active role in sociophysical types of games, and (h) extending play therapy routines to children's positive behaviors learned during therapy for healthy living and ego development.

The chapters across Parts 1 and 2 of the volume make application to settings and thereby aid understanding of the "powers of play" with young children. The explanations and applications of child's play for development, learning, and therapy enable those in the helping professions to work better with children. In following through with principles and techniques detailed in the chapters, the adults in the helping professions, as noted by Paul Harvey, a famous commentator, "become the rest of the story."

Thomas D. Yawkey
*The Pennsylvania State University*
*University Park, Pennsylvania*

Anthony D. Pellegrini
*The University of Georgia*
*Athens, Georgia*

# ACKNOWLEDGEMENT

The editors of this volume are indebted to many professionals for the successful initiation and completion of this work. The authors of the various chapters and introductory narrations have given a great deal of their professional expertise and energies to this volume. The editors also acknowledge the assistance of Anthony A. Deraco, Production Manager and Louise Kahan, manuscript editor for Technomic Publishing Company.

**Part I**

CHILD'S PLAY AS DEVELOPMENT AND LEARNING

# CHILD'S PLAY
# AS DEVELOPMENT AND LEARNING

Maria P. Guccione and Thomas D. Yawkey

Mullen's chapter is entitled "Motor development and children's play." It explains the importance, relationships, and effects of movement development on the major learning domains. Movement and/or psychomotor development is the means by which a child can explore his surrounding world; it is used to bring into concrete terms the more abstract features of a child's world. Learning through movement is a more natural process for children. Movement generates a greater interest by the child, leading to increased learning. Movement education is equally important to the child's affective development. Movement experiences help enhance a child's perception of himself, as well as the way he views his peers.

Mullen feels that a child knows his abilities and acts according to his self-perceptions. Consequently, positive situations which challenge, yet, which are in the child's range of abilities are best. Providing positive experiences leads to a positive self-concept. Mullen notes that as the child develops his psychomotor abilities, he is enhancing his cognitive and affective domains. These three domains are interchangeable facets of the entire learning process and are enhanced by movement beginning in infancy.

Mullen categorizes movement into three broad categories: stability; locomotor; and fundamental manipulative abilities. Each of these categories encompasses developmental movement areas which are sometimes overlapping and which permeate movement throughout the life cycle. Adults who work with children should develop and use appropriate and meaningful movement experiences with them in order to enhance growth. In this context, Mullen emphasizes the distinction between physical and motor fitness skills.

In this chapter, Phelps adds to the understanding of play by (a) explaining its relation to motor growth, (b) describing self-concept as basic to motor activity, and (c) identifying appropriate motor experiences for young children. Mullen concludes that play is not a "waste of time" but vital to development.

Caster's chapter, "The young child's play and social and emotional development," examines elements of socioaffective growth. In this area, theorists define and describe play quite differently. Some define play as a simple dichotomy between play versus non-play; others recognize it as intermediate steps in the process of "pure play." Several others categorize play into developmental hierarchical categories. Each category becomes more specific and requires greater cognitive and social development.

In addition, Caster notes that the social developmental aspects of play have also been arranged into categories which appear to be hierarchical in nature. However, much controversy exists concerning the frequency and appearance for each of the social play categories. For example, several studies reveal that a child progresses through all of the social categories, while others indicate that categories may be skipped. Other studies reveal that social economic status and sex may be confounding factors.

Controversy also exists concerning the nature of the play the child demonstrates—i.e., complex, simple, social, or non-social. And, different types of play materials relate to the type of play a child demonstrates. These studies also suggest that the same material may be used quite differently by different age and sex groupings. Environmental studies limiting the availability of toys tend to encourage more complex play; larger indoor play areas tend to lead to a greater amount of social play. Restricting outdoor equipment, however, tends to increase undesirable behaviors while at the same time increasing social play.

In summary, this chapter aids understanding of play as a socioaffective entity. These understandings include (a) pinpointing relationships between play and social and emotional growth, (b) identifying the variables of age and sex and their roles in selection and use of materials, and (c) developing learning environments which minimize anxiety but encourage cognitive and social growth.

In Yawkey and Diantoniis' chapter on "Relationships between child's play and cognitive development and learning in infancy birth through age eight," play is viewed as a voluntary activity in which the child becomes engaged. Yawkey and Diantoniis stress that what appears to be simple imitation of the child's adult world is, in actuality, a complete learning process. Play requires the use of the thinking processes and involves social interaction. As a child experiences success or failure in interacting with other children or contemplates several solutions to a given play situation, he is involving his social and intellectual skills. In this context, many show support for the importance of play in child development.

Since play involves the child's interaction with his environment, it becomes quite obvious that different social environments will illicit different behaviors from children. Cultural and economical influences do affect the quality and quantity of a child's play. For example, lower socioeconomic children tend to display a greater amount of fantasy play, yet a decrease in pretend play. This is extremely important. It is at this point, when fantasy begins to decrease, that children become cognitively ready to understand symbols in reading. Hence, the children experience great difficulty in reading. Sociodramatic play can enhance communication processes of disadvantaged children. Yawkey and Diantoniis describe several of these studies which support that hypothesis. In addition, the factors of birth order and sex are described.

In summary, several significant contributions made by this chapter include (a) viewing play as fundamental to cognition, (b) showing alternative play patterns useful with disadvantaged children, (c) linking play with reading successes, and (d) describing the development of play as a function of birth and sex. In conclusion, Yawkey and Diantoniis note that play forms the foundation for all academic and social behaviors useful in present and later living.

Pellegrini's chapter is "Children's play with language: Infancy through early childhood." It explores speech play which is defined as a process by which young children explore and manipulate their language system. It is a subset of play which leads to metalinguistic awareness. During speech play there is little concern for conveying a message. Rather, the emphasis is on the speaker's manipulation of the language system. This characteristic of speech play greatly parallels those researchers who define play as an activity which is more important than the end product. Through playful manipulation of language activity, individuals gain knowledge of the rules governing their language system.

Pellegrini notes that several authors and researchers view play as involving a conscious manipulation of language rules. Metalinguistic awareness is a correct unconscious use of the language system. In this regard, play with language and the acquisition of language vary with age and experience. Speech play occurs in a hierarchical order, and Pellegrini divides speech play into three categories: (a) phonology, which includes babbling, gibberish, and a switch from solitary to social speech; (b) syntax; and (c) semantics which involve reduction and expansion techniques and include activities such as substitution and replacement games. Pellegrini maintains that, as the child gets older and increases his cognitive development, he will demonstrate a switch from syntagmatic to pragmatic replacements. Consequently, the hierarchical order can be very beneficial to adults working with children. By observing a child's language play, adults gain insight into the child's cognitive development. However, these proposals of hierarchical categories do not indicate a causal relationship between play and acquisition. A child who demonstrates phonological play first will not necessarily acquire phonological language first.

For years, the primary goal of schooling has been literacy. "Literate oral language" is a precursor to literacy. Through "literate oral language," children must convey messages by the use of words and without any reliance on contextual or assumed knowledge. Consequently, by developing "literate oral language," children are forming the foundation of skills which are necessary for reading and writing. Research supports social dramatic play and role-playing as increasing a child's ability to use explicit language. Pellegrini feels that adults can aid the process of language development by implementing sociodramatic play in the classroom and by providing materials which require the use of explicit language. In addition to language development, sociodramatic play decentralizes a child from himself and makes him more aware of the viewpoints of others.

The evidence which shows a definite positive relationship between speech play and achievement in reading and writing cannot help but maintain the importance of child's play in language development. Play as an intrinsic motivation for children to explore includes symbolic representations which are important for reading.

In summary, Pellegrini's chapter contributes to several important ideas for understanding play as language. These include (a) describing hierarchical ordering of speech play, (b) examining the switch from syntagmatic to pragmatic replacements, (c) viewing "literate oral language" for reading and writing development, and (d) explicating sociodramatic play for growth in "literate oral language."

In "Fill and dump play: Mastery of handling skills and object permanence," Mann investigates the notion that play with objects is motivated by a desire to achieve mastery. In this chapter, play is defined as effectance motivation. In the study, Mann analyzes and assesses "fill and dump" play as a means of substantiating play as effectance motivation.

Prior to providing the details of his study, Mann describes object permanence and relates it to cognitive development. He hypothesizes a parallel between the development of object permanence as described by Piaget and the development of mastery in "fill and dump" play. Mann then categorizes mastery attempts into five developmental stages: (a) from birth through 10 months of age mastery attempts are rare; (b) between 10 and 12 months mastery attempts are uncommonly observed; (c) between 13 and 18 months mastery attempts are very common; (d) between 19 and 24 months mastery attempts remain high; and (e) beyond 24 months mastery attempts decrease due to mastery of object permanence and a search by the child for a more challenging play activity.

The experimental study consisted of 36 infants from middle class homes, 19 boys and 17 girls between the ages of 10 to 34 months. The population was divided into six groups according to age. The procedures in the experiment permitted each child to manipulate three toys during each of two separate visits which occurred within 10 days of each other. The visits took place in an observation room with minimal distractions. A play session for a given toy consisted of either 30 minutes of contact time or three trials. This time procedure was repeated for the next two toys. With observation using a 15-second interval scale, an inventory was compiled for each of the three toys. Mann defines mastery as density or the occurrence of three observations of a specific behavior within a one minute interval. The results indicate that, through "fill and dump" play, subjects practice such skills as removing objects from containers, filling containers, posting objects through lid holes, and lifting. Also, the period during which mastery attempts are found in "fill and dump" play correspond closely to the theorized ages for development of object permanence. Lastly, the measure of mastery attempts was found to possess discriminant, concurrent, and predictive validity.

In summary, this chapter makes several important contributions to the understanding of play as development. These include (a) defining play as effectance motivation, (b) describing and experimenting with parallels between object permanency and "fill and dump" play, and (c) identifying and explaining five stages in the development of "fill and dump" play.

# Motor development and children's play

**Marie R. Mullan**
*The University of Georgia*

## INTRODUCTION

Parents and teachers of young children are becoming increasingly aware of the importance of providing their children with meaningful movement experiences. There is a growing realization among early childhood educators, special educators, and physical educators that the so-called play experiences engaged in by preschool and primary-grade children play an important role in learning to move and learning through movement. For young children, movement is the very center of their life. It permeates all facets of their development, whether in the psychomotor, cognitive, or affective domains of human behavior. In this part, we will take a cursory look at the contributions that movement can make to each of these domains.

## MOTOR DEVELOPMENT

The primary contribution of movement programs for young children is in the development of psychomotor competencies. Psychomotor development is the very heart of the movement education program and should be viewed as an avenue by which both cognitive and affective competencies can be enhanced. Psychomotor development refers to learning to move with control and efficiency through space. It is often referred to simply as motor development (the terms will be used interchangeably) and is subdivided here into two aspects, namely, movement abilities and physical abilities.

With preschool and primary-age children, the term "movement ability" refers to the development and refinement of a wide variety of fundamental movements. These movement abilities are developed and refined to a point where children are capable of operating with considerable ease and efficiency within their environment. As they mature, the fundamental movement abilities that were developed when they were younger are applied to a wide variety of games and sports that, hopefully, are engaged in as a part of their daily life experiences. The fundamental movement abilities of striking an object in an underhand, sidearm, or overarm pattern, for example, are elaborated upon and found in numerous sport and recreational pursuits such as golf, tennis, and softball.

The term "physical abilities" refers to the young child's ever-increasing ability to function and operate within the environment with regard to his or her level of physical fitness and motor ability. Children's physical abilities are influenced by a variety of health and performance related factors that in turn influence their movement abilities.

Movement behavior may be categorized into three broad and sometimes overlapping classifications. These classifications represent the primary focus of the motor development specialist when working with children in a movement education program. The first and most basic of these movement classifications is referred to as stability. Stability abilities are those developing patterns of movement that permit young children to gain and maintain a point of origin for the exploration that they make through space. Stability abilities are sometimes referred to as nonlocomotor movements because they involve such stationary activities as bending, stretching, twisting, and turning. They also include activities in which a premium is placed on maintaining equilibrium such as with inverted supports (handstand or headstand) and rolling movements (forward, backward, and sideward rolls).

At the time when stability abilities are developing, fundamental locomotor abilities are also enhanced. Locomotion involves projection of the body into external space by altering its location in either a vertical or horizontal plane. Such activities as running, jumping, skipping, and galloping are commonly thought of as locomotor in nature. It is through locomotion that children are able to explore the world about them effectively.

The third classification of developing movement abilities in young children involves the development of fundamental manipulative abilities. Gross motor manipulation involves imparting force to objects such as in throwing, catching and trapping, and stacking toys. It is through the manipulation of objects that children are able to come into actual physical contact with objects in their world.

MOVEMENT EDUCATION

The movement education of preschool and primary-grade children involves the development of fundamental locomotor, manipulative, and stability movement abilities. Upon closer examination of movement behavior throughout the life cycle, we find that these three categories permeate human movement from infancy through adulthood. That is, locomotor, manipulative, and stability movement activities are experienced at all levels in the total life experience which may be classified motorically into developmental stages.

The first stage of motor development is represented by the reflexive movements of the fetus and newborn. Reflexive behaviors are subcortically controlled. They precede and operate concurrently with the development of rudimentary movement abilities. Rudimentary movements, or the second stage, begin developing in the infant shortly after birth to approximately two years of age. Some locomotor activities are creeping, crawling, and, walking; manipulative experiences include reaching, grasping, and releasing objects and also involve the stability movement of gaining control of the head, neck, and trunk while learning how to sit and stand unattended.

The third stage of motor development is referred to as the fundamental movement abilities phase. Developing fundamental movement abilities involves attaining acceptable levels of performance in a variety of basic movement skills beginning around the second year of life and continuing through the preschool years and primary grades to about the age of seven years. This age range is commonly referred to as early childhood.

Boys and girls in the intermediate grades (third, fourth, and fifth grades) are considered in middle childhood, and the stage of development it gives rise to is the general movement abilities phase. General movement abilities closely resemble the fundamental movement abilities of the preceding phase because they often involve many of the same movements. The difference, however, lies in the fact that, at the earlier stage, the rudimentary movement was generalized to the pattern. As an example, striking at the earlier stage was the task of imparting force to objects (balls, balloons, yarn balls), and, in this stage, it is approached as the general sport skill of striking a softball, tennis ball, or hockey puck and applied to individual, dual, and small group activities rather than the official sport of softball, tennis, or hockey.

A fifth stage of development is the specific movement abilities phase, which corresponds to the developmental phase of later childhood and preadolescence (sixth, seventh, and eighth grades). This stage of motor development is similar to the previous one except that the child is developmentally more mature and more capable of coping with the physical and psychological demands brought about through greater emphasis on form, skill, and accuracy in the performance of the more advanced game and the official sport itself.

The final phase of motor development is the specialized movement abilities stage, beginning around high school and continuing through adulthood. The specialized skill phase involves application of the knowledge gained in the preceding phases to a selected few lifetime activities, engaged in on either a recreational or competitive level.

We must *not* view young children as miniature adults who can be programmed to perform in Little League and Pee Wee Activities with potential high-pressure, physiologically and psychologically, but rather, view children as children and structure meaningful movement experiences appropriate for their particular development level. The age ranges for each stage of motor development are in general terms. Children will often be seen to function at different stages within the same age level, accountable by experiential background and heredity makeup.

The physical development aspect of the psychomotor domain may be classified as either physical fitness or motor fitness. These terms, however, are elusive and difficult to define to the mutual satisfaction of experts in the field. Physical fitness is generally considered to be the ability to perform one's daily tasks without undue fatigue. It is also a state in which ample reserve of energy should be available for recreational pursuits and to meet emergency needs. Components of physical fitness are generally considered to be muscular strength, muscular endurance, cardio-respiratory endurance, and flexibility. On the other hand, the concept of motor ability or "motor fitness" is classified by some experts as being part of physical fitness.

Hockey (1973:6) best summarizes the debate in this paragraph:

Many factors associated with the development of skill have erroneously been referred to as physical fitness components. It should be kept in mind that only factors that relate to the development of health and increase the functional capacities of the body should be classified as physical fitness components. Those that are necessary for skillful performance of an activity should be classified as motor ability components.

Components of motor ability (motor fitness) are then generally thought of as one's performance abilities as influenced by speed, agility, balance, coordination, and power.

Another important outcome of a well-rounded movement education program for young children is the enhancement of fundamental cognitive concepts. Throughout the history of man, philosophers, psychologists, and educators have indicated that a relationship exists between the functioning of the body and the mind. From the Greek philosophers, Socrates and Plato, to the educational theorists of the twentieth century, there has been a great deal of philosophical support. The fact is, however, that little had been done of an experimental or practical nature prior to the 1960's to put this philosophical construct into operation. Not until the growth in popularity of the works of Jean Piaget has there been a true shift in favor of recognizing the importance of movement in the development of both psychomotor and cognitive aspects of the child's behavior. Piaget emphasizes the tremendous importance of movement as an information-gathering device for children to learn about themselves and their world. Educators are now recognizing that important perceptual-motor skills and fundamental academic concepts can be dealt with together. This is not to imply that movement is the primary or sole mode by which cognitive abilities can be developed. It is, however, meant to say that movement can, through good teaching, be effectively used as a tool for enhancing children's cognitive awareness of themselves and the world about them.

The proper use of "teachable movements," along with the emphasis placed on the development of cognitive concepts of why, what, how, and when, in relation to one's movement, can play an important role in helping children get ready for learning by supplementing and reinforcing information that is dealt with in the traditional setting of classroom and nursery schools. There are two primary aspects of cognitive development that may be dealt with effectively through the movement education portion of the child's day. The first of these aspects is the various perceptual-motor concepts involving the development of body awareness, spatial awareness, directional awareness, and establishment of an effective time-space orientation. The second aspect of cognitive development involves the development and reinforcement of increased understanding and appreciation of fundamental academic concepts involving science, mathematics, the language arts, and social studies through the medium of movement. The bulk of available evidence indicates that both types of cognitive concepts, whether perceptual-motor or academic in nature, may be enhanced through active involvement in carefully selected and directed movement activities. It should be noted, however, that there is little support for the notion that increased movement abilities will have a correspondingly positive effect on the native intelligence.

The process of interacting with our environment is a combination of perceptual and motor processes, which are not independent of one another, as is often assumed. The dash that appears in the term "perceptual-motor" signifies the interdependence of one on the other. This becomes apparent when we recognize that efficient and effective movement is dependent on accurate perceptions of ourselves and our world and that the development of one's perceptual abilities is dependent, in part, on movement.

The development of perceptual-motor abilities is a process of both maturation and experience, and as a result, all children develop at their own individual rate. Not all children are at the same ability level upon entering school, and although nothing can be done about the maturational component of this process, parents and teachers can have an important influence on the experience component.

The development of perceptual-motor abilities involves the establishment and refinement of kinesthetic sensitivity to one's world through movement. This kinesthetic sensitivity involves the development and refinement of an adequate space structure and temporal (time) structure. All movement occurs in space and involves an element of time, and the development of these structures is basic to efficient functioning in a variety of other areas. In order to enhance children's knowledge of their spatial world, we should involve them in movement activities designed to contribute to their body awareness, directional awareness, and spacial awareness. The temporal world of children may be correspondingly enhanced through activities that involve synchronizing rhythm and the sequencing of movements. Also, selected visual, auditory, and tactile abilities may be reinforced through movement in a variety of carefully selected activities.

Movement activities for young children can enhance the understanding of fundamental academic concepts when they are integrated with material dealt with during the academic portion of the day. Textbooks by Humphrey (1974), Werner (1979), Cratty (1971), and others have presented in operational terms how specific types of activity might be effectively used to enhance the acquisition of language-arts competencies, basic mathematical operations, social studies concepts, and science concepts. There are a variety of indirect and direct reasons why this occurs. Among them is the fact that active participation is fun. It is often a more natural approach that more closely approximates the needs and interests of children. Active participation in a game in which academic concepts are being dealt with makes it difficult for a child's attention to be diverted by extraneous stimuli. Also, active learning through movement activities enables children to deal in concrete terms with their world, rather than the abstract (Cratty, 1973:123). However, not all children benefit best in the enrichment of their academic abilities through active participation in movement activities. There is evidence that indicates that the traditionally silent and relatively immobile form of thought is quite effective for many students. The point to be made is that some children benefit greatly from a program that integrates movement activities with academic concepts development and that most children will probably realize at least some improvement.

The third important, but often overlooked, outcome of a good movement education program for young children is enhancement of the affective domain. Affect development involves dealing with the children's increasing abilities to act, interact, and react effectively with other people as well as with themselves. It is often referred to as "social-emotional development," and its successful attainment is of crucial importance to preschool and primary-grade children. The movement experiences engaged in by young children play an important role in children's perceptions of themselves as individuals as well as how they are able to relate to their peers and utilize their free time. Alert parents and teachers will recognize the vital importance of balanced social-emotional growth. They will understand the developmental characteristics of children and gather the necessary information of behaviors in at least the following two areas—(1) self-concept and (2) peer relations and play. This knowledge will enable them to encourage and structure meaningful movement experiences that will strengthen children's social-emotional growth and be in accordance with their developmental needs, interests, and capabilities.

## MOVEMENT EXPERIENCES

Preschoolers and primary-grade children are active, energetic, and emerging beings. They are engrossed in play and utilize play experiences as a means of finding out about themselves and their bodies. The important beginnings of self-concept as "self-esteem," as it is often termed, is found in the preschool years. Young children generally view themselves on one end of two extremes in all that they do. Their egocentric nature does not permit them to view themselves objectively in light of their particular strengths and weaknesses. They are unable to fully grasp the concept that one's ability to do things lies somewhere between these self-limiting poles. The "right-wrong" and "good-bad" world that children live in plays a big role in how they view themselves. Since their world is one of play and vigorous activity, the successes and failures that they experience play an important role in the establishment of a stable self-concept. If children experience repeated failure in their play world and are unable to perform the fundamental movement tasks of early childhood, they are likely to encounter difficulties in the establishment of a stable positive concept of themselves.

Based on this knowledge, it becomes important for people working with children to structure meaningful movement experiences that are within children's developmental capacities—ones that reduce the failure potential, thereby enhancing the success potential. The possibility and risk of failure must be gradually introduced to children in a manner that is educationally appropriate. We must endeavor to instill the concept that each person is a unique individual with a variety of limitations as well as capabilities. Positive feelings about oneself will help form the basis for developing the concept.

Movement experiences that permit exploration and problem solving on the part of children are very worthwhile. They permit children to solve movement problems or challenges within the limits of their own abilities and do not require the emulation of a predetermined criterion of performance. In this way, each child is permitted to achieve a measure of success bound only by the limits of his or her capabilities.

Movement experiences that have an adventure or "pseudo-danger" element to them are of value in enhancing children's self-concept. Activities, such as those that permit children to climb trees or apparatus on creative playgrounds or "play scapes," balance several feet off the ground on a rope ladder or bridge, or crawl through tunnels, incorporate an element of adventure in which children must overcome their natural fears and uncertainties to accomplish a "dangerous" task. The feelings of exhilaration and self-satisfaction with accomplishing such a task helps to promote an "I can" attitude and "I am" within the children to enhance their self-esteem.

While children are engaged in learning about themselves and their world, they are also involved in learning how to interact with peers. Children gradually move through various stages in the establishment of successful relations with members of their peer group. Prior to age five, children are egocentric and content to play alone. At about age five, children enter the group-play stage which is characterized by the ability to play in small groups for increasing periods of time. This is followed by the ability to play in large groups in cooperative/competitive team-type efforts by age seven or eight years.

Movement serves as a primary vehicle by which children progress through each of the play stages. The wise adults will recognize that wholesome peer relations are a developing phenomena. They will be careful to view children's difficulties with sharing, playing together, and concern for others' feelings as factors that must be dealt with understandingly in light of each child's developmental level. Through wise guidance, movement can be used as an effective tool in helping children develop each of these abilities.

The world of preschool and primary-grade children is a play world. Play serves as a primary vehicle by which they learn about themselves and the world around them. If asked, "What did you do today?" young children characteristically respond by saying, "Play." Care must be taken not to view such a response as a frivolous remark or unnecessary part of their daily task. Play must be viewed in the perspective that it is the work of children. Through play, whether individual or group, active or quiet, children develop fundamental understandings of the world around them.

The development of fundamental movement abilities contributes to children's use of leisure time. The ability to perform a wide variety of locomotor, manipulative, and stability-type activities in an acceptable manner enables children to pursue a variety of play-type activities. Children who do not do as well are hindered in their pursuit of leisure-time activities that involve the use and development of their movement abilities. As a result, a negative cycle that witnesses poor movement abilities being formed, due to lack of opportunity or encouragement, is established. The constructive use of leisure time can be enhanced through the possession of efficient movement abilities. Although gross motor activities are only *one* way of engaging in leisure, they are important for most children and adults.

The opportunity for active movement in the outdoor play spaces should go well beyond the traditional recess period characterized by mass confusion, boredom, and fighting. The outdoor play area should, first of all, be designed for children in such a way that it stimulates their interest, imagination, and large muscle development. As simple as this sounds, one need only to look at the majority of outdoor play spaces at the nursery-school, elementary school, and home yard areas to see that they are not designed for children. All too often, the outdoor play space is constructed with its primary objectives being to amuse children and require minimum upkeep rather than encouraging motor development. As a result, a typical outdoor play space of this type is characterized by areas of blacktop and galvanized, colorful swing sets, teeter-totters, and slides.

Outdoor equipment and structures should be selected to invite creative expression and imaginative interpretation by the children. The outdoor equipment should be abstract or neutral in its sculpture form in order to stimulate the child's imagination. It should stimulate a variety of locomotor, manipulative, and stability activities. Although individualistic in nature, outdoor play materials and equipment should encourage social contact. They should also stimulate imagination and cognitive processes through media that invite physical exploration and enjoyment.

In planning outdoor play space the following questions should be addressed: Is it safe? Is it developmentally appropriate? Is it practical and economically feasible? Can it be maintained with minimum maintenance? Can it be easily supervised?

The outdoor movement center is easily incorporated into the total outdoor play space. There should be ample space for children to move freely. Ideally, there will be a large grassy area or hillside for running, jumping, sliding, and rolling. There will also be a hard surface for riding wheel toys and for activities with bouncing objects. Trees should be an integral part of the movement center, not only to provide shade, but to encourage climbing. A variety of equipment that encourages gross motor activities should also be located in the outdoor play space. Climbing, striking, and balancing equipment should be an integral part of an outdoor area.

## CONCLUSION

In conclusion, the movement activities engaged in by young children play a very important role in the development of their psychomotor, cognitive, and affective abilities. Young children are involved in the important and exciting task of learning to move effectively through their world. They are developing a wide variety of fundamental movement abilities, enhancing their physical abilities, and learning to move with joy and control. Children also learn through movement. Movement serves as a vehicle by which they explore all that is around them. It aids in developing and reinforcing a variety of perceptual-motor and academic concepts. It also serves as a medium for encouraging affective development in which effective and efficient movement contributes to enhancing a positive self-concept, wholesome peer relationships, and the worthy use of leisure time through constructive play.

## REFERENCES

Arnheim, D. and Pestolesi, R. *Elementary Physical Education: A Developmental Approach.* St. Louis: C. V. Mosby (1978).

Corbin, C., ed. *A Textbook of Motor Development.* Dubuque, IA: W. C. Brown (1980).

Cratty, B. J. *Active Learning: Games to Enhance Academic Abilities.* Englewood Cliffs, NJ: Prentice-Hall (1971).

Cratty, B. J. *Intelligence in Action.* Englewood Cliffs, NJ: Prentice-Hall (1973).

Cratty, B. J. *Perceptual and Motor Development in Infants and Children.* New York: Collier-MacMillan Co. (1970).

Dauer, V. and Pangrazi, R. *Dynamic Physical Education for Elementary School Children.* Minneapolis: Burgess (1979).

Gallahue, D. L. *Understanding Motor Development in Children.* New York: John Wiley and Sons (1982).

Gerhardt, L. A. *Moving and Knowing: The Young Child Orients Himself to Space.* Englewood Cliffs, NJ: Prentice-Hall (1973).

Graham, G., et al. *Children Moving.* Palo Alto, CA: Mayfield (1980).

Hockey, R. V. *Physical Fitness.* St. Louis: C. V. Mosby (1973).

Hoffman, H., et al. *Meaningful Movement for Children: A Developmental Theme Approach to Physical Education.* Boston: Allyn and Bacon (1981).

Humphrey, J. *Child Learning.* Dubuque, IA: W. C. Brown (1974).

Kritcherisky, S. and Prescott, E. *Planning Environments for Young Children.* Washington DC: NAEYC (1977).

Logsdon, B. J., et al. *Physical Education for Children: A Focus on the Teaching Process.* Philadelphia: Lea and Febiger (1977).

McClenaghan, B. A. and Gallahue, D. L. *Fundamental Movement: A Developmental Approach.* Philadelphia: W. B. Saunders Co. (1978).

Piers, M. W., ed. *Play and Development.* New York: W. W. Norton and Company (1972).

Rarick, G. L. *Physical Activity: Human Growth and Development.* New York: Academic Press (1973).

Ridenour, M. V., ed. *Motor Development—Issues and Applications.* Princeton, NJ: Princeton Book Co. (1978).

Riggs, M. L. *Jump to Joy.* Englewood Cliffs, NJ: Prentice-Hall (1980).

Riley, M., ed. *Play as Exploratory Behavior.* Beverly Hills, CA: Sage (1974).

Schurr, E. L. *Movement Experiences for Children.* Englewood Cliffs, NJ: Prentice-Hall (1980).

Seidel, B. L., et al. *Sport Skills: A Conceptual Approach to Meaningful Movement.* Dubuque, IA: W. C. Brown (1980).

Werner, P. H. and Burton, E. C. *Learning Through Movement: Teaching Cognitive Content Through Physical Activity.* St. Louis: C. V. Mosby (1979).

# The young child's play and social and emotional development

**Tonja Root Caster**
*The University of Georgia*

## INTRODUCTION

Garvey (1977) described play as being pleasurable and enjoyable; it has no extrinsic goal but has an intrinsic goal of enjoying the process rather than the end product. Second, it is voluntary and spontaneous. Third, it includes active involvement. Finally, it seems to relate to cognitive and social phenomena, such as creativity, problem-solving, language development, and the development of social roles.

Play seems only to occur when children do not feel anxious or threatened (Weisler and McCall, 1976) and after they have become familiar with an object through the processes of exploration (Garvey, 1977; Hutt, 1979). Exploration, as Hutt defined it, is one of the epistemic behaviors of play; through exploration, a child gains information and knowledge about an object by examining its physical characteristics. Consequently, during exploration, the child assumes a literal orientation to the object. For example, a child, upon seeing a toy boat for the first time, might stop by it, look at it, and handle it. By exploring an object, a child might attempt to discover what the object can do. With the toy boat, a child might move the wheel or wind the paddle. After exploring the object, a child might practice doing different things with it. A child might move the toy boat across a table, build a house for it, or put it in water.

Play with objects occurs after exploration of those objects. Play, a ludic behavior, relates to and relies upon past experiences and upon previous exploration of the object. During play, the child assumes a nonliteral orientation to the object. He or she focuses not on what the object can do, as in the example, but on what he or she can do with the object. The transition between exploration and play is bidirectional. The child alternates between exploration and play in such a manner that there is no clear definite transition from one to the other.

Garvey (1977) used the term "nonplay" to refer to the child's literal orientation towards the object. To be considered play, the activity must include some nonliteral interpretation of the object or situation. Distinguishing between play and nonplay requires that one observe more than just the activity in which the child is engaging. It requires the observer to determine the child's orientation to the object or situation with which he or she is involved. "All play requires the players to understand that what is done is not what it appears to be" (Garvey, 1977, p. 7).

Kransor and Pepler (1980) provide a different definition of play. They described their concept of "pure play" as the overlap of four components of play: nonliterality; positive affect; intrinsic motivation; and flexibility. Positive affect refers to the pleasurable sensations a child receives through playing, which he or she expresses through smiling, laughing, and giggling. A child is intrinsically motivated to play; that is, he or she plays because of a desire to play, not because of external forces. Flexibility refers to the child using an object in many different ways during play.

"Pure play," as noted previously, requires the simultaneous occurrence of all of the four components. Behavior which is not "pure play," but could be considered "more or less" play contains some, but not all, of these components. In this way, Kransor and Pepler's concept of play contrasts with play as defined by Garvey, Rubin, Hutt, and others who view behavior as either play or nonplay and recognize no intermediate categories.

There are several ways of categorizing different types of play; one can subdivide play into hierarchical categories. Piaget (1962) has divided play into three categories: sensorimotor play; symbolic play; and games with rules. Smilansky (1968) elaborated on this system by outlining four categories: functional play; constructive play; dramatic play; and games with rules. During functional play, children manipulate objects, try to repeat actions, and imitate actions as they explore the immediate environment.

Constructive play is an extension of functional play. After children learn uses of play objects during functional play and lengthen their concentration span, they begin to set and reach goals for themselves. Instead of only manipulating objects, as was characteristic during functional play, they begin to create things with those objects during constructive play. Thus, children begin to build structures with blocks and paint pictures of objects or people (rather than drawing only lines or scribbles) with brushes, paints, and paper.

During dramatic play, the third stage, children become cognizant of the relationship between their play and the objective world. While children learn to create things during constructive play, dramatic play allows children to develop their creativity further by giving them opportunities to substitute objects, actions, and language for realistic props. In addition, children develop their social skills as they interact socially and verbally with other players during dramatic play.

The last category is games with rules. Children begin developing socially negotiated rules during dramatic play. The games with rules stage furthers this development as children learn to accept and adjust to games with prearranged rules.

Thus far, the characteristics of play have been described and discussed. Play has been described as pleasurable, as having an intrinsic goal to enjoy the process of playing, as being voluntary and spontaneous, and as including active involvement. Play requires that the child has previously become familiar with the object through exploration. There is disagreement as to what constitutes play. Hutt says the transition between play and exploration is not definite; instead, the child alternates between the two. Garvey views exploration as nonplay. Play requires a nonliteral orientation; that is, focus not on what the object can do but on what he or she can do with the object. Kransor and Pepler take the position that a behavior need not be dichotomized as either play or nonplay but that a behavior should be considered "more or less" play when it contains one or more of four components: nonliterality; positive affect; intrinsic motivation; and flexibility.

This section concluded with a description of Smilansky's four categories of play: functional play; constructive play; dramatic play; and games with rules. Children manipulate objects during functional play and create things with those objects during constructive play. During dramatic play, children substitute representational objects for realistic props. Children learn to accept and adjust to games with prearranged rules.

## SOCIAL PLAY

Social play has been defined as an engagement among two or more children in which the "successive, nonliteral behaviors of one partner are contingent on the nonliteral behaviors of the other partner(s)" (Garvey 1974, p. 163).

Just as cognitive aspects of play have been subdivided into developmental hierarchical categories, so have the social aspects of play. Parten (1932) defined six categories of social participation: unoccupied behavior; onlooker; solitary independent play; parallel activity; associative play; and cooperative or organized supplementary play. Unoccupied behavior is described as watching something momentarily, glancing around the room, standing or sitting without apparent reason, or playing with one's own body. An onlooker observes the play of other children, often talking with them and giving them suggestions, but never engaging in their play. Solitary independent play is described as play which a child does alone, without regard to the activities of other children. Parten considered these first three categories as types of nonsocial play.

In contrast, Parten regarded the last three categories (parallel activity, associative play, and cooperative or organized supplementary play) as indices of social participation. During parallel activity, a child plays independently, but with toys that are similar to those that children near him or her are using. Associative play was defined as playing with other children involved in similar, if not identical, activities. Children may try to control other children, but each child acts as he or she wishes. Children's conversations indicate that they are more interested in associations with the other children than in the play activities. During cooperative or organized supplementary play, children belong to a group in which one or two members direct the activities of others. The group is organized for some purpose, such as social dramatic play or making some product.

Parten (1932) found that these six social participation categories were hierarchical and that there was a correlation between the preschool children's ages and the social participation categories. Unoccupied behavior was observed in only the youngest children, two to three years of age. Solitary play was most prevalent at the age of two-and-one-half. Onlookers were most common among children two-and-one-half to three years old. Parallel activity was most often observed among two-year-olds. Associative and cooperative play were most prevalent among the children who were four- to four-and-one-half years old. While only a few children were observed in the unoccupied category, most children engaged in solitary play, onlooker situations, and associative play. Parallel activity was the most prevalent of all the categories of social participation. Parten inferred that the children who engaged in parallel activity and/or solitary play were not usually the same ones who participated in either associative or cooperative play. Thus, she included these two categories (parallel activity and solitary play) among those describing other nonsocial types of play in which the youngest children engage.

There has been some controversy, however, regarding parallel play. Smith (1978) found that preschool children's parallel play occurred less frequently than group and solitary play, rather than occurring most frequently as found by Parten (1932). He also found that social involvement for the older children (ages 34 to 48 months) most often progressed from solitary play to group play, whereas the social involvement for the younger children (ages 28 to 33 months) most often progressed from solitary through parallel to group play. He concluded that "a phase of predominantly parallel behavior is a sign of a younger or perhaps a less mature child" (Smith, 1978, p. 523). Smith suggested, therefore, that parallel play is an optional stage in a child's social development.

Bakeman and Brownlee (1980) observed the play of preschoolers (ages 32½ to 42 months) and categorized the play as unoccupied, solitary, together (with other children but not occupied in play), parallel, and group. They found that the children engaged in parallel play the most frequently of the five categories. They also found that children participated most often in together or group play after parallel play and that every child moved from parallel to group play more than once. Bakeman and Brownlee concluded that children use parallel play as an opportunity to increase their socialization with those nearby and to assess the situation to which they are close.

There is another controversy relating to Parten's (1932) findings. Barnes (1971) found that only 25 percent of the play of the three- and four-year-olds in his study was associative and cooperative. Parten had found that about 40 percent of the preschoolers' play was associative and cooperative. Barnes concluded that children are much less socially oriented in their play activities than were children in 1932. Rubin, Maioni, and Hornung (1976), however, disagree with Barnes' conclusion. Rubin and associates found that the data from their study on the middle-class preschoolers supported Parten's (1932) findings, as their middle-class preschoolers participated in associative and cooperative play approximately 40 percent of the time. Rubin and associates (1976) also supported Barnes' findings, as their lower-class preschoolers engaged in associative and cooperative play about 27 percent of the time. They concluded that these findings suggest that the preschoolers in Barnes' study were predominantly from lower-class background, though this information had not been reported in Barnes' study, and that children have not become less socially oriented in their play.

Rubin, Maioni and Hornung (1976) studied the relationship between Parten's social hierarchy (1932) and Smilansky's cognitive hierarchy (1968) and the differences between the free play behaviors of middle- and lower-class preschoolers. Middle-class children participated in more constructive, associative, and cooperative play, and less parallel and functional play than their lower-class peers. More specifically, middle-class preschoolers engaged in more associative play that was functional than did the lower-class children. This finding supports the findings of Feitelson, Weintraub, and Michaeli (1972) who found that advantaged preschoolers in homogeneous schools engaged in more cooperative activities with their peers than did disadvantaged preschoolers in heterogeneous schools.

Rubin, et al. (1976) also found that females participated in more solitary and parallel play and less associative-dramatic play than did the male preschoolers. The data of all the preschoolers together revealed that Parten's social play categories occurred in the following order of frequency, from most to least frequent: solitary play; associative play; parallel play; and cooperative play. The frequencies of Smilansky's (1968) cognitive categories were hierarchically arranged as follows, from most to least frequent: functional and constructive play; dramatic play; and games with rules.

Though nonsocial play has not been viewed by many as aiding social or cognitive development, Rubin (1982) found that at least one form of nonsocial activity is useful and adaptive. In his study of four-year-olds, he found that children who engaged in parallel-constructive activities (such as artwork, puzzle, or block construction) solved both social and nonsocial problems well, were popular with their peers, and were viewed as socially competent by their teachers. Rubin inferred that teachers viewed these children as socially competent since the teachers encouraged parallel-constructive activities. The children's problem-solving abilities were also related to the children's participation in parallel-constructive activities.

Another study has shown that solitary play, a form of nonsocial play, may contribute to cognitive development. In studying the solitary play of kindergarten children, Moore, Evertson, and Brophy (1974) found that goal-directed activities and educational play accounted for almost 50 percent of the solitary play observed. The authors concluded that solitary play is not a result of social immaturity but is a positive and desirable form of play. These findings are supported by those of Rubin, Maioni, and Hornung (1976). Rubin and associates concluded that parallel, not solitary play, was the least mature type of play for three- and four-year-olds. Children who engaged in parallel play may want the company of other children but may not have the social skills that associative and/or cooperative play require, while children who engage in solitary play may have chosen to play alone, away from other children.

Thus far, this section has described Parten's six hierarchical categories of social participation. She considered the first four categories as nonsocial types of play. These categories were unoccupied behavior, onlooker, solitary play, and parallel activity. The last two categories, associative and cooperative play, she considered as social types of play. Though Parten stated that each child progressed through each category, Smith contended that his study on preschoolers suggested that parallel activity is an optional stage. Bakeman and Brownlee concluded from their study that children use parallel play as an opportunity for socialization and to assess situations. Rubin, Maioni, and Hornung showed that parallel, not solitary, play was the least mature type of play for three- and four-year-olds.

Relating to the benefits of nonsocial types of play, Rubin found that children who engaged in parallel-constructive activities were good problem-solvers, were popular with their peers, and were viewed as socially competent by their teachers. Moore, Evertson, and Brophy found that another type of nonsocial play, solitary play, was also a positive form of play, as almost half of the play included goal-directed and educational activities.

Though there has been some disagreement, the studies of Parten and of Rubin, Maioni, and Hornung have shown that the middle-class preschoolers participated in associative and cooperative play more often than the lower-class preschoolers.

## ENVIRONMENTAL VARIABLES

A number of researchers have explored the relations among environmental variables, such as the play materials available to children and the types of play in which children engage (e.g., Parten, Updegraff and Herbst, Rubin and Seibel, Quilitch and Risley, Montes and Risley, Rosenthal, and Smith and Connolly). These studies suggest that different types of materials relate to different types of play and also that a given type of material may be used differentially according to ages and sex. Additionally, they show a number of other environmental variables, such as social and spatial density in the play area affecting the frequency of social play.

Parten (1933) evaluated the social value (the tendency to elicit social play categories) of toys for preschool children ages two to four-and-one-half. Play with blocks was related to each type of social play (solitary, onlooker, parallel, associative, and cooperative) with almost equal frequency, though cooperative play with blocks was the most frequent. House and dolls were related to the most cooperative play. Play with vehicles was about equally related to parallel, associative, and cooperative play. Parallel play was observed in sandbox, cutting paper, clay, swings, beads, and paints activities. Finally, the use of trains was observed about equally during solitary and associative play but were used less frequently during the remaining types of social play. Parten rated these ten games and toys according to their social value, from the highest to the lowest, as follows: house and dolls; vehicles; clay; blocks; scissors and paper; sand; paints; swings; beads; and trains.

Parten also found that the social value of an activity was different for children of different ages. She found that sandbox activity was more social among the older than younger children. Two- and three-year-olds engaged in solitary play during house and doll activity, while the play of older children (generally over three years of age) was more socially complex. Boys participated in house and doll activity almost as frequently as girls. For the younger children, play with trains was seldom social, while the older children played with trains associatively and cooperatively. Boys engaged in most of the train play. Vehicles seldom encouraged social play from the younger children, while from older children, they elicited cooperative play. Girls, most of whom were under three, played with vehicles only about a fourth of the time. The swings were generally used by the older girls. Girls used scissors and paper, beads, and paint more frequently than the boys. Boys played with the blocks almost three times as much as girls.

Updegraff and Herbst (1933) observed the play of pairs of two- and three-year-old preschool children using clay and blocks. The two-year-olds watched their partners (as onlookers) and gave more new use suggestions when playing with clay than when playing with blocks. More of the children's conversation was about the play material when they played with blocks than when they played with clay. Play with clay elicited more sociability (defined as showing interest in other children's activities, seeking their companionship, and making contact with them) and more cooperativeness (defined as engaging in activities with others without submitting to them) than did play with blocks.

Rubin and Seibel (in press) observed preschoolers' (ages 37½ to 60 months, mean age of 4.9 years) in 11 activities over a three-month period. Most preferred free play toys and corresponding activities (vehicles, playdough, painting, art construction, houseplay, puzzles, sand and water play, blocks, letters and numbers, and science). Each child's behavior was classified along cognitive (either functional, constructive, dramatic, or games with rules) and social continua [either solitary or parallel (nonsocial play) or group (social play)]. The cognitive aspects of play were very consistent across the three-month observation period. They changed for only one of the 11 activities; play for block activities went from no significant differences among the amounts of functional, constructive, or dramatic play to constructive play being preferred over both functional and dramatic play. In addition, when children were engaged in dramatic play with blocks, their play was usually social, yet when they played constructively with blocks, their play was usually nonsocial. Rubin and Seibel found three activities encouraged nonsocial-functional play: playdough; sand and water; and science. Six activities encouraged nonsocial-constructive play: painting; art construction; puzzles; blocks; letters and numbers; and construction toys. Rubin and Seibel also assessed sex differences among toy and activity preferences of the preschool children. They found that the males participated in more vehicle play (parallel-dramatic), in more sand and water play, and in less painting and art construction (parallel-constructive) than did the female preschoolers. They concluded that social-dramatic play was inhibited by sand and water, puzzles, science, and art activities.

In another study, Rubin (1977b) examined how younger children (mean age of 3.87 years) engaged in ten of their most preferred activities (cutting and pasting, painting and crayoning, playdough, houseplay, store, doctor and fireman, vehicles, sand and water, blocks, science materials, books, and puzzles) during a 30-day period. Males played more frequently with vehicles and blocks than did females, while females played with puzzles more frequently than did males. Non-social play (which included solitary and parallel play) was elicited more than social play by painting and crayoning, playdough, sand and water, and puzzle activities. Social play occurred most frequently during houseplay, vehicle play, and reading activities. Playdough and sand and water activities were more often functional than constructive, dramatic, or games with rules. Constructive play occurred most frequently during painting and crayoning, reading, and puzzle activities. Houseplay was most often dramatic play.

Quilitch and Risley (1973) studied the effects of "isolate" toys (gyroscope, crayons, tinker toys, jig saw puzzle, Farmer Says Talking Book, and playdoh) and "social" toys (Don't Spill the Beans, Pick Up Stix, checkers, and playing cards) on the play of seven-year-old children. In both the short (45 minutes during one day) and longer experiment (15 minutes during each of nine days), children played much more socially when presented with the social toys than when presented with the isolate toys.

Another important issue is the manner in which teachers make materials available to children. Montes and Risley (1975) studied the effects of two procedures for allowing children the access to toys (preschoolers aged four and five). During the free access condition, children selected their own toys, and all children helped clean up at the end of the free play period. During the limited access condition, children had to ask for permission from the teacher to check out toys, and the teacher encouraged children to return toys not being used. They found that the two conditions did not differ in the amount of time children spent playing with toys, selecting toys, interacting with the teacher, and cleaning up. However, in the limited access condition, children's socio-dramatic play was more complex to the extent that the children more frequently engaged in make-believe in relation to situations and actions, and the children talked more about the play episode than they did during the free access condition. Although allowing children free access to toys and materials may appear to aid children's development, in that it gives children opportunities to make decisions, limiting free access to toys appears to encourage more complex play.

Rosenthal (1979, in Kounin) studied various preschool settings and their social interaction potential as defined by the population density of that area. In the puzzle, clothing, and vehicle areas, children engaged in solitary play more than half of the time. Small groups of two or three children played with sand, science props, climber, and books. Large groups of six or more children played (less than a fourth of the time) in the art, large blocks, and music centers.

Smith and Connolly (1980) studied three groups of preschoolers (age range 32 to 55 months, mean age of 43.7 months) to determine the effects of two different spacial densities on children's play. The spacially crowded conditions allowed exactly 15 square feet per child, while the large space condition allowed about 60 square feet per child. They found that there was more parallel play, less group play (consisting of two or more children), and a smaller mean group size playing together in the spacially crowded condition than in the large space condition. Children also played with the Wendy house, books, sand, water, and clay more often in the spacially crowded condition than in the large space condition.

The findings of the previously mentioned studies generally indicate that play with sand, clay/playdough, and water is generally nonsocial and functional. Other nonsocial activities include painting (constructive), puzzles, art, science, and reading (unless interaction has been encouraged by an adult). The activities which encourage the most social play include play with blocks, vehicles, and house and dolls (dramatic). Spacially crowded classrooms appear to encourage parallel play while discouraging group play. In the spacially crowded classrooms, there was also more play with materials which were found to be associated with social play (only the Wendy house). These findings should help teachers construct learning environments which encourage social growth.

As materials used inside a preschool stimulate different types of play indoors, so playground equipment also influences children's play outdoors. Johnson (1935) studied the effects of a reduction of playground equipment on the play of a group of children ages three to five years. Exercise (e.g., swinging, running, jumping, talking, walking, standing, and looking) and play with vehicles, shovels, balls, rocking boat, and building materials decreased in amount after the removal of play equipment (e.g., slides, swings, stair climbing apparatus, jungle gym, and sandbox), while play with materials (e.g., tricycles, wagons, wheel barrows, saw horses, planks, shovels, rakes, and balls), sand and dirt, and games, and contacts with the teacher increased. Social play increased in play with materials, sand and dirt, undesirable behavior (teasing, crying, quarreling, and hitting), and games, while it decreased in exercise when playground equipment was reduced. Concerning sex differences, a reduction in playground equipment elicited more exercise, use of materials, and undesirable behavior from boys than from girls. Girls engaged in more games, and boys engaged in more undesirable behavior. Boys made more social contacts than did girls, particularly in exercise and play with materials, while girls made more social contacts than boys in games. When Johnson compared the play of children of different ages, she found that five-year-olds participated in more exercise than did three- or four-year-olds before the reduction of playground equipment. However, the five-year-olds participated the least in exercise after the playground equipment reduction. Four-year-olds played with materials almost with equal frequency before and after playground equipment was reduced, while three- and five-year-olds played with materials with slightly greater frequency after the reduction of playground equipment. Johnson concluded that less equipped playgrounds seem to encourage more social and non-material play than do more equipped playgrounds.

In a second study, Johnson (1935) analyzed the effects of an increase of playground equipment on the play of two different groups of children with mean ages of 60 and 63 months. Contrary to the first study, she found that the amount of exercise decreased, while the amount of play with materials increased after the introduction of more playground equipment. In agreement with the first study, Johnson found that undesirable behavior and games decreased in frequency after the change in equipment. Sex differences were consistent with those found in the first study. Johnson concluded that individual (nonsocial) play can be increased while undesirable behavior and social contact decreased by introducing more equipment.

Smith (1974) studied the effects of different types of playground equipment on the play of children aged three to four-and-three-quarters in a playground setting. Each of the two groups of children was observed playing during three conditions: (1) apparatus only (including chairs, tables, toy chests, climbing frame and slide, doll's house, baby carriage, tricycle, and rocking boat); (2) toys only (including chairs, tables, jigsaw puzzles, beads and string, doll, teddy bear, dress-up clothes, tea set, musical instruments, doll's house, sandbox and toys, easel and paints, books, blocks, and telephone); and (3) control condition (including all of the apparatus and toys listed in the other two conditions). Smith found that the children's play was more active, sociable, and creative when they played in the apparatus only condition. Children talked more with one another, came into physical contact with others more frequently, and used play materials in a greater variety of ways than in the toys only condition. In comparison with the control condition, children during the apparatus only condition engaged in more cooperative play and in less solitary and parallel play. This was not a result simply of a reduction in the amount of equipment which would require more sharing (see Smith and Connolly, 1973). Children also played more creatively, using familiar objects in new and unusual ways during the apparatus only condition, as compared with the control condition. Comparing the toys only condition with the control condition, the play in the toys only condition consisted of more object manipulation and less automanipulative and stereotypic behaviors (e.g., eye-rubbing and hand fumbling). These results may have been caused by the novelty of the two experimental conditions—apparatus only and toy only. Instead of playing with the objects, the children were exploring them, using the objects in new and unusual ways in order to gain information and knowledge about their physical characteristics. In comparing the two experimental conditions (apparatus only and toys only), the apparatus only condition elicited more smiling, laughing, walking, pushing, climbing, and sliding. During the toys only condition, children more often watched the playground staff, were in a large group with an adult, and played with objects. The frequencies of all these behaviors in the control condition were between their frequencies in the two experimental conditions. However, aggressive behaviors and thumb sucking occurred less frequently in the control condition than in the two experimental conditions. Smith suggested that the novelty of the two experimental conditions might account for this observation. Again, instead of playing in the two experimental conditions, the children were exploring. Hutt suggests that in an unfamiliar environment where children are apprehensive, it is more difficult for children to play. They must explore the environment before they can play. The children in this study, however, were playing in a familiar environment and exploring in an unfamiliar environment. It appears that the children were less apprehensive playing in a familiar environment than exploring in an unfamiliar one. Smith concluded that "temporarily reducing freedom of choice in play activities by reducing the amount or variety of equipment, may lead to greater levels of conflict or stress, but also to greater levels of sharing or creative activities" (Smith, 1974, p. 62).

## IMPLICATIONS

The studies reviewed in this chapter generally adopted one of two research strategies—observational or experimental. Each strategy has strengths and weaknesses which limit the types of conclusions the researcher can draw from the study. These limitations also restrict the ability of the teacher/therapist to apply the findings to an actual setting.

Most of the studies reviewed in this chapter were observational. These include Parten (1932), Smith (1978), Bakeman and Brownlee (1980), Barnes (1971), Rubin, et al. (1976), Rubin (1982), Moore, et al. (1974), Parten (1933), Rubin and Seibel (in press), Rubin (1977b), and Quilitch and Risley (1973). Observational studies focus on describing what exists, though the findings may also be related to existing theories or used to develop new theories. For example, Parten (1932) described six hierarchical categories of social participation and then tested her theory through observations. Researchers who use observational studies cannot conclude that one thing caused something else to occur; they can only state that the two things happened simultaneously. Rubin and Seibel (in press) stated that nonsocial-functional play occurred when children played with playdough, sand and water, and science, but they could not say that those materials caused nonsocial-functional play. The teacher/therapist who intends to apply the findings of observational studies must read carefully to avoid misinterpreting observed relationships as cause-effect relationships.

A few of the studies reviewed in this chapter were experimental. These include Feitelson, et al. (1972), Updegraff and Herbst (1933), Montes and Risley (1975), Smith and Connolly (1980), and Smith (1974). Experimental studies attempt to hold constant variables except one or more which they are deliberately manipulating or allowing to vary. Controlling extraneous variables (aspects of the experiment which the researchers do not intend to vary) allows researchers to conclude that the observed differences (e.g., differences in play behaviors) appear to be directly related to changes in the experimental variables (specific variable(s) being deliberately manipulated). Most educational research, however, controls for some, but not all, of the relevant variables, so some precision of experimental research is lost. For example, Smith (1974) observed the play of two groups of children in a playground during three conditions (apparatus only, toys only, and control). He then compared the play of each group separately for each of the three conditions. By having the same group of children in each condition,

Smith controlled for individual differences among children that would have existed if he had compared the play of different groups of children for each of the three conditions. In designing an experimental study, the researcher may have to create situations which are novel to the subjects. Smith (1974) created a novel situation by having the two groups of children play in a playground which had three different sets of equipment. He suggested that the novelty of the two experimental conditions (apparatus only and toys only) might account for some of the behaviors observed. It is sometimes difficult to determine whether the results were influenced by the variable(s) manipulated or by the situation to which the subjects were unaccustomed. Teachers/therapists should be alert to the difficulty of employing the findings of experimental studies to real situations.

The research findings offer several implications for teachers/therapists who wish to encourage children's social play. Play appears to occur only when children do not feel anxious or threatened. Teachers/therapists should strive to create an environment where children feel safe to try new things and where they feel they have the support of those adults around them. The teacher/therapist might encourage a child to engage in a new activity while being close by to help physically and/or to give verbal support.

Indoors, materials available for use by children may alter the social aspects of their play. Materials which encourage the most social play, such as blocks, vehicles, doll houses, dolls, and dress-up materials, need to be in abundant supply and readily available for children to use during play. Other materials which seem to encourage non-social forms of play and thus inhibit social play need to be available less frequently. These materials include sand, clay/playdough, water, puzzles, science, reading, painting, and other art activities.

Additionally, play seems to occur only after children have become familiar with their environments. Thus, while it is important to have available materials which encourage social play, it is also important that the same materials remain available for an appropriate length of time so that children have opportunities both to explore and to play with them.

The manner in which materials are available to children also affects the quality of children's play. Limiting children's access to toys encourages more complex play. Teachers/therapists should consider a procedure whereby children have to check out the materials they wish to play with from the teacher/therapist.

In addition to regulating the availability of materials for indoor play, teachers/therapists should encourage social play with materials not usually used for this kind of play (e.g., sand, clay/playdough, water, and reading), but which children enjoy exploring and playing with, and which encourage cognitive growth. This can be done through modeling, in which the professional becomes an active member of the group. For example, children become socially active participants in discussiong books if encouraged by a teacher.

Playground equipment available for use by children outdoors may also alter the social aspect of their play. Playgrounds with less equipment encourage more social play which is accompanied by more undesirable behavior (teasing, crying, quarreling, hitting). The equipment which is available for outdoor play should include more apparatus (e.g., climbing equipment, slides, tricycles, rocking boats) and fewer toys (e.g., dolls, sandbox and toys, art materials, books, blocks) if teachers/therapists want to encourage more creative social play.

## REFERENCES

Bakeman, R. and Brownlee, J. R., "The strategic use of parallel play: A sequential analysis," *Child Development, 51,* 873-878 (1980).

Barnes, K. E., "Preschool play norms: A replication," *Developmental Psychology, 5,* 99-103 (1971).

Feitelson, D., Weintraub, S., and Michaeli, O., "Social interactions in heterogeneous preschools in Israel," *Child Development, 43,* 1249-1259 (1972).

Garvey, C. *Play.* Cambridge, Massachusetts: Harvard University Press (1977).

Garvey, C., "Some properties of social play," *Merrill-Palmer Quarterly, 20,* 163-180 (1974).

Hutt, C., "Exploration and play," in *Play and Learning,* B. Sutton-Smith, ed. New York: Gardner Press (1979).

Johnson, M. W., "The effect on behavior of variation in the amount of play equipment," *Child Development, 6,* 56-68 (1935).

Kounin, J. S. and Sherman, L. W., "School environments as behavior settings," *Theory into Practice, 18,* 145-151 (1979).

Krasnor, L. R. and Pepler, D. J., "The study of children's play, Some suggested future directions," in *New Directions for Child Development* (No. 9), K. H. Rubin, ed. San Francisco: Jossey-Bass, Inc., Publishers (1980).

Montes, F. and Risley, T. R., "Evaluating traditional day care practices: An empirical approach," *Child Care Quarterly, 4,* 208-215 (1975).

Moore, N. V., Evertson, C. D., and Brophy, J. E., "Solitary play: Some functional reconsiderations," *Developmental Psychology, 10,* 830-834 (1974).

Parten, M. B., "Social participation among preschool children," *Journal of Abnormal and Social Psychology, 27,* 243-269 (1932).

Parten, M. B., "Social play among preschool children," *Journal of Abnormal and Social Psychology, 28,* 136-147 (1933).

Phyfe-Perkins, E., "Children's behavior in preschool settings—The influence of the physical environment," in *Current Topics in Early Childhood Education* (Vol. 3), L. G. Katz, ed. Norwood, NJ: Ablex (1980).

Piaget, J. *Play, Dreams, and Imitation in Childhood.* New York: Norton (1962).

Quilitch, H. R. and Risley, T. R., "The effects of play materials on social play," *Journal of Applied Behavioral Analysis, 6,* 573-578 (1973).

Rubin, K. H., "Fantasy play: Its role in the development of social skills and social cognition," in *New Directions for Child Development* (No. 9): *Children's Play,* K. H. Rubin, ed. San Francisco: Jossey-Bass, Inc., Publishers (1980).

Rubin, K. H., "Non-social play in preschoolers: Necessary evil?" *Child Development, 53,* 651-657 (1982).

Rubin, K. H., "Play behaviors of young children," *Young Children, 32* (6), 16-24 (1977a).

Rubin, K. H., "The social and cognitive values of preschool toys and activities," *Canadian Journal of Behavioral Sciences, 9,* 382-385 (1977b).

Rubin, K. H., Fein, G. G., and Vandenberg, B., in *Carmichael's Manual of Child Psychology: Social Development,* E. M. Hetherington, ed. New York: Wiley (1983).

Rubin, K. H., Maioni, T. L. and Hornung, M., "Play behaviors in middle- and lower-class preschoolers: Parten and Piaget revisited," *Child Development, 47,* 414-419 (1976).

Rubin, K. H. and Seibel, C. G., "The effects of ecological settings on the cognitive and social play behaviors of preschoolers," in *Proceedings of the Ninth Annual International Inter-disciplinary Conference of Piagetian Theory and the Helping Professions,* in press.

Singer, J. L., "Some practical implications of make-believe play," in *The Child's World of Make-believe: Experimental Studies of Imaginative Play*, J. L. Singer, ed. New York: Academic Press (1973).

Smilansky, S. *The Effects of Sociodramatic Play on Disadvantaged Preschool Children.* New York: Wiley (1968).

Smith, P. K., "Aspects of the playgroup environment," in *Psychology and the Built Environment*, D. Canter and T. Lee, eds. England: Architectural Press (1974).

Smith, P. K., "A longitudinal study of social participation in preschool children: Solitary and parallel play reexamined," *Developmental Psychology, 14,* 517–523 (1978).

Smith, P. K. and Connolly, K. J. *The Ecology of Preschool Behavior.* New York: Cambridge University Press (1970).

Smith, P. K. and Connolly, K. J., "Toys, space and children," *British Psychological Society Bulletin, 26,* 167 (1973).

Updegraff, R. and Herbst, E. K., "An experimental study of the social behavior stimulated in young children by certain play materials," *Journal of Genetic Psychology, 42,* 372–391 (1933).

Weisler, A. and McCall, R. B., "Exploration and play: Resume and redirection," *American Psychologist, 31,* 492–508 (1976).

# CHAPTER 3

# Relationships between child's play and cognitive development and learning in infancy birth through age eight

**Thomas D. Yawkey[1] and Joseph M. Diantoniis**
*The Pennsylvania State University*

## INTRODUCTION

Pretend or fantasy play is the intellectual ability of children to change themselves into people, objects, or situations other than themselves, as shown through their verbal expression and/or motor movement (Greene and Yawkey, 1982). The study of pretend play and its relationships to children's development and learning has gained respectability as a worthwhile endeavor and activity just within the past 15 years (Yawkey, 1980). The fact that play is just recently regarded as important for development and learning is rather curious. Considering that infants, preschoolers, pre-adolescents, adolescents, and adults all perform the mysterious act called play, pretending and imagining are rather commonplace activities and actions. Although the quality and quantity of thinking structures used in play differ across ages, child's play is regarded as necessary for cognitive development and learning (Ellis, 1973; Piaget, 1962). However, the power of play and its potential for development for the young child, birth through eight, is virtually an untapped area for research (Neuman, 1971).

The purpose of this chapter is to examine the untapped reservoir of play for developmental purposes from a number of perspectives. First, characteristics of pretend or fantasy play, relative to thinking and social processes of young children, are described and applied to learning settings. Second, factors which influence and affect play are discussed. These factors are derived from results of research studies and include cultural and economic conditions and communication processes. Third and finally, fantasy or pretend play as a cognitive developmental phenomena is explained.

[1]The senior author's research and writing on constructivist play, cognition, and communication are supported, in part, by grants from The United States Department of Education, The Margaret M. Patton Foundation, Kittanning, Pennsylvania and Penn State's Division of Curriculum and Instruction, Dr. Fred H. Wood, Head. The views expressed in this and other documents are those of the authors and do not represent the funding agencies.

## THINKING AND SOCIAL PROCESSES:
## SOME INGREDIENTS OF PLAY

Based on general research results from a number of studies, several characteristics of pretend or fantasy play can be observed. First, children freely select and change activities—perhaps running on the playground, then swinging, then hopping. For children, play is a free activity. Children desire but are not required to play. Second, play is an activity that is limited only by space and the time in which it takes place. Third, the outcomes or products of play are not important to the child. The child has no objective in playing on the swing or drawing a picture, except to have fun. Fourth, children's play is not production of goods or materials, but learning about themselves, others, and the environment. The child may repeat activities over and over as he investigates and verifies information from the environment. Fifth, play involves rules made by the child. The rules are unique to each imaginative play situation. Finally, play has a make-believe characteristic. A block may become a "fire engine" or a "doll," and a broom becomes a horse which speaks. A closer examination of these characteristics reveals important processes that are related to intellectual, social, and language development.

As children are observed in actual play, two essential elements or ingredients of play become apparent, which are (a) the involvement of the thinking processes and (b) the repetition of social interactions. Children who are role-playing as they try on old clothes are actually interpreting information from their surroundings and comparing it to what they already know. One child may try on a dress, identifying it as an object worn by mother. Perhaps she may use imaginative play in home experiences, such as cooking eggs, to verify what was previously observed. Also, for example, Tom sits on a large block busily imitating the sounds of a fire engine. Tom is mentally reproducing past knowledge about fire engines and applying it to another object. In both instances, what appears to be random spontaneous activity is, upon closer examination, the use of thinking. In fact, all play activities can be observed to involve thinking processes, such as comparing, classifying, predicting, and verifying. But, in addition to the thinking processes, social interaction also accompanies play.

A multitude of play activities involving several children doing things together can be observed. Three children playing at a nearby table communicate verbally and nonverbally as they play. Another group of children at the sliding board discuss who takes the next turn. Indeed, interaction among children occurs in much of play. As youngsters experience success and failure in these group activities, several things happen! Language develops; social skills evolve; and children learn about their social and physical worlds.

There is also a connection between thinking and talking in group play. Thinking takes place in a social environment. Greta may want to use a car that Mark has. Greta wants to pretend she is driving the car. She asks Mark for the car, and if he hands it over, Greta evaluates the situation as successful. If Mark doesn't give her the car, Greta evaluates the situation differently and may think over other strategies to obtain the car, or she may decide to forget the whole thing. Perhaps Mark may tell Greta where to obtain another car, and both can pretend they are driving. Mark and Greta have learned from the social occasion through play. Both have used their thinking processes in the activity. In another example, several children are playing house and roles have been divided. Mary is the mother, and Roel is the father. Cues for their verbal exchanges are given by one another.

Through many observations of children playing in group situations, the development of the thinking processes in a social setting is observed. Play then sets the foundation for the child as a constructive, intelligent, and social citizen. The contributions of play to the development of thinking processes are the foundation of academic learning. Correspondingly, the foundation for social behavior and feelings of success, which are needed for dealing with other persons throughout life, are acquired in play.

## APPLYING THE DIMENSIONS OF PLAY AS THINKING AND SOCIAL PROCESSES

Can the concrete effects of play on children be observed? How can play enhance a child's growth? The answers to these questions help to make important use of play in assisting growth and showing the need for play as a critical component in learning and development. First, learning and growth result from involvement with the environment. As children imagine and fantasize, they are making important contacts with their environment. The youngsters, in turn, are trying to master, interpret, and understand the environment within their own context. People, objects, and situations are important parts of this environment. As they play ball with peers or play house, children are making important social discoveries. They are learning how to use language as a tool to deal with their surroundings. Whether arguing over a toy or building a castle in the sand with a peer, children are using thought processes to select appropriate behaviors, evaluate their response to situations, and make associations. When children are successful in their relations with others, they feel good about it. They learn that they are good and worthwhile. Many social successes enable them to get over occasional rough spots. Social situations are critical to children's learning about and interacting with their environments. The effects of pretend play as a thinking and socializing agent is based on a number of factors. Based on research results, these factors are examined below.

## FACTORS INFLUENCING PLAY

*Cultural and Economic Influences.* Singer (1973) suggests that cultural background, socioeconomic level, intelligence, verbal facility, and ability to control impulses and delay gratification are directly related to the development of imaginative thinking. The results of anthropological research of Whiting (1963) support marked differences in the extent to which children engage in sociodramatic play across cultures. Cultural differences seem to have a direct relationship within cultures upon make-believe, as well as their requirements for early work. Societies which demonstrate less work demands upon children have greater tendencies toward imaginative play behaviors (Singer 1973).

Prior to the past 15 years, it was assumed that play occurred naturally in all children at about the same age and regardless of their cultural or economic background. However, the results of recent research show that economic and environmental conditions do affect the quality and quantity of children's imaginative play. Areas of recent investigations include the following: (a) amount of space; (b) availability of play materials in the environment (e.g., John and Goldstein, 1967; Valentine, 1938; Van Alstyne, 1932); (c) development of language processes (e.g., Lovinger, 1964; Korchin, Mitchell, and Meltzoff, 1950); and (d) effects upon cognitive processes (e.g., Rosen, 1974; Freyburg, 1973; Smilansky, 1968). Each of the areas as they relate to imaginative play through economic conditions is discussed.

Within the first area of research, amount of space available to children, Gulick (1920) examines the factor of space and describes an absence of play among lower-class children in crowded metropolitan areas. Hetzer (1920) also proposes a lack of play among urban children due to the lack of space. Both Gulick and Hetzer support the belief that the idylic conditions of rural life assist the growth of play (Feitelson and Ross, 1973).

Second, research has also investigated the availability of materials as a contributing factor for the growth of play (Van Alstyne, 1932), as well as the conditions characteristic of optimal play environments (Valentine, 1938). Futhermore, through extensive work within lower-class, John and Goldstein (1967) discovered that the lack of available toys, or even household objects for play, result in stimulus deprivation.

The third area of research addresses economic influences from a language perspective. Studies by Lovinger (1964) and Korchin, Mitchell, and Meltzoff (1950) indicate differences in communicative abilities resulting from economic influences. Lovinger (1964) investigated the possibilities of (a) using sociodramatic play to increase verbal interactions and (b) whether the increased use of language in play would be transferable to cognitive tasks. Lovinger hypothesized that increased verbal interaction would transfer to cognitive tasks, as shown by children's overt abilities to use concepts and language they had developed internally.

Lovinger's study uses nonstructured interaction by (a) following, adding to, and enriching the natural play of children, (b) using experiences the children played out, and (c) creating a play situation and encouraging the children to become involved. Experimental children were trained to rehearse realistic experiences and stories through sociodramatic play, and those in control performed arts and crafts experiences. Results support Lovinger's hypotheses that sociodramatic play with preschool disadvantaged children results in an increased use of language and greater ability in dealing with cognitive tasks (as shown by significantly higher scores by the experimental over the control groups).

Lovinger proposes that the mere chance to become involved in sociodramatic play allows children conceptually to join disparate ideas and experiences. In the end, this produces the development of the flexibility which Smilansky (1968) feels is crucial to cognitive functioning and is extremely lacking within populations of disadvantaged children. From a similar language perspective, research results of Korchin, Mitchell, and Meltzoff (1950) also note language differences between children raised in differing economic environments. Within the study, middle-class children produce significantly longer fantasy stories than lower socioeconomic children.

The final area of research deals with the effects of socioeconomic influence upon cognitive abilities. In conducting the study, Smilansky (1968) compared the effects of play between 140 Israeli low-income children and middle-class nondisadvantaged youngsters between the ages of three and six. The results indicate that lower-class youngsters engage in much less dramatic and sociodramatic play than middle-class children. Smilansky supports the use of play training by stating that there is a need to provide children with additional knowledge, skills, and experiences not received within the home, by assisting them to use their already existing experiences and isolated concepts. Smilansky emphasizes that learning necessary skills and materials is insufficient to promote intellectual functioning. Rather, a method to accept, integrate, and process already existing information in a more effective and productive manner is necessary.

Smilansky proposes that play training, particularly in the form of role-playing, would enable children to develop new conceptual schemes from which additional information and experiences could be more meaningfully used in learning. Since deficiencies in play are results of children's inability to reorder segments of play episodes, the use of play training would overcome the deficits and lead to the use of problem-solving alternate modes of functioning. Smilansky states explicitly that the economically disadvantaged children lack the flexibility necessary to alter and resequence play episodes.

Based upon differences in play between children from high and low socioeconomic (S.E.S.) groups, Smilansky (1968) trained children of low S.E.S. on play behaviors reflective of high S.E.S. children. After only 67 hours of training, results showed that the lower S.E.S. children improved in both play behaviors and on mean frequences of (a) words used in a sentence, (b) contextual words, and (c) non-repeated words as compared to baseline language samples recorded prior to training. Smilansky supports Lovinger's (1974) hypothesis of sociodramatic play as a contributor to increased verbal abilities. Improvements in sociodramatic play lead to increases in verbal abilities (Lovinger, 1974). Several other studies also indicate an absence of pretend play among children representative of lower socioeconomic groups (e.g., Rosen, 1974; Freyberg, 1973).

Rosen (1974) attempted to see if Smilansky's (1968) findings would be generalizable in the United States, given differences in populations between the two studies. In addition to differential culture influences, the disadvantaged families studied by Smilansky were male-dominated and intact. The families in Rosen's study were single parent and primarily female-dominated. Rosen's findings support Smilansky to the extent that a sample of low income black kindergarten children engage in less sociodramatic play than white or black middle-class kindergarten children.

Further, Freyberg (1973) focused on experimental treatments of playlike behaviors and the relationship of play to cognitive functioning. Freyberg's population was 80 five-year-old black children from a lower socio-economic urban area. As a major result of eight 20-minute training sessions over a period of one month, the experimental group increased in the quantity of imaginative play. Freyberg concludes that (a) performance of these children on various measures could be increased through sociodramatic play and (b) their acquisition of cognitive and language skills could be facilitated by play training.

Research conducted by Griffing (1974) was similar to both Smilansky's (1968) and Freyberg's (1973) studies. Similar to Freyberg's population, the children were low and middle-class urban black children. In addition, Griffing defines play in accordance with Smilansky's definitions and protocols. Griffing's (1974) results show a significant relationship existing between socioeconomic status and play performance. Griffing's study further substantiates the influence of the economic variable upon children's play behaviors.

In summary, the previous research studies show the influences of cultural and economic factors upon children's play behaviors. Second, the results of these studies with disadvantaged populations support the use of imaginative play to overcome their observed developmental and learning deficits.

*Age Differences.* The influence of age was previously viewed as relationships between increasing age, the acquisition of the cognitive maturity, and essential intellectual functioning, prerequisite to the development of sociodramatic play. In this sense, age is a major factor that influences sociodramatic play.

Relevant to sociodramatic play and role-playing, Shantz (1975) notes that children below the age of six could not be expected to achieve the cognitive process of role-taking because of their intellectual immaturity. It is assumed, however, that even before the onset of the cognitive ability to role-take, play based upon role-playing would still be appropriate and beneficial toward the enhancement and facilitation of learning and development of young children.

Although age differences affect children's choices of role adoptions, the influence of sex differences is more prevalent throughout recent research. The following section discusses the variable of sex differences relative to role-playing and imaginative play.

*Sex Differences.* The influence of sex differences is reported in various research studies (e.g., Yawkey, 1979; Garvey, 1977; Pulaski, 1973; Singer, 1973; Hartley, et al., 1952).

Garvey (1977) describes three types of roles which children assume in sociodramatic play. They are (a) functional, (b) family, and (c) character roles—both stereotyped and fictional. The influence of sex is evident particularly in regard to the adoption of family roles. Garvey reports that both boys and girls tend to adopt male and female roles. Sex-typed choices are practically absolute in mixed-sex pairs. However, Garvey notes that within some all-male pairs, a few boys adopted functional roles generally played by girls, such as shopper or server, but never adopted female family roles. Similarly, females in same-sex pairs preferred to adopt female roles and exhibited little versatility, except to be a doctor, or in a few occasions, assumed the functional role necessary to repair a broken car.

Similarly, Hartley, et al. (1952) discuss the origins of sex differences as related to functional roles in dramatic play as early as three years of age. They observe role preferences between the sexes. The role of girls in play revolves around domestic themes where those of boys are wider, broader, and more varied. Erikson (1963) also reports differences in play behaviors on the basis of sex. The most significant sex difference was the tendency of males to erect structures, buildings, towers, or streets when playing with blocks. In contrast, females tended to play on tables as the interior of houses and showed little use of blocks. Males' play with blocks is further characterized by height, downfalls, and strong motions, while females showed static interiors which were open and peaceful.

Furthermore, Pulaski (1973) notes that males show a greater overt enjoyment in fantasy play than females. Low-fantasy males demonstrated a greater degree of motility than females. Pulaski also suggests that predisposition to fantasy is a stronger indicator than differences in sex in a determination of children's play behaviors. Sex differences appeared only on measures on which fantasy level had no strong effect (Pulaski, 1973).

Yawkey (1979) also reports sex differences in imaginative behaviors and on reading readiness measures. The results from the Singer Imaginativeness Inventory, which is an assessment of the level of imaginative predispositions in young children, showed that females score significantly higher than males on imaginative behaviors. Furthermore, Yawkey (1979) notes that females outperformed males on formal reading readiness in the study.

In sum, significant sex differences favoring females was reported in the (a) variety of roles assumed, (b) measurement of imaginative predisposition, and (c) assessment of reading readiness. In addition, Cicirelli (1972) and Staub (1971) provide indirect evidence that role-taking is more advanced in first-born older females, as compared to males. Further influences of birth order upon children's play are discussed in the following section.

*Influence of Birth Order.* Shantz (1975) proposes that family constellation is another factor that influences role-taking. Family constellation means the sex, age, and birth order of children. Although studies of role-taking and birth order tend to be biased, in that parental and sibling influences are often confounded by differential interactions of parents to first-born compared to later-born children, the fact remains that a number of studies agree that birth order does influence the growth and development of play.

Flavell (1968) speculates that children who interact with younger siblings have increased opportunities for role-taking and role-enacting. Similarly, Rubin, Hultsch, and Peters (1971) report decreased role-taking abilities in later-born children but increased abilities in first-born children. Singer (1973) notes further that high-fantasy participants have fewer older and more younger siblings. Further, a child with no other brothers or sisters in the family tends to develop greater role-playing abilities than youngsters with many siblings in the family unit (Rubin, et al., 1971). Similarly, Singer (1973) also reports a greater frequency of only children within the high-fantasy groups. All of the preceding research studies suggest that play development is related to decreased opportunities for peer contact typified by earlier birth order.

*Influences of Communication Processes.* Several studies (e.g., Yawkey, 1978; Wolfgang, 1974; Levin, 1973) focused on the importance of play and communication processes such as reading. To the extent that the cognitive skills are required in the development of reading abilities, it could be assumed that play could contribute toward the overall development of reading. As a result of the application of cognitive skills to reading, the following section examines particular studies which emphasized the development of various aspects of readings through imaginative play.

According to Wolfgang (1977), when children attain the level of operational thinking around the age of six or seven, symbolic play tends to assume the form of drama with predetermined scripts. The transition in thinking occurs at the time when fantasy begins to decrease and the children are cognitively ready to understand signs and symbols in reading. The rationale for play training in the area of reading development is that training in play behaviors would aid in the growth of communication skills which enable children to comprehend the highly arbitrary and complex rules of a formalized reading process (Wolfgang, 1974).

From a communication perspective, Yawkey (1978) finds that imaginative play strategies, used as a part of reading readiness activities, significantly facilitate the young child's initial oral language performance.

Yawkey (1978) further proposes that the addition of imaginative play to reading readiness and reading could result in a more effective teaching methodology to begin reading instruction.

Wolfgang (1974) also examined the importance of imaginative play and reading development and further substantiated the facilitative aspects of play training upon the development of reading abilities. The results show that imaginative play in its various forms of random activity, simple and complex symbolic and diagnostic symbolic, facilitate reading abilities. Furthermore, advanced readers in the study used higher levels of imaginative play than readers classified as disabled. Wolfgang draws a parallel between the components of play and initial reading. The playing child, through his toys, conceptualizes and conveys meaning that shows internalized thinking patterns. In reading, social signs or words replace toys as symbols, and the youngster uses a similar internalized thought process to give meaning to the sign. Thus, in both reading and imaginative play, there is the signifier (i.e., concrete) and the signified (i.e., abstract) object. The parallel implies that those children who develop the capacity to use high levels of integrated symbolic play later display success in using signifiers as signs in reading. In contrast, those who did not play symbolically reflect delays in their ability to utilize signs in reading. In addition, Wolfgang's research study was designed to compare the relationship between the cognitive aspects of reading and certain aspects of play in first-grade boys. The results indicate that, although the advanced readers achieved high levels of play, they were below the delayed readers in their ability to sustain play at the dramatic play level and to select a number of toys. Wolfgang suggests that while the advanced readers attained an equilibrium between assimilation (play) and accommodation, which assisted their advanced reading, the delayed readers were still assimilating freely in imaginative play. This appeared to interfere in their accommodation to reading "signs" or using "signifiers." Based upon the results, Wolfgang (1974) proposes that imaginative play can be used as a tool to facilitate reading abilities.

Similarly, in agreement with Wolfgang's findings, Fein (1978) also sees imaginative play as separating meaning from action and object. Here, imaginative play helps youngsters to develop and use a system of signifiers to represent meaning. Fein also suggests that play provides an opportunity to use signifiers to organize higher levels of meaning.

A study conducted by Levin (1973) assumed that reading comprehension requires the reader to use complex organizational strategies. The organizational strategies allow the reader to reduce meanings and interrelationships in the reading materials. Levin draws a distinction between two types of poor readers, which are (a) those who exhibit deficits due to a lack of prerequisite skills and (b) those readers who show problems due to differences in reading habits rather than a lack of skills. Levin proposes that adding imagery strategies to reading would facilitate comprehension. The findings were that (a) attention to visual imagery and thematic content produces dramatic improvements in the comprehension of poor readers and (b) adding visual imagery only produced an increase in those children with "differences" in comprehension, not "deficits." The results suggest that children without adequate prerequisite reading skills would not benefit from the additional strategies to increase reading comprehension through the role-playing.

In addition, the results of Saltz and Johnson (1974) showed that children who received training in sociodramatic play improved in reading skills, such as sequencing, reconstruction events, identifying causal relationships, and making inferences. In a second study, Saltz, Dixon, and Johnson (1977) reported increases in intelligence, as measured by standardized I.Q. tests, in the ability to distinguish reality from fantasy in those children who received, compared to those who did not receive, play training.

In summary, the selected factors of economic and cultural conditions, birth order, and communication processes show how fantasy play can be influenced. In the final section of this chapter, play as a thinking and socializing agent is described as a developmental phenomena.


PROCESSES IN PLAY

Having discussed the characteristics of and factors influencing imaginative play earlier in this chapter, the remaining section describes related developments in cognition and play. Learning is indeed child's play. Through play, children learn from and about their world. It provides one of the most natural opportunities for them to use their knowledge and abilities and, in turn, reflects their level of cognitive development (Lowe, 1975; Yawkey, 1983, in press).

Before children learn to distinguish their thought about something from the thing itself, objects that are not present physically cease to exist mentally (Bruner, 1973). Only while observing or interacting with their environment are children able to think about it. For them, objects out of sight are out of mind. Consequently, they are limited by sensorimotor thought to sensorimotor play.

Gradually, children learn to separate thought and object by cognitively representing (i.e., internalizing) their observations and interactions. This is a significant cognitive development because it enables children to imagine or think about objects that were encountered previously (Lefrancois, 1976). Play is now limited only by their imagination. Rosenblatt's (1977, in Tizard) analysis of toy play and Smilansky's (1968) study of sociodramatic play identify developments in play that parallel developments in representational thought.


DEVELOPMENTS IN TOY PLAY

Children do not intuitively know how to play with toys (Rosenblatt, 1977, in Tizard). Figure 1 shows that prior to 13 months of age, a toy provokes the same indiscriminate and investigative sensorimotor responses, regardless of its physical attributes or functional relations. For instance, 13-month-old Timmy will mouth, bang, and wave his teddy bear as readily as one of his blocks.

By the time they are 13 months old, children go beyond sensorimotor to representational toy play. They demonstrate the ability to separate thought and object by using a toy "as if" it were the real object (Yawkey, 1983, in press). Timmy, for example, will push his matchbox car along the floor or pretend to eat from a toy spoon.

These initial developments are gradually complemented by increasingly imaginative toy representations. At 16 months of age, nearly half of a child's toy play has its origins in representational thought. Timmy now drives his car up walls, on furniture, and over his body. In addition, he gracefully maneuvers his spoon through the air "as if" it is an airplane.

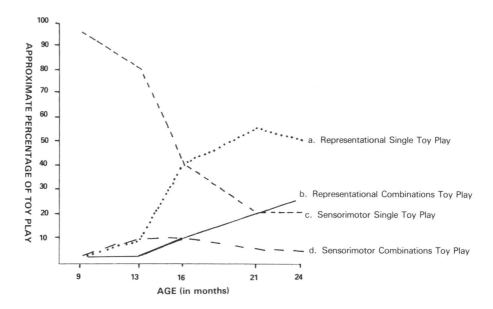

a. Representational Single Toy Play
b. Representational Combinations Toy Play
c. Sensorimotor Single Toy Play
d. Sensorimotor Combinations Toy Play

a.      Representational Single Toy Play—a toy is used "as if" it were another object
b.  Representational Combinations Toy Play—two or more toys are used "as if" they were other objects.
c.      Sensorimotor Single Toy Play—a toy provokes the same indiscriminate and investigative responses regardless of its physical attributes or functional relations
d.  Sensorimotor Combinations Toy Play—two or more toys used simultaneously provoke indiscriminate and investigative responses regardless of their physical attributes or functional relations

*Figure 1.* Description of Toy Play from 9 to 12 Months. Adapted and modified from Rosenblatt (In Tizard, 1977).

By 21 months, children begin to use two or more toys simultaneously "as if" they were the real objects. For instance, Timmy parks his race car in a shoebox garage and even lands his 747 spoon on a meterstick runway. Combining objects on the basis of their physical properties or functional purposes is the last significant development preceding role-play (Yawkey, 1983, in press).

## DEVELOPMENTS IN ROLE-PLAY

Children engage in role-play when they use actions and language to represent other people, objects, actions, or situations (Curry and Arnaud, 1974). Smilansky (1968) identifies four different representations performed by children during role-taking. These representations are (a) imitative actions and words, (b) imaginary object, (c) imaginary action, and (d) imaginary situation. Each type of representation is explained in the following paragraphs.

First, pretending becomes increasingly apparent by two years of age (Valentine, 1942; Piaget, 1962). As a result, children use actions and verbal descriptions to imitate familiar people and objects (Curry and Arnaud, 1974; Brainerd, 1978). Timmy, for example, likes to act "as if" he is Mr. Becker, the mailcarrier, or run about the yard "as if" he is a fire engine. Moreover, he is capable of enacting these roles simply by declaring that he is the mailman or a fire truck. By the time children are two-and-one-half years old, they are able to portray purely imagined experiences as well (Brainerd, 1978). It is now possible for Timmy to imitate what Mr. Becker might do when confronted by a growling dog or what a fire engine looks like after helping firemen battle a fire. Eventually, role-taking progresses from the mere imitation of people and objects to include the use of imaginary objects, actions, and situations.

The second type of representation is imaginary object. Three-year-olds do not require numerous props to add credence to their roles. Smilansky (1968) and Yawkey (1978) state that children elaborate their portrayals by using actions or words to represent real objects. Quite similar to pantomime, Timmy acts "as if" he has a pet tiger by pretending to feed it, pet it, and take it for a walk. If confronted by a bully, Timmy, for example, might boldly declare that Kitty, his pet tiger, does not like strangers. Make-believe actions and situations are also made possible through the use of language.

Third, words are internal representations for actions and situations (Lefrancois, 1976). So, by verbally creating actions and situations, children demonstrate their ability to use representational thought. For instance, Timmy pretends "as if" he is playing basketball by boasting about his great passes, fancy dribbling, or game-winning score.

The final cognitive representation evidenced during role-taking is the ability to use language to represent various play situations. This allows children to develop play themes for enacting their preferred roles (Yawkey, 1978). While throwing a ball, Timmy pretends that he is playing for the world championship or that he is the league's most valuable player by verbally expressing his role.

By the age of seven or eight, children's thought and play become dominated by increasingly realistic themes (Smilansky, 1968). This change results from intellectual, as well as other social, emotional, and environmental factors described in the first two sections of this chapter. At this age, children want to participate in activities that parallel reality as closely as possible (Curry and Arnaud, 1974). Games with rules, the next stage of play development, satisfies this requirement by providing an imaginative, but more structured, form of diversion.

In summary, children's pretend play and cognitive development are interrelated in a number of definite ways. Thinking and social processes form some of the basic ingredients in child's pretend play. In applying the dimensions of child's play, social situations are critical to his learning and development of ego continuity and group awareness. Cultural and economic influences and birth order contribute to the interrelationships between children's play and cognitive development. In considering this relationship, the various types and kinds of representations must also be described. These four different representations are imitative actions and words, imaginary objects, actions, and situations.

The success or failure of most efforts must be judged in terms of their usefulness. In response, this chapter is offered so that others will use play to help children develop a love for knowledge and a love for learning.

REFERENCES

Bandura, A. and Walters, R. H. *Social Learning and Personality Development.* New York: Holt (1963).

Barker, R. G., Dembo, L., and Lewin, K. "Frustration and regression: An experiment with young children," *University of Iowa Studies in Child Welfare, 18,* No. 386 (1941).

Blohm, P. J. and Yawkey, T. D. *Language and Imaginative Play Experience Approach (LIPEA) to Reading: Fact or Fantasy?* Unpublished manuscript, University of Wisconsin-Madison (1977).

Brainerd, C. J. *Piaget's Theory of Intelligence.* Englewood Cliffs, NJ: Prentice-Hall (1978).

Bruner, J. S. *Beyond the Information Given.* New York: Norton (1973).

Caplan, F. and Caplan, T. *The Power of Play.* Garden City, NY: Doubleday (1973).

Chauncey, J., ed. *Social Preschool Education* (Vol. 2). New York: Holt, Rinehart, and Winston (1969).

Cicirelli, V. G., "The effect of sibling relationship on concept learning of children taught by child-teachers," *Child Development, 43,* 282–287 (1972).

Curry, N. E. and Arnaud, S. H., "Cognitive implications in children's spontaneous role play," *Theory Into Practice, 13,* 273–277 (1973).

Elder, J. L. and Pederson, D., "Preschool children's use of objects in symbolic play," *Child Development, 44,* 500–504 (1978).

El'Konin, D., "Symbolics and its function in the play of children," *Soviet Education, 8,* 35–41 (1966).

Ellis, J. J. *Why People Play.* Englewood Cliffs, NJ: Prentice-Hall (1973).

Erikson, E. H. *Childhood and Society.* New York: Norton (1963).

Fein, G. *Play and the Acquisition of Symbols.* Unpublished manuscript, The Merrill-Palmer Institute (1978).

Fein, G., "A transformational analysis of pretending," *Developmental Psychology, 11,* 291–296 (1975).

Feitelson, D., "Developing imaginative play in preschool children as a possible approach to fostering creativity," *Early Child Development Care, 1,* 181–195 (1972).

Feitelson, D., "Patterns of early education in the Kurdish community," *Megamot, 5,* 95–109 (1954).

Feitelson, D. and Ross, G. S., "The neglected factor—play," *Human Development, 16,* 202–223 (1973).

Flavell, J. H. *The Development of Role-taking and Communication Skills in Children.* New York: Wiley (1968).

Freud, S., "Creative writers and daydreaming," in *The Standard Edition of the Complete Psychological Works of Sigmund Freud* (Vol. 9), J. Strachey, ed. London: Hogarth (1959).

Freyberg, J. T., "Increasing the imaginative play or urban disadvantaged kindergarten children through systematic training," in *The Child's World of Make-believe,* J. L. Singer, ed. New York: Academic Press (1973).

Garvey, C. *Play.* Cambridge, MA: Harvard University Press (1977).

Gebert, W. L. and Yawkey, T. D. *The Effects of Imaginative Play and Role Strategies on Language and Reading Learning and Development in Young Children.* Unpublished manuscript, The Pennsylvania State University (1980).

Gottlieb, S., "Modeling effects upon fantasy," in *The Child's World of Make-believe,* J. L. Singer, ed. New York: Academic Press (1973).

Greene, R. and Yawkey, T. D., eds. *Growth, Abuse, and Delinquency and their Effects on the Individual Family and Community.* Lancaster, PA: Technomic Publishers, Inc. (1982).

Griffing, P., "Sociodramatic play among young black children," *Theory Into Practice, 13,* 257–66 (1974).

Guick, Z. A. *Philosophy of Play.* New York: Schribner (1920).

Hartley, R. E., Frank, L. K., and Goldenson, R. M. *Understanding Children's Play.* New York: Columbia University Press (1952).

Hetzer, H. *Kindheit and Armut.* Hirzel, Leipzig (1929).

John, V. P. and Goldstein, L. S., "The social context of language acquisition," in *The Disadvantaged Child,* M. Deutsh, ed. New York: Basic Books (1967).

Johnson, J. E., Ershler, J., and Bell, C., "Play behavior in a discovery-based and a formal-education preschool program," *Child Development, 51,* 271–274 (1980).

Kelly, M. L. and Yawkey, T. D. *An Investigation of Crossties and Non-Crossties Programs and Sex Differences on Selected Abilities in Five-year-old Children.* Unpublished manuscript, The Pennsylvania State University (1978).

Korchin, S. J., Mitchell, H. E., and Meltzoff, J. A., "A critical evaluation of the Thompson Thematic Apperception Test," *Journal of Projective Techniques, 14,* 445–452 (1950).

Lefrancois, G. R. *Adolescents.* Belmont, CA: Wadsworth (1976).

Leiberman, J. N., "Playfulness and divergent thinking: An investigation of their relationship at the kindergarten level," *Journal of Genetic Psychology, 107,* 219–224 (1965).

Levin, J. P., "Inducing comprehension in poor readers. A test of a recent model," *Journal of Educational Psychology, 65,* 19–24 (1973).

Lovinger, S. L., "Sociodramatic play and language development in preschool disadvantaged children," *Psychology in the Schools, 11,* 313–320 (1974).

Lowe, M., "Trends in the development of representational play in infants from one to three years; an observational study," *Journal of Child Psychology and Psychiatry, 16,* 33–47 (1975).

Neumann, E. *The Elements of Play.* New York: MSS Corporation (1971).

Nicolich, L., "A longitudinal study of representational play in relation to spontaneous imitation and development of multiword utterances," *ERIC,* 103–133 (1975).

Pederson, F. A. and Wender, P. H., "Early social correlates of cognitive functioning in six-year-old boys," *Child Development, 39,* 185–193 (1968).

Piaget, J., "Piaget's theory," in *Carmichael's Manual of Child Psychology* (Vol. 1), P. H. Mussen, ed. New York: Wiley (1970).

Piaget, J. *Play, Dreams and Imitation in Childhood.* New York: Norton (1962).

Pulaski, M. A., "Toys and imaginative play," in *The Child's World of Make-believe,* J. L. Singer, ed. New York: Academic Press (1973).

Rosen, C. E., "The effects of sociodramatic play on problem-solving behavior among culturally disadvantaged preschool children," *Child Development, 45,* 920–927 (1974).

Rosenblatt, D., "Developmental trends in infant play," in *Biology of Play,* B. Tizard and D. Harvey, eds. London: Spastics International Medical Publications (1977).

Rubin, K. H., Hultsch, D. F., and Peters, D. I., "Non-social speech in four-year-old children as a function of birth order and interpersonal situation," *Merrill-Palmer Quarterly, 17,* 41–50 (1971).

Saltz, E., Dixon, D., and Johnson, J., "Training disadvantaged preschoolers on various fantasy activities on cognitive functioning and impulse control," *Child Development, 48,* 367–380 (1977).

Saltz, E. and Johnson, J., "Training for thematic-fantasy play in culturally disadvantaged children: Preliminary results," *Journal of Educational Psychology, 6,* 623–630 (1974).

Sears, R. R., "The influence of methodological factors on doll play performance," *Child Development, 18,* 190–197 (1947).

Shantz, C., "The Development of social cognition," in *Review of Child Development Research* (Vol. 5), E. M. Hetherington, ed. Chicago: University of Chicago Press (1975).

Sigel, I. E., "Developmental theory in preschool education: Issues, problems, and implications," *Early Childhood Education.* Yearbook of the National Society for the Study of Education, Chicago: University of Chicago Press, 13–31 (1972).

Singer, J. L. *The Child's World of Make-believe.* New York: Academic Press (1973).

Smilansky, S. *The Effects of Sociodramatic Play on Disadvantaged Preschool Children.* New York: Wiley (1968).

Staub, E., "The learning and unlearning of aggression," in *The Control of Aggression and Violence,* J. L. Singer, ed. New York: Academic Press (1971).

Sutton-Smith, B., "The role of play in cognitive development," in *Child's Play,* R. E. Herron and B. Sutton-Smith, eds. New York: Wiley, 252–260 (1971).

Valentine, C. W. *The Psychology of Early Childhood.* London: Methuen (1942).

Valentine, C. W., "A study of the beginnings and significance of play in infancy," *British Journal of Educational Psychology, 8,* 188–200 (1938).

Van Alstyne, D. *Play Behavior and Choice of Play Materials of Preschool Children.* Chicago: University of Chicago Press (1932).

Volpe, R., "Developing role-taking activity," *Child Study Journal, 9,* 61–68 (1979).

Volpe, R., "Orthopedic disability, restriction and role-taking activity," *Journal of Special Education, 10,* 311–381 (1976).

Vygotsky, L. S., "Play and its role in the mental development of the child," *Soviet Psychology, 5,* 6–18 (1967).

Yawkey, T. D., "More on play as intelligence in children," *Journal of Creative Behavior, 13,* 247–262 (1979).

Yawkey, T. D., "Pretend play of young children with make-believe companions," in *Child's Play: Developmental and Applied,* T. D. Yawkey and A. D. Pellegrini, eds. Hillsdale, NJ: Lawrence Erlbaum Associates (1983, in press).

Yawkey, T. D. and Fox, F. D., "Evaluative intervention research in child's play," *The Journal of Research and Development in Education* (1981, in press).

Yawkey, T. D. and Gebert, W. L. *An Identification of Selected Parenting Needs and Models for the Community Component of the 1979 Cycle of the Penn State Teacher Corps Project in Rural Appalachian Central Pennsylvania.* Research presentation delivered at the American Educational Research Association, Boston (April 1980).

Yawkey, T. D. and Gebert, W. L., "Role-playing and imaginative behaviors: Their effects on the child's learning and development," in *Early and Middle Childhood: Growth, Abuse, and Delinquency and their Effects on the Individual, Family, and Community,* R. Greene and T. D. Yawkey, eds. Lancaster, PA: Technomic Publishers, Inc. (1982).

Yawkey, T. D. and Silvern, S. *Investigation of Types of Play and Aural Language Growth in Young Children.* Research paper presented at the American Educational Research Association, San Francisco (April 1979).

# Children's play and language: Infancy through early childhood

**Anthony D. Pellegrini**
*The University of Georgia*

## INTRODUCTION

Recent research on the development of children's oral and written language has stressed the role of play with language, or speech play, as a correlate of language development (e.g., Cazden, 1974; Kirshenblatt-Gimblet, 1976; Pellegrini, 1981). This recent body of research will be reviewed in this chapter. First, speech play will be defined as a subset of play which facilitates children's metalinguistic awareness. The second section outlines specifically how children's play with the phonological, syntactic, semantic, and pragmatic aspects of language affects oral language development and metalinguistic awareness. Third, specific activities for implementing a speech play curriculum in school or institutional settings are suggested. Fourth, play as a basis for teaching literacy (i.e., reading and writing) will be outlined.

## PLAY WITH LANGUAGE

Play has been defined by Garvey (1977) as a spontaneous and pleasurable process with no extrinsic goal; the *process* of the play activity is more important than the *product*, or outcome, of the activity. Play with language, or speech play, has the speaker manipulating the phonological, syntactic, semantic, and pragmatic aspects of language, with little concern for the traditional goal of language, conveying a message to an interlocutor. Jakobson (1960) has described speech play as serving a poetic function (i.e., focusing upon the aspects of language, not upon the goal of language's instrumental function, i.e., the conveyance of a message). Through the process of playfully manipulating the aspects of language, young children gain a knowledge of the linguistic rule system. For example, through a word substitution game such as:

The car is here.
The house is here.
The garage is here.

children systematically manipulate words in one syntactic category, a class of nouns which can be used in the syntactic subject. Jakobson has observed children engaging in such forms of solitary speech and argued that these forms of play are not unlike the pattern drills used by adults to learn a second language. For example, a Vietnamese adult learning English might be exposed to the following drill:

The tree is brown.
The car is red.
The dog is fat.

This type of speech play, or drill, provides the child with an opportunity to discover syntactic rules of the language.

Children's awareness of the rules of their linguistic system has been labelled metalinguistic awareness (Cazden, 1974; C. Chomsky, 1979; Gleitman and Gleitman, 1979). Metalinguistic awareness is often an end product of speech play because, in play episodes, the rule system of language itself is manipulated. Cazden (1974) has stated that in speech play, the elements of the rule system are opaque; that is, the rules of the language system are the focal point of activity, whereas the conveyance of meaning is transparent or not focused upon. In typical discourse settings, structural elements are transparent. In discourse, speakers concentrate on conveying a message. In play, speakers explore the elements of language.

C. Chomsky (1979) has described varying degrees of children's metalinguistic awareness. Metalinguistic awareness means, according to Chomsky, having conscious, or explicit, access to the rule system governing language. Conscious access involves being able to discriminate between well formed and unacceptable words and utterances. In contrast, an implicit, or unconscious, knowledge would have children using the language correctly and manipulating the aspects of language in play but not being conscious of the rules which govern these manipulations. The extent to which players are consciously aware of the linguistic rules typically varies with age and with their varied experiences with the language system.

Children's conscious access to the different rule systems of language, as Chomsky stated, is limited by developmental status. Chomsky's research has shown that children in kindergarten through fourth grade have conscious access to the rules of the sound system of language (i.e., phonology) (Chomsky, 1979). Chomsky found that kindergarteners were consistently aware of phonological rules, such as the rule that one written letter represents many different sounds. She did not find conscious access to syntactic rules, rules relating to the ordering of words in a sentence, until children were in fourth grade. That is, children younger than fourth graders could not discriminate between grammatical and ungrammatical utterances. The Gleitmans' (1979) research extends Chomsky's results to the extent that they too found that kindergarteners did not detect violations of syntactic rules. They also found seven-year-olds were able to detect syntactic anamolies but were unable to detect semantically implausible sentences. Metalinguistic awareness of the rules governing different aspects of language seems to develop from phonological to syntactic awareness to semantic awareness.

Speech play, then, like other forms of play, is a mode whereby young children explore and manipulate the many aspects of their language system. From infancy, children engage in speech play, initially alone, then in social settings, in an effort to master the different aspects of their language system. Metalinguistic awareness is one end product of speech play. Chomsky hypothesized that if children were metalinguistically aware, they should be more adept users of their whole language system; that is, they should be more fluent readers and writers.

## PLAY WITH ASPECTS OF THE LANGUAGE SYSTEM

Researchers have found that children play with aspects of language in hierarchic order (Kirshenblatt-Gimblet, 1976). That is, children tend to play with phonological aspects before they play with syntactic or semantic aspects. The social, or pragmatic, aspect is the last aspect to be played with. In this section, play with each aspect of language will be discussed separately, in the order in which each appears. A word of caution first. First, Cazden (1977) has warned that describing speech play in terms of separate categories should not be taken to mean that each category develops independently. Secondly, because children play with one aspect of language before another aspect, it does not mean that the former developmentally precedes the latter. For example, that children play with sound before meaning does not mean that phonological development precedes, or is independent of, semantic development. Bruner's (1974, 1975) recent research has shown that infants convey meaning to their caretakers through gestures, without the use of sounds, even though phonological play is observed before semantic play.

Children are first observed playing with phonology or the sound system of language (Garvey, 1977). During the babbling period, from birth to approximately ten months of age, infants explore all the sounds in the human linguistic system. Gradually, they limit their sound play to manipulation of only the sounds of their native language (DeStefano, 1978). These repetitive and rhythmic vocalizations usually are generated when prelinguistic children are in pleasurable states. During this time, they learn the "shape" of their language by experimenting with stress and intonation patterns present in the language they hear. Such speech play is characterized by chanting sequences of nonsense syllables which have the same stress and intonation patterns as words in their native language. This type of speech play is typically generated by children to accompany their solitary play actions.

Children two years of age and older play with the phonological aspects of language in social settings (i.e., in the presence of adults or other children). The play of two-year-olds with the phonological aspects of language is exemplified by use of conventional noises, through syllable repetition, to identify actions, events, and objects (e.g., *ruff-ruff, vroom*). Gibberish is another common form of play with phonological aspects of language in social settings. In gibberish, children talk to each other or generate rhymes with utterances governed only by phonological rules, such as *Deema dima doma nig* (Kirshenblatt-Gimblet, 1976). Gibberish is contrasted with jabberwacky, the form of phonological play engaged in by older children. Jabberwacky uses both phonological and syntactic rules to generate utterances, such as *Twas brillig and slithy tones* (Kirschenblatt-Gimblet, 1976). More common phonological play for school age children has them jointly reciting rhymes to accompany games and actions (e.g., jump rope rhymes).

Spontaneous play with the phonological aspects of language not only helps children master the rules of their native language's system, but it also helps them prepare for the reading process. Phonological play often involves children exploring relations between graphemes (written letters) and phonemes (groups of sounds). Through play, children become aware of the sounds which correspond to certain letters.

Between two to three years of age, children have been observed playing with the syntactic and semantic aspects of language (Garvey, 1977; Weir, 1962). Play with syntax, or how words are ordered in utterances to convey meaning, has children manipulating whole sentences or syntactic categories within sentences. For example, children have been observed changing declarative sentences into interrogatives. In such cases, children explore the syntactic transformations causing these changes. Weir's son Anthony manipulated whole sentences through reduction/expansion techniques (for example, *Here it is. Here it is now. Here.*). Anthony also explored acceptable words for individual syntactic categories through word substitution games (e.g., *He runs fast. He swims fast.*). Noun to pronoun substitution games were also observed (e.g., *John is here. He's here. Who's here?*).

Word placement games also have a semantic, or meaning, dimension. Weir found that Anthony's replacement games differed qualitatively from games of older children and adults. Anthony's first word replacement games consisted of using words which were syntagmatically related (for example, *The mat is here. The cat is here.*). Syntagmatic classifications are based on superficial, perceptual associations between stimuli such as phonetic similarity between words. Syntagmatic groupings co-occur naturally in children's speech and physical environments. Older children's replacements tend to be conceptually, or paradigmatically, related (for example, *The pin is here. The needle is here.*). Paradigmatic groupings consist of words from the same conceptual category. This qualitative shift from syntagmatic to paradigmatic grouping reflects the different conceptual systems of younger and older children. Ability to use words that are paradigmatically related in word replacement games is a result of children's general cognitive development.

Other forms of semantic play involve narratives and rhymes which accompany action games such as jump rope or hop-scotch. Preschoolers' narratives and rhymes are quantitatively different from the narratives of school-aged children. Younger children's narratives are generally shorter than older children's because of memory limitations. Young children use concatention, or the joining together of a series of rhymes and lists to lengthen their narratives and rhymes. *Ninety-nine bottles of beer on the wall* is a good example of using lists to lengthen a rhyme.

As was stated above, children's play with the various aspects of language is limited by children's cognitive make-up (for example, the child's use of syntagmatic, as opposed to paradigmatic, word replacements). Given this, teachers and/or caretakers can use the child's word play to gain insight into his/her cognitive processes and developmental status. For example, if his/her semantic word play does not group conceptually related words (paradigmatic grouping), he/she may not be able to group items conceptually; he/she may only be capable of grouping items which they observe together (syntagmatic groupings).

Children initially explore the various aspects of language while engaged in solitary word play. At two to three years of age, the main arena for children's speech play changes from a solitary to a social contest. Speech play in social contexts involves not only explorations of the structural aspects of language (i.e., phonology, semantics, and syntax) but also explorations of the pragmatics of language or how language is used in a social context. Successful play with the pragmatics of language involves children being able to discriminate between situations which will support or not support such speech play. Players must be able to determine the appropriateness of using a particular form of language in a particular setting; that is, they must use a form of speech play which will elicit a response from other interlocutors. Interlocutors must be able to recognize the rules of the particular form of speech play in order to respond to speech play overtures. If the interlocutor does not recognize the form of language used, the play initiator will have to explain the form or the rules of the speech play if the play episode is to be sustained (Pellegrini, 1982). When the children are in a situation where interlocutors do not respond to their speech play overtures, they can elicit a response only if they are able to explain the rules of the speech play event so that interlocutors know how to respond appropriately. In the case of preschoolers' dramatic play, the initiator of a play episode may have to clarify his opening line in a play episode, "Hi, Jane," to his playmate by stating, "I'll be the husband, and you be the wife." In short, successful pragmatic speech play involves players not only matching contextual markers with appropriate forms of play, but also necessitates their clarifying players' roles when communication breaks down.

Contextual markers which can help children determine the appropriateness of initiating speech play in certain settings include the activity engaged in by the group and the composition of the group itself. Specific activities of groups of children are typically accompanied by a specific form of speech play. For example, jump rope is accompanied by a set repertoire of rhymes. A child familiar with the speech repertoire for a specific game could move into a group playing that game if he/she knew the form of speech acceptable for that game. Children could move into or initiate social dramatic play (Smilansky, 1968, 1971) episodes based on a similar context, corresponding-speech repertoire relationship. For example, a child moving into a dramatic play context where other players were "playing school" would have to adopt the language of a student or a teacher. If the student used language characteristic of another play context (e.g., cops and robbers), the teacher-student play context would be disrupted. Players must use a speech repertoire which is acceptable in a certain context if the play episode is to be sustained.

The second contextual marker which helps speakers identify the most appropriate speech repertoire to use is the social composition of the play group itself. Bernstein (1971) has shown that when speakers who know each other very well get together, the meaning of their language is highly implicit. That is, when a group shares a common knowledge base, they will use a form of language whose meaning is clear to them but may be unclear to listeners who do not share their common body of knowledge; different social groups use different codes of language.

Groups of children often consciously use language which only their peers can understand. The use of different types of idiosyncratic language often distinguishes social cliques from each other. For example, Labov (1968) observed different New York City gangs using distinctly different forms of slang. The form of slang used by a gang member marked his gang membership.

Bernstein stated that individual groups may use their own forms of jargon or even secret language to reinforce the solidarity of the group.

Obscure jargon or secret languages has been used by youth groups to conceal secrets from rival groups or adults (e.g., *nadset,* the teenage language of Burgess' *Clockwork Orange,* 1962, French backward talk, Sherzer, 1977, or pig-latin). Children often judge whether to use a particular form of language in a certain group, depending on whom constitutes the group.

Play with the pragmatic aspect of language relates directly to the speaker's ability to communicate in a social context. In order for players to be competent communicators in different settings, they should have direct or various experiences with a number of different types of communicative contexts. That is, children should use language in many different settings (e.g., student-teacher, peer-peer, doctor-patient, judge-defendant). These varied experiences can be provided by way of field trips, dramatic play, and children's literature.

These pragmatic skills are obviously applicable in non-play discourse contexts. The ability to use situationally appropriate language and to switch speaking styles according to contextual demands has been labelled communicative competence by Hymes (1972). Children from preschool to high school levels can be exposed to different forms of social dramatic play so that they can become more adept at manipulating the pragmatic aspects of language. Older children may benefit from role-playing episodes involving job interview role-playing. Nonstandard English speakers (e.g., Blacks and Appalachians) would benefit from role-playing episodes whereby they must switch from nonstandard to standard dialects, and vice versa, according to context. In this way, practice is gained at matching contextual variables with the situationally appropriate forms of language.

## SPEECH PLAY IN AN EDUCATIONAL CURRICULUM

Speech play should be viewed as one component of an educational curriculum whose goal is to facilitate children's metalinguistic awareness and communicative competence. Such a curriculum should include activities which encourage children to use language to convey meaning as well as the poetic function of language (i.e., playing with language). These different uses of language complement each other as general facilitators of metalinguistic awareness.

As young children mature, they play with language less easily and less frequently (Cazden, 1974). Adults tend to be mostly concerned with the instrumental function of language. That is, adults tend to minimize the importance of playing with language as a vehicle for developing metalinguistic awareness. Biber (1975) has suggested that teachers of young children will support speech play in the curriculum only if they can see traditional educational payoffs from using speech play. That is, if speech play is to become part of the curriculum, they must see a positive relation between speech play and achievement in reading and writing and between language production and comprehension. The previous sections of this chapter on speech play and language development provided some of that evidence. Other empirical studies have found strong relations between various forms of speech play and performance on standardized language, reading, and writing achievement tests. Pellegrini (1980), for example, found that children who engage in dramatic play are better readers and writers than children who engage in functional and constructive play.

## PLAY AND TEACHING LITERACY

A primary goal of formal schooling in modern society is to teach literacy. Literacy typically involves the ability to produce (through writing) and comprehend (through reading) written language. It has been suggested by a number of researchers (e.g., Olson, 1977; Cook-Gumperz, 1977; Pellegrini, DeStefano, and Thompson, 1983) that the ability to use "literate oral language" is a necessary precursor to attaining literacy. As a result, teaching children to use literate, or explicit, language is an implied goal of schooling. The intent of this section of the chapter is to show how children's use of literate oral language is related to reading and writing. Next, a technique to teach the use of literate language, social dramatic play, will be outlined.

Literate oral language, or explicit language, conveys information solely by means of words; meaning is lexicalized or encoded into words. That is, all the information to be supplied to a listener is encoded verbally (lexicalized). The speaker does not rely on contextual cues or shared assumptions about meaning to convey the meaning of his/her oral text. For example, a child requesting a crayon from another child in explicit language would say, "I need that red crayon," not "I need that" and point to the red crayon. In the second utterance, the speaker is relying on contextual information to convey meaning; the contextual information is the pointing gesture to the specific crayon that both speaker and listener are looking at. For meaning to be conveyed in the latter utterance, the listener must be physically present to see the speaker point to the crayon; only then can the listener understand the referent for *that*. If the listener does not share the contextual cues, the speaker's utterance will be ambiguous; the listener will not know the exact referent for *that*. In the explicitly encoded utterance, the speaker's conveyance of meaning is dependent on the text alone because the referent for *that* is defined verbally as a *red crayon*. A listener can comprehend this utterance without having access to contextual cues. The speaker is conveying meaning solely by lexicalizing the meaning. Ambiguity often arises between a speaker's intended meaning and the listener's comprehension of the text when the speaker assumes that the listener is attending to a specific contextual cue. If this assumption is not met, ambiguity results.

Another source of possible ambiguity in conveying a message is where the speaker assumes that he/she and the listener share common experiences and then relies on these common assumptions to help convey the message. The literate speaker does not rely on shared assumptions of meaning with listeners to convey information. Contrast "The movie was great" with "*Superman II* was great." In the first utterance, the speaker's opinion of the movie could be conveyed only if the speaker and listener shared prior knowledge, the correct referent for *the movie*. If the listener had a different movie in mind, the message would not have been conveyed successfully. In this case, the speaker's assumption about a shared common experience with the listener was not valid, and ambiguity resulted. In the second utterance, the speaker makes no such assumptions of shared knowledge. The specific title of the movie is verbally encoded; as a result, possibilities for ambiguity are minimized. Literate oral language, therefore, can be characterized as language which conveys meaning textually or with words. It does not convey meaning contextually or by relying on shared knowledge assumptions. All information is lexicalized. When speakers rely on contextual cues or assumptions about shared knowledge, the possibility for miscommunication exists because of the ambiguity of this text. These assumptions can only be met when speakers and listeners share the same physical space and are from very similar backgrounds.

The ability to produce and comprehend explicit oral language is very similar to reading and writing, respectively. The writer of an informative text assumes that he/she and the reader will not be sharing the same physical space when the reader is processing the text; thus, gestures cannot be used to convey meaning. Similarly, the writer assumes that people who read his/her text will not share a large common body of knowledge. Thus, in order to convey the information maximally and avoid ambiguity, the writer must lexicalize all his/her relevant assumptions. He/she should not assume that the reader has implicit access to these assumptions. Verbally encoding the assumptions makes them explicit. Reading comprehension is similar to gaining meaning from explicit oral language. The listener/speaker can get meaning only from text. The "you know what I mean" assumption is replaced with an explicit "I mean the following—" statement. Meaning is made explicit, and implicit assumptions are minimized.

Given this similarity between conveying and comprehending literate oral language and reading and writing, it will be suggested here that a program which stimulates the use of explicit oral language be incorporated into schools' literacy training curricula. The specific pedagogical technique to be outlined here, social dramatic play (Smilansky, 1968, 1971), has been shown to be an effective facilitator of children's using explicit language in preschool and elementary school settings (Pellegrini, 1980, 1982; Pellegrini and Galda, 1983). The relation between children's use of explicit oral language in social dramatic play and literacy (the ability to write and read) has been clearly documented (Pellegrini, 1980). Further research (Pellegrini and Galda, 1983) has established a causal link between children engaging in social dramatic play and their ability to answer questions and retell stories they enacted in play.

Social dramatic play, as defined by Smilansky (1968), includes the following criteria: imitative role play (e.g., "I'll be the mommy."); make-believe in regards to objects (e.g., a broom represents a guitar.); actions (e.g., eating with an invisible spoon); and situations (e.g., "Let's play school."). These criteria relate specifically to children's ability to use explicit oral language. More specifically, the symbolic (imitative role-playing and make-believe) and the social interactive aspects of social dramatic play necessitate players' using explicit language if play is to be successfully initiated and sustained.

In order for children to meet the symbolic criteria for social dramatic play (imitative role-play and make-believe), they must symbolically transform roles, objects, and actions from their functions in the real world to their play functions. For example, John is transformed into Daddy, and a cardboard box is transformed into a car. The meaning of play roles, actions, and objects are something other than what they appear to be. For this reason, prospective players cannot understand the fantasy functions of roles and objects by their being merely physically present in the play arena. Sharing of realistic contextual cues with other players is not sufficient for meaning to be conveyed because the context has been re-defined according to a fantasy theme. The ability of children to understand one child's play initiation is typically the result of the play initiator's ability to verbally define the symbolic transformations (e.g., "I'll be the doctor, and you be the patient."). If the play initiator does not use explicit language to introduce the episode, ambiguity over role and setting definition often results (e.g., "This is good," when the child is pretending to eat paper). Where play initiations are ambiguous, other children typically ask for clarification of the ambiguous utterance (e.g., "What's good?"). The play initiator then usually will be more specific about the fantasy transformation (e.g., "This is my cake."). Thus, because of the symbolic nature of social dramatic play, children must make their assumptions explicit about role and prop transformations by verbally defining them (Pellegrini, 1982).

Children are motivated to generate explicit language in social dramatic play because they enjoy it. As was shown in the above example, the children themselves help players lexicalize meaning by asking for clarification when ambiguity arises.

The teacher can help children in the symbolization process by varying children's play props. For example, children who have trouble sustaining fantasy play may need realistic props to guide their play. The teacher may provide a baby doll to be used in the housekeeping corner. After children sustain play with the realistic prop, the teacher should replace it with a more ambiguous prop (e.g., a rolled-up towel). In order to sustain play around the towel/baby prop, children will have to make the transformation explicit (*letting the towel be the baby*). Finally, the teacher should remove the prop altogether so that players will have to rely totally on a linguistic representation for baby. The children will no longer be able to rely on context to convey meaning.

The sustained social interactive aspect of social dramatic play also helps children develop the ability to use decontextualized oral language. Observers of children's play (e.g., Piaget, 1965; Rubin, 1980) suggest that children become sociocentric in direct proportion to their engagement in social dramatic play. When they engage in play with their peers, children's individual concepts of the play episode often conflict or vary. For example, two children may want to play the same role, or they may disagree as to the sequence of story events. When children's viewpoints conflict with each other, they become aware, often abruptly, that there are ways of viewing the world other than their own. Their self-centered, egocentric perspectives must be compromised if the specific episode is to be sustained. Through play, children learn that they must begin to value others' perspectives. If they do not, they will begin to find that they are less welcomed in social groups. Thus, through social dramatic play, they are motivated to become more sociocentric.

Sociocentricity is related directly to one's ability to use literate language. Sociocentric children will encode, verbally, assumptions they are trying to convey because they realize that different people may have different perspectives and, consequently, interpretations of a text. It is the egocentric child that assumes that others know implicitly what he/she is trying to convey (e.g., "You know what I mean?").

To summarize, it has been suggested that, by engaging in social dramatic play, children will develop the ability to encode information explicitly in words. The symbolic aspect of play necessitates the use of explicit language because the play roles and props are being defined somewhat idiosyncratically; each play episode may have different play role/prop assignments. If these roles are not defined, other children will not understand the play episode being initiated. The social interaction aspect of play helps children become sociocentric beings. In play and its resultant role/theme/prop conflicts, children must learn to accept other players' views of the world. This ability to recognize perspectives other than one's own is necessary if children are to be motivated to make explicit their assumptions about the definitions of the play themes.

Smilansky (1971) suggests specific ways in which teachers can implement a social dramatic play program. She stated that children's play should meet all symbolic and sustained social interaction criteria outlined above. She suggests that the teacher or teacher's aide help children meet the criteria in one of two ways. First, the adult, as an observer of children's play, can help children meet criteria they fail to meet by posing questions or suggestions relevant to those specific criteria. For example, "Oh nurse, can you please help this child?" can be used as a suggestion to facilitate children's social interaction. Second, the adult, as an actual player, can help children meet criteria. For example, "I'm the nurse, may I help you?" can be used to help children meet the criterion, make-believe in regard to roles. Note that in both forms of intervention, the adult addresses children in their play roles; it is important not to break the play mode.

The intent of this section was to outline a rationale for including social dramatic play in the school curricula. Social dramatic play, as defined here, should help the teaching of literacy skills; in that reading and writing and the oral language generated by children in play have children relying on lexicalization to convey meaning. This advocation of play as a valuable mode of teaching literacy has been documented in the educational (e.g., Pellegrini, 1980, 1982) and psychological literature (e.g., Saltz, Dixon, and Johnson, 1977). Hopefully these "hard" data will be used to document the utility of play in school. The studies show that play is not a waste of time and does have "traditional" educational payoffs, as has been suggested.

The ability to use symbols to present concepts is a process which undergoes rapid development in young children. This symbolic process can be observed in children's everyday actions. For example, in the housekeeping corner of a school, a child may use a shoe to represent a telephone receiver. In this instance, the shoe is a symbolic representative for another object, a telephone. It is a symbolic representation because the shoe is not a direct copy of the telephone. The symbolic process becomes more abstract when the child does not use a concrete prop to represent the telephone. He/she can symbolically represent a phone by making a ringing sound and holding an invisible receiver to his/her ear. Children are beginning to use highly abstract symbols (such as an invisible telephone) during the early childhood period.

The language skills taught in most early education programs require children to use symbolic processes. More specifically, in learning to read and write, children must recognize the symbolic relations between a written word (a sign) and word meaning (the concept a sign refers to). This relation is an abstract relation because the form of the word representing the concept (for example, *cat*) is in no way related to the reference for the word. *Cat* has come to denote a pet because speakers of English have agreed upon this meaning. Any other combination of sounds (e.g., *goot*) could represent cat if it were socially agreed upon.

Research has shown that children's abilities to write and read individual words is related to their ability to engage in symbolic play (Pellegrini, 1980). Teachers can facilitate children's symbolic development by encouraging them to use abstract props in dramatic play episodes. As children develop, teachers should encourage them to use words to represent play props and concepts. In this way, children gain practice in using words to represent concepts. This process is basic in order for children to use written words to represent concepts.

Just as young children's use of props in dramatic play becomes more abstract (e.g., shoe then should represent a phone), so too does their use of written signs to represent concepts. Various researchers have shown that children's initial efforts at conveying meaning through the written medium is undifferentiated scribble (Clay, 1975; Luria, 1977). Luria (1977) stated that during this beginning phase of writing, children do not realize that specific written words convey a specific message. Children in the next stage have this realization; they use pictographs to convey meaning. Pictographs are picture-forms which represent objects. Toward the middle of the kindergarten period, children use adult-like written word forms to convey meaning. These written signs are sometimes idiosyncratic to the extent that children often use invented spelling in word construction.

The remainder of this section on literacy will discuss a procedure by which teachers can guide children through the writing continuum described above. The goal of this procedure, partially derived from Luria (1977), is to help children realize the symbolic relations between specific written word forms and specific word meaning. Word writing skills can be facilitated by using a procedure whereby children use written words as a memory aid. To develop this skill, young kindergarteners should be told to try to write down words that the teacher dictates to them. For example, a teacher dictates a list of five words. Children should attempt to write down each word as they are dictated. Young kindergarteners typically use undifferentiated scribble to represent each word. After the dictation, the teacher should ask each child to tell the meaning of each scribbled word. In this way, children realize that specific written forms represent specific concepts.

If some children are reluctant to attempt to write the dictated word, they should be seated next to a student who does scribble after each word. The children who are reluctant to write will eventually model this behavior. Through such activities, children begin to recognize that written words correspond to a meaningful referent.

To complement this activity, teachers should also work on other aspects of children's symbolic functioning, activities wherein young children practice encoding meaning into different media. More specifically, a teacher can use a real baseball as a basic referent object. Children can be made to realize that different symbols can represent a baseball. They can be shown the following symbols which represent the ball: a photo of the ball; a drawing of the ball; and the word *ball*.

In order to move children from scribble to the stage of meaningful written representation, Luria (1977) recommended that teachers vary words according to quantity of the words to be written. For example, children should be asked to write: five cows; three cows; four dogs; six dogs. In this way, the specific content of children's scribble will vary specifically according to a specific referent. After this type of activity, scribble will be more meaningful for children, in that they will vary the content of the scribble according to the concept to be represented.

Teachers can further facilitate the development of content specific forms of writing by dictating names of "conspicuous objects" (Luria, 1977). Conspicuous objects vary according to size, color, or shape. An example of such objects might be a large house and a small house, a blue car and a red car, and a square pool and a round pool. By having to use writing to encode these object pairs, children are forced to reflect on the *form* (or content) of the medium.

Children should use pictographs to record words dictated by the teacher in order to develop further the notion that specific words have a specific content. At first, the words dictated should be words that can be represented with pictures easily (e.g., *house*). Children should be encouraged to draw general pictures for each word. They should read their completed lists back to the teacher and/or peers. The result of this type of activity is twofold. First, they realize that specific written forms convey specific meaning. Second, they realize that written forms convey meaning to others; written symbols are read.

The next, and final stage of children using written symbols to represent concepts has them using adult-like words. Children are moved out of the pictograph stage by having them attempt to write words that cannot be pictorially represented (e.g., *hungry*). They should be given written lists of words from which to choose. More specifically, a teacher dictates a list of abstract words. Students choose what they think is the appropriate word from a teacher-provided list of written words. Students should then copy each word from the list. After the dictation is complete, students and teachers should match the appropriate written words with the dictated words.

The writing process outlined in this section of the chapter was meant to supplement activities which facilitate children's more general symbolic development. The instructional processes outlined here, enabling children to use written words to represent concepts, follows this developmental continuum. Children are motivated to write because they see it as useful; it helps them remember, and it helps them communicate to others. Their writing of individual words, however, only gradually approximates adult forms. Researchers (e.g., Read, 1975) have found that early elementary school students are still acquiring the adult-forms; their spelling of individual words become conventionalized. Teachers can best facilitate children's writing by having them experiment with different symbolic media along with the written medium.

REFERENCES

Bernstein, B. *Class, Codes, and Control, Vol. I.* London: Routledge & Kegan Paul (1971).

Biber, B., "Awareness in the learning process: A comment," in *Dimensions of Language Experience*, C. Windsor, ed. New York: Agathon Press (1975).

Bruner, J., "The ontogenesis of speech acts," *Journal of Child Language, 2,* 1–19 (1974).

Bruner, J., "From communication to language—A psychological perspective," *Cognition, 3,* 255–287 (1975).

Burgess, A. *A Clockwork Orange.* New York: Ballentine (1962).

Cazden, C., "Play with language and metalinguistic awareness: One dimension of language experience," *The Urban Review, 7,* 23–39 (1974).

Cazden, C., Review of *Speech Play.* Kirschenblatt-Gimblet, B., ed. Philadelphia: University of Pennsylvania Press (1976), in *Harvard Educational Review, 47,* 430–435 (1977).

Chomsky, C., "Consciousness is relevant to linguistic awareness." Paper presented at International Reading Association Seminar on Linguistic Awareness and Learning to Read. Victoria, British Columbia (June 1979).

Clay, M. *What did I Write?* Aukland, New Zealand: Heinemann (1975).

Cook-Gumperz, J., "Situated instructions," in *Child Discourse*, S. Ervin-Tripp and C. Mitchell-Kernan, eds. New York: Academic (1977).

DeStefano, J. *Language, the Learner, and the School.* New York: Wiley (1978).

Erickson, E. *Childhood and Society.* New York: Norton (1950).

Garvey, C. *Play.* Cambridge: Harvard (1977).

Gleitman, H. and Gleitman, L., "Language use and language judgement," in *Individual Differences in Language Ability and Language Behavior,* C. Fillmore, D. Kempler, and W. Wang, eds. New York: Academic Press (1979).

Hymes, D. Introduction to *Functions of Language in the Classroom,* C. Cazden, V. John, and D. Hymes, eds. New York: Teachers College Press (1972).

Jakobson, R., "Linguistics and poetics," in *Style in Language,* T. Sebeok, ed. Cambridge: MIT (1960).

Kamii, C. and DeVries, R. *Physical Knowledge in Preschool Education.* Englewood Cliffs, NJ: Prentice-Hall (1978).

Kirshenblatt-Gimblet, B., ed. *Speech Play.* Philadelphia: University of Pennsylvania Press (1976).

Labov, W., Cohen, P., Robins, C., and Lewis, J. *A Study of the Non-Standard English of Negro and Puerto Rican Speakers in New York City, Vols. I and II.* Washington, DC: U.S. Office of Education (1968).

Long, J., Pellegrini, A., and Horwitz, S., "An empirical investigation of the ESEA Title I evaluation system's no treatment expectation." Paper presented at the Annual Meeting of the AERA, San Fancisco, CA (April 1979).

Luria, A., "The development of writing in the child," *Soviet Psychology, 17,* 65–114 (1977).

Olson, D., "From utterance to text," *Harvard Educational Review, 3,* 257–281 (1977).

Pellegrini, A., "Establishing and assessing goals and objectives in early childhood education programs," *Journal of Instructional Psychology, 8,* 15–19 (1981).

Pellegrini, A., "Identifying causal elements in the thematic-fantasy play paradigm," *American Educational Research Journal* (in press).

Pellegrini, A., "Preschoolers' generation of cohesive text in two play contexts," *Discourse Processes, 5,* 101–107 (1982).

Pellegrini, A., "The relationships between kindergarteners' play and reading, writing and language achievement," *Psychology in the School, 17,* 530–535 (1980).

Pellegrini, A., DeStefano, J., and Thompson, D., "Saying what you mean: Using play to teach literate language," *Language Arts, 60,* 380–384 (1983).

Pellegrini, A. and Galda, L., "The effects of thematic fantasy play training on the development of children's story comprehension," *American Educational Research Journal, 19,* 443–452 (1983).

Piaget, J. *The Moral Development of the Child.* New York: Free Press (1965).

Piaget, J. *Play, Dreams, and Imitation.* New York: Norton (1962).

Read, C. *Children's Categorization of Speech Sounds in English.* Urbana, IL: NCTE (1975).

Rubin, K., "Fantasy play," in *Children's Play,* K. Rubin, ed. San Francisco: Jossey-Bass (1980).

Saltz, E., Dixon, D., and Johnson, J., "Training disadvantaged preschoolers on various activities: Effects on cognitive functioning and impulse control," *Child Development, 48,* 367–380 (1977).

Sanches, M. and Kirshenblatt-Gimblet, "Children's traditional speech play and child language," in *Speech Play,* Kirshenblatt-Gimblet, B., ed. Philadelphia: University of Pennsylvania (1976).

Sherzer, J., "Play languages," in *Speech Play,* Kirshenblatt-Gimblet, B., ed. Philadelphia: University of Pennsylvania (1976).

Smilansky, S., "Can adults facilitate play in children?" in *The Child Strives Toward Self-Realization,* S. Arnaud and N. Curry, eds. Washington, DC: NAEYC (1971).

Smilansky, S. *The Effects of Sociodramatic Play on Disadvantaged Preschool Children.* New York: Wiley (1968).

Tallmadge, G. and Wood, C. *User's Guide.* Mountain View, CA: RMC Research Corp. (1976).

Weir, R. *Language in the Crib.* The Hague: Mouton (1962).

# Fill and dump play: Mastery of handling skills and object permanence

**Bruce L. Mann**
*Cornell University*

## INTRODUCTION

In an influential paper, Robert White (1959) first introduced the notion of an innate drive to master the environment. White suggested that this need to competently interact with the environment is responsible for such early achievements as grasping, crawling, walking, acts of focal attention, memory, and the exploration (and manipulation) of novel objects and places. His conceptualization of what he called "effectance motivation" was in response to a growing discontent in the realms of both psychoanalytic ego psychology and behavioral learning theory with motivational explanations involving primary drives and tension-reduction. Although early psychoanalytic theory had focused on the instinctual and unconscious energies underlying the personality, by 1959, theorists had begun placing substantial emphasis on the adaptive functions of the ego in order to account for effective ego development. Similarly, learning theorists were becoming more and more dissatisfied by the continual need to invoke secondary reinforcement as an explanation for most human behavior.

According to traditional psychoanalytic theory, the infant's persistent exploration of and play with objects is motivated by a need for tension-reduction. White argued that the healthy young child plays with objects, not to neutralize instinctual energies, but because that interaction is, in itself, gratifying. Further, he asserted that effectance motivation can be found in its purest form in the exploration and play of young animals and children. He wrote,

> The infant's play is indeed serious business. If he did not while away his time pulling strings, shaking rattles, examining wooden parrots, dropping pieces of bread and celluloid swans, when would he learn to discriminate visual patterns, to catch and throw, and to build up his concept of the object? When would he acquire the many other foundation stones necessary for cumulative learning? (pp. 224–225).

In the infant's exploratory play with small objects, White found the purest example of the drive toward mastery. However, more than 20 years later, the research community has yet to satisfactorily document the presence of effectance motivation in object related play. Nor has there been much success in developing a measure enabling us to distinguish behavior motivated by a desire for mastery from behavior enacted for other reasons.

The general purpose of this study is to assess White's notion that the infant's play with objects is motivated by a desire to master the objective environment. More specifically, the focus will be on a commonly observed, but rarely discussed, type of play called "fill and dump play." Fill and dump play, in its simplest form, involves the repetitious dropping of small objects into a container, after which the container is emptied, and the process is begun over again. Three questions will be addressed: (1) How can the presence of effectance motivation be determined? (2) What physical skills (if any) are mastered through fill and dump play? (3) What cognitive skills (if any) are mastered through fill and dump play?

## MEASURING EFFECTANCE MOTIVATION

Weisler and McCall (1976), in a widely read review of the literature on exploration and play, complain that "despite the frequency of discussions on the function of play, there is almost no research on these issues." They go on to ask, "What is the role of effectance behaviors in play?" (p. 503). Yarrow (1981) similarly notes that almost no research has been devoted to the issues involved in the measurement of mastery behavior. He attributes the lack of research to the difficulties inherent in translating higher order concepts, which seem to have a face validity (e.g., intelligence, altruism), into measures which index them. In short, although very appealing as a concept, mastery has neither precise definition nor accepted methods of measurement.

A substantial contributor to the problem has been the variable, unpredictable nature of play behavior. At least four types of inconsistencies have frustrated those researchers who have attempted to identify the regularities in play suggestive of mastery attempts. First, the instability of the structure of the behavioral sequences in play stands out in comparison to the stability of behavioral sequences in, for example, exploration (Hughes, 1979). Second, there seems to be very little cross-situational consistency (Rubenstein, 1967). Third, there is only minimal cross-age consistency in children's play behavior (Cox and Campbell, 1968). Lastly, given toys similar in appearance and function, there is little cross-toy consistency in the frequencies of behaviors (Mann, 1981). McCall (1974), despite an ambitious effort, failed to reduce play behavior to any underlying factorial dimensions. He argues for the need for multivariative approaches in studying free play and concludes, "Although it raises serious but not insoluble methodological problems," the theoretical importance of the issues justify the effort (p. 81).

In his germinative paper, White suggested what one might look for in attempting to quantify the presence of effectance motivation. Mastery behavior is "directed, selective and persistent" (p. 217).

> The urge toward competence is inferred specifically from behavior that shows a lasting focalization, and that has the characteristics of exploration and experimentation, a kind of variation within the focus (p. 222).

The latter characteristic, "variation within the focus," has been documented and, as earlier discussed, has frustrated attempts to generalize about the play process. However, the idea of a "lasting focalization" in effectance motivation has produced some results of interest.

McCall (1974) found "density of manipulative exploration" to be the play variable which correlated highest with other indices of developmental maturity. Density, "the extent to which the infant spends his time in concentrated manipulation of the objects with relatively little time wasted in looking around," was related to longer periods of play, greater rates of manipulation with visual regard, more circular responses, and more parallel play. Two additional findings point to density as an effective index of mastery behavior. First, highly dense play was more common with complex toys (e.g., blocks) than simple toys (e.g., rattle). Second, between 8.5 and 11.5 months of age, play became denser. As will later be discussed, this period is also when infants begin attempts at mastering the physical world around them (Piaget, 1967).

Yarrow (1981) found four indices of mastery motivation useful in assessing whether individual subjects were relatively strong or weak on a mastery motivation trait. The four indices were persistence, task completion, latency to task involvement, and positive affect. One of those indices, persistence, closely resembled McCall's density variable. Yarrow defined persistence as the length of time spent in task-directed behavior, and suggested that maintenance of attention reflects the extent to which subjects felt challenged by a task.

Thus, some empirical support does exist for White's claim that infant play behavior with objects is related to mastery of objective reality. Further, the research seems to support White's assertion that mastery is behavior which is directed, selective, and persistent. This study will similarly use a measure of behavioral density to identify those play behaviors motivated by mastery needs. In response to Yarrow's (1981) criticism that previously used measures of mastery are lacking in even the most elemental psychometric criteria, this study will present evidence validating the measure before proceeding to conclusions about the presence of mastery in object play.

## FILL AND DUMP PLAY

Very little is known about the developing relationship between infant and object, except that the relationship is of tremendous importance to the infant. Burton White (1978), in his famous studies of the infancy period, estimated that, on the average, eight-month-old infants spend 20 percent of their time manipulating small objects. At 20 months, infants average 18 percent of their time in play with small objects, and at 30 months, still average 14 percent. To put these percentages in perspective, at 30 months, the child still spends twice as much time in object-related behavior as he does in socially related behavior. Given these numbers, the lack of research on object play is puzzling. Yet, as Weisler and McCall (1976) note, "there is a need for the measurement of qualitatively different behaviors, their time course, and their sequence as a function of even the most elementary parameters (e.g., age, sex, toy characteristics, etc.)" (p. 502).

Yarrow (1981) was able to distinguish three types of object-related behaviors where mastery motivation was present: (1) manipulating objects to produce effects or to secure feedback (e.g., shaking a rattle); (2) practicing skills just emerging (e.g., discrimination of shapes and the fine motor skills required to place the shapes in the proper holes); and (3) solving detour or barrier problems. B. White (1978) theorizes that there are two major types of exploratory play—exploration of all the attributes of new objects and mastery experiences or the practice of simple skills on objects.

> One of the simple skills they practice as early as Phase V (5.5 to 8.0 months) is the emptying of objects out of containers, one at a time. Once those objects are all emptied out, they may very well be systematically returned, one at a time, with the child pausing to examine them as he does so (p. 123).

R. White's (1959) seminal article also keys on "fill and dump play" as involving the practice of skills. According to R. White, fill and dump play is behavior leading to the effective grasping, handling, and letting go of objects.

Prior to R. White's article, Gesell and Ilg (1943) had published some age norms for fill and dump play. At six to nine months, infants will drop objects into a container; by 12 months of age, they enjoy filling, emptying, and refilling containers with blocks; and by 18 months, they will put up to 10 blocks in a container. Elsewhere (Braga and Braga, 1974; Arnold, 1955) are reports of fill and dump play with a plastic cup between 6 and 12 months of age, with cereal bowls from 9 through 12 months, with baskets from 9 through 16 months, and with plastic jars with lids from 13 through 21 months. Tasks involving fill and dump play are included on the Gesell, the Bayley, and the Cattel tests of infant development.

Despite these age norms, there have been no attempts to document the mastery of handling skills through fill and dump play. This study will attempt to identify mastery attempts, detail those physical skills being developed, and examine the order of their development. Further, practice of skills is by no means limited to the physical realm. We can expect that at the same time that the infant is perfecting his grasping skills, he is also learning much about the nature of the objective world and perfecting his object-concept.

## OBJECT PERMANENCE AND FILL AND DUMP PLAY

If little is known about the emergence of physical skills through play, less is known of the emergence of cognitive skills which are less observable or quantifiable. Weisler and McCall (1976) point to this topic as being of singular importance.

> Despite the fact that the child's mental development should be revealed in the nature of this play, this has rarely been studied. Of major interest would be charting the sequence of qualitative acts during the same period and the relationship between the emergence of certain cognitive skills and specific acts during play (p. 504).

However, as noted earlier, it is difficult to identify even the presence of mastery attempts in free play. Documenting a link between those mastery attempts and cognitive skills further complicates the matter, especially given disagreement as to the course of development of those cognitive skills.

There exists a substantial amount of face validity to the hypothesis that fill and dump play is related to the development of object permanence. In fill and dump play, the infant repetitively brings into sight objects which were hidden in a container, only to remove them from sight by returning them to the container. The operation is often repeated dozens of times and is easily elaborated upon if provided with a lid (with or without holes) or a nesting arrangement of objects. Indeed, in repeating this operation over and over, the infant seems to be repeating those adult behaviors which had earlier puzzled him. In the daily life of the infant, the first object permanence problems confronted are likely to arise from watching adults put things away or leave the room. In fill and dump play, are infants working on an object permanence problem?

There is heated disagreement on the ages associated with the varying degrees of competency of the infant's object concept. Piaget's (1967) classical formulation of the development of object permanence has been assaulted by, among others, Gibson (1966) and Bower (1974). These researchers have typically presented simplified tasks to infants and found Piaget's age ascriptions too conservative. Other researchers (Dodwell, et al., 1976; Goldberg, 1976), however, have failed to replicate these findings, and others (Acredolo, 1977; Bremner and Briant, 1977) have produced findings supportive of Piaget's original claims which are now largely accepted.

This study will attempt to relate the development of object permanence to mastery attempts in fill and dump play by comparing the frequency of mastery attempts at different ages to the frequencies which would be expected given the theorized ages at which infants acquire a sense of object permanence. Thus, it is first necessary to detail the course of development of object permanence as described by Piaget.

At 10 to 11 months of age, the infant first begins to achieve a sense that objects have a permanence outside of his own perceptual experience. This sense, however, is far from perfect. At this age, infants will look for an object only in the most likely place, even if the object is hidden elsewhere before their eyes. Significantly, this is the first age that infants are commonly observed in fill and dump play (White, 1978), even though at six months, they are capable of putting a small block in a cup (Gesell and Ilg, 1943).

Between 12 and 18 months of age, the infant makes great strides in acquiring a sense of object permanence. Piaget calls this the period of "tertiary circular reactions and discovery of new means by active experimentation." This period is characterized by highly repetitive explorations of objects. During this time, the infant learns to look for objects in the position resulting from the last visible placement. Still, invisible displacement of toys typically confound the infant. LeCompte and Gratch (1972) and Saal (1975) found that it was not until 18 months of age that infants are surprised by an invisible change of objects and search for the missing toy. There is general agreement that by 24 months of age, infants can find objects hidden by invisible displacement and that the object-concept is perfected.

Given this course of development for object permanence, if fill and dump play involves mastery of object permanence, the following predictions seem reasonable:

1. Until 10 months of age, mastery attempts in fill and dump play will be very rare. This holds especially true, given the expectation that mastery appears in free play well after a capacity appears in a testing situation.
2. Mastery attempts will be uncommonly observed betwen 10 and 12 months. As the infant is just starting to develop a sense of object permanence, the repetitive practice and experimentation characteristic of mastery play will be beyond the reach of most infants.
3. Mastery attempts will be commonly observed between 13 and 18

months. During this time, the infant makes great strides in solidifying his object concept. He tests his newly formed understanding on a variety of objects and in a variety of situations. Mastery attempts should peak during this period.

4. Mastery attempts will remain high between 19 and 24 months of age. During this time, the object concept is perfected; the infant finally becomes liberated from his immediate perceptions.

5. Beyond 24 months of age, there will be a substantial drop in the number of mastery attempts. Having achieved a sense of object permanence, mastery is attempted at new challenges in the child's environment. Fill and dump play loses its purpose.

## HYPOTHESES

Summarizing, the general purpose of this study is to assess White's notion that play with objects is motivated by a desire to achieve mastery. Since mastery is thought to occur on both the physical and cognitive levels, two hypotheses are proposed:

Hypothesis 1: Fill and dump play leads to the mastery of emerging physical skills, such as removing objects from containers one at a time, dumping objects from containers, placing objects in a container, lid fitting, and posting objects through holes in a lid.

Hypothesis 2: The period of mastery for fill and dump play will closely correspond to the period during which object permanence is mastered (as suggested by Piaget). Similarity in mastery periods will be seen as evidence that fill and dump play is the infant's attempt to achieve object permanence.

It was deemed necessary to validate the measure of mastery before confidence could be placed in the findings pertaining to the above hypotheses. Thus, analyses will be reported concerning the discriminative, concurrent, and predictive validity of the measure of mastery attempts which was used.

## SUBJECTS

Thirty-six subjects between 10 and 34 months of age (mean=20.2 months) comprised the sample for this study. Subjects were broken down into six age groups for purposes of data analysis: 10 to 12 months (mean=11.5); 13 to 15 months (mean=14.3); 16 to 18 months (mean=17.3); 19 to 23 months (mean=20.5); 24 to 28 months (mean=27.2); and 29 to 34 months (mean=31.3). Each subject saw each of the three toys during two visits. All 36 subjects returned for their second visit within ten days of the first. The order of toy presentation was counterbalanced.

All subjects were from middle class homes; 19 were boys, and 17 were girls. Although attempts were made to select only subjects who did not have any of the experimental toys at their homes, the popularity of one of the selected toys made this very difficult, especially as it was also seen as important not to bias the sample in favor of subjects who did not like toys. Thus, five subjects had prior experience with Baby's First Blocks, and two had prior experience with Balls In A Bowl.

## SELECTION OF TOYS

Three toys were chosen for study. Three criteria were used in selecting those toys: (1) toys must be intended for fill and dump play; (2) toys must be recommended for similar age ranges; and (3) toys must physically meet high quality standards. The toys chosen were:

1. Balls In A Bowl (BIAB); Johnson & Johnson Baby Products. This toy consists of a yellow tinted transparent bowl and three clear plastic balls with spinners inside. The bowl is open at the top, and despite there being a lip around the opening, infants can squeeze both hands inside the bowl. BIAB is recommended for ages 7 to 28 months.
2. Baby's First Blocks (BFB); Fisher-Price Toys. This toy consists of a bright yellow, cylindrical container and 15 blocks. The cylinder is 15 inches in height and 7 in diameter and also includes a lid that snaps on and has three differently shaped holes through which blocks can be posted. The blocks vary in shape (round, square, and rectangular) and in color (red, green, and blue). BFB is recommended for children between 6 and 24 months of age.
3. Box and Blocks (B&B); Johnson & Johnson Baby Products. This toy consists of a square red container (5 inches per side), a nesting arrangement of six open-ended blocks, and a lid with two holes (round and square). Two blocks are cylindrical, and four are rectangular. The rectangular blocks come in two very different sizes. The cylinders are open at both ends, the rectangles at one end. The open end of the blocks are grooved to permit snug end-to-end fitting. The different sizes and open ends permit blocks to be put inside other blocks, as well as inside the container. B&B is recommended for children between 10 and 34 months of age.

## ASSESSMENT ENVIRONMENT

Testing took place at the Environmental Programs, Inc., observation laboratory, a small carpeted room (about 12 feet by 12 feet) equipped with a one-way mirror. The laboratory room was kept devoid of all furniture to minimize distractions.

## PROCEDURE

Setting the rules: Upon entering the laboratory room, the basic format and purposes of the project were explained to the parent. Only one adult was permitted in the testing room with the child. The parent was told that she should not interfere in her child's play except (1) to take care of the child's comforting, feeding, or toileting needs, (2) in the case of a very young infant, to help the child get a toy which was slightly out of reach, or (3) to restrain play if it became aggressive beyond the bounds permitted at home. The parent was told that if the child handed them the toy, they should accept it but remain a passive participant allowing the child to govern the play episode.

Demonstrating the toys: The testing sessions began with the introduction of the first toy, accompanied by a demonstration of the capabilities of the toys. Upon concluding the demonstration, the toys were placed within easy reach of subjects. Each toy was given virtually the same demonstration at the start of each of three trials.

Timing Procedure: Subjects were given three trials with each toy. On the first trial, subjects were given as much time as they needed to make contact with the toy. Once contact with the toy was initiated, a stopwatch was started. If contact was lost, the stopwatch was stopped until the infant reestablished contact with the toy. If contact was not reestablished for a period of 45 seconds, that trial ended, and a new trial was initiated. Following demonstrations on the second and third trials, subjects were given only 45 seconds to reinitiate contact with the toy.

A play session with a given toy was terminated either after 30 minutes of recorded contact time or after three trials had ended. The first toy was then removed, the second toy brought into the room, and the timing procedure repeated.

Behavior Inventories: An inventory of behaviors was compiled for each of the three toys. For two of the toys, the inventories were developed using, as a basis, the written observational records made during testing of the Johnson and Johnson toys when they were prototypes. The inventory for BFB was based on expected behaviors and then slightly modified after an initial round of testing.

Observation Procedure: Observations were made every 15 seconds using a one-zero sampling procedure. Behaviors occurring within each 15 second interval were recorded. This procedure has been shown to yield accurate estimations of both the frequency and duration of behaviors (Goodenough, 1928; Wright, 1950; Kummer, 1971; Hutt, 1966; Hinde, 1964; Suomi, 1971; Smith and Connally, 1972).

Mastery Attempts: The behavior inventories yielded frequency scores for each of the fill and dump behaviors studied. Of those behaviors, three are "simple" fill and dump play behaviors—removes object from container singly, dumps objects from container, and puts objects in container. One of the behaviors studied, posting objects through holes in the lid, is an elaboration on simple fill and dump play requiring a higher degree of fine motor control and an awareness of different shapes. The final behavior studied, lid fitting (and removing), is behavior which is complementary to fill and dump play in the sense that lids go with containers. Also, lid fitting is a necessary part of posting objects through the lid, since the lid must be removed to take the blocks out of the container and then fit back on to permit the fitting of blocks through the holes.

Unfortunately, the easily obtained observation frequency scores for each of these behaviors do not necessarily reflect the frequency of attempts at mastery. Based on the procedure used in this study, it seems reasonable to expect behavior frequencies to reflect not only spontaneous age appropriate mastery attempts, but also behavior enacted in the service of mastering other behaviors (e.g., being necessary to first remove the objects from the container before it is possible to attempt mastery at dropping them in) and nonspontaneous imitations of the toy demonstrations. Thus, some way of deriving mastery attempt frequency scores was needed. Following R. White (1959), McCall (1974), and Yarrow (1981), behavioral mastery attempts were determined by identifying dense occurrences of a given behavior. Density of behavioral enactment was operationally defined as three observations of a given behavior in an interval of one minute. The only exception to this rule was "dumping." Only two observations of dumping per minute was necessary for a mastery attempt to be scored, since to repeatedly dump objects from the container, it is necessary to first refill the container. Later, an empirical look will be taken at the relationship between frequency of behaviors and frequency of mastery attempts.

Reliability: The interrater reliability of the observational procedure was determined by correlating the frequency of behaviors obtained by Observer 1 with the frequencies obtained by Observer 2 on a subset (17 percent) of the play sessions. The obtained coefficient of agreement was a more than satisfactory .86. The two sets of scores substantially differed for only one session (r=.37). The discrepancy between observations 1 and 2 lay in confusion as to whether six instances of dropping were instead six instances of throwing. With agreement on this point, the coefficient for that session becomes .95.

## VALIDITY OF THE MEASURE

The first order of business was to validate the measure quantifying mastery attempts. Three types of evidence bearing on the issue of validity will be examined: (1) discriminant validity will be determined by examining the relationship between behavioral frequency and the frequency of behavioral mastery attempts; (2) concurrent validity will be assessed by examining the Spearman Rank-Order correlations between the empirically obtained "Average Age of Mastery Attempts" (AAMA) for each of the behaviors and judges, rankings of the difficulty of mastering each behavior relative to the others; and (3) predictive validity will be determined by examining Kendall's Tau coefficient of relationship between a ranking of the behaviors based on AAMA and the pattern of the behaviors at which individual subjects showed mastery attempts. The tendency should be for subjects to show mastery attempts at only those behaviors similar in levels of difficulty.

Discriminant Validity—Behavioral Frequency and Mastery Attempts: As was discussed in the previous section, the observed frequency of a given behavior includes not only mastery attempts, but imitation of demonstrations and enactment of behaviors in the service of mastering other behaviors. Thus, only particularly dense episodes of a behavior (defined as three or four recorded occurrences per minute, except for dumping) were identified as mastery attempts. Two of the behaviors "Dumps Objects—BFB" and "Dumps Objects—B&B" were eliminated from all further analyses because mastery attempts did not occur with enough frequency (more than once per subject in any given group).

Pearson Product-Moment presents correlations between frequency of behaviors and mastery attempts, both within age groups and within behavioral categories. Each age group reveals a relationship which is between .88 and .94, a consistency suggesting that, while certainly not independent of behavioral frequency, frequency of mastery attempts assesses something slightly different. In other words, a similar amount of variance in behavioral frequency scores is accounted for by frequency of mastery scores in each age group.

The greater variability of correlations within behavioral categories than within age group categories is also of interest. On the one hand, mastery attempt scores for "Removes Object Singly—B&B" exhibited almost no (r=.09) relationship to frequency scores; on the other hand, mastery attempt scores for "Posting Through the Lid—BFB (and B&B)" exhibited almost a perfect linear relationship with frequency scores (r=.99 and .97). The low correlation makes sense, given that B&B is a more complex toy, and removing the blocks is likely to occur mostly in the service of other behaviors. The high correlations for "posting through the lid" make sense, given that it was the latest developing behavior. Therefore, any attempts were likely to be mastery oriented.

A close look at the curves for frequency and mastery attempts shows that mastery attempt scores improve on behavioral frequency scores in three ways. First, there is one behavior category for which mastery attempt scores and behavior frequency scores peak at different ages and show entirely different curves. Most commonly, however, although both the curves and peaks for frequency of behavior and frequency of mastery attempts were similar, the mastery attempt scores showed far greater delineation of peaks and valleys. This sharper delineation of age group trends suggests that the measure of mastery attempts succeeded in accentuating the dynamic, developmental nature of the behaviors under study.

Concurrent Validity—Average Age of Mastery Attempts (AAMA) and Judged Rankings of Behavioral Difficulty: For each age group, the number of mastery attempts for each behavior was multiplied by the mean ages, then summed across age groups and divided by the total number of mastery attempts. The purpose of this procedure was to obtain average ages of mastery attempts for each behavior. Table 1 presents a ranking of the 11 behaviors by AAMA's and includes the averages themselves. The AAMA's will later be looked at as interesting in their own right. The purpose here is to establish further credibility to the measure of mastery attempts by demonstrating that it possesses concurrent validity, that is, agreement with other ways of determining an order of difficulty for the behaviors under study. The validation measure chosen for comparison was rankings made by three judges of the difficulty of each of the 11 behaviors. All three judges, although unaware of mastery scores, had participated heavily in the data collection phase of this study, and thus, had a substantial store of casual impressions upon which to draw in determining their rankings. Judges were instructed to order the behaviors according to their difficulty, in other words, which behavior-object combinations they thought would develop first, second, etc.

*Table 1. Ranking of behaviors by average ABE of mastery attempts and correlations with judges ranking of behaviors.*

| Behavior | Average Age (Mo.) of Mastery Attempts | Ranking by AAMA | Ranking by Judge 1 | Ranking by Judge 2 | Ranking by Judge 3 |
|---|---|---|---|---|---|
| ROS-BFB | 15.11 | 1 | 2 | 1 | 1 |
| ROS-BIAB | 16.67 | 2 | 1 | 1 | 2 |
| ROS-B&B | 18.11 | 3 | 3 | 3 | 2 |
| LF-BFB | 18.40 | 4 | 5 | 10 | 6 |
| FC-BIAB | 19.79 | 5 | 4 | 4 | 5 |
| FC-BFB | 20.81 | 6 | 6 | 4 | 4 |
| LF-B&B | 20.93 | 7 | 8 | 11 | 8 |
| FC-B&B | 21.62 | 8 | 7 | 6 | 9 |
| DO-BIAB | 23.28 | 9 | 9 | 7 | 7 |
| PTL-BFB | 24.78 | 10 | 10 | 8 | 10 |
| PTL-B&B | 25.21 | 11 | 10 | 9 | 11 |
| Spearman Rank Order Correlation (x = .85) | | | .97 | .64 | .93 |

Key
ROS = Removes Objects Singly
  LF = Lid Fitting
  FC = Fills Container
  DO = Dumps Objects
 PTL = Posts Through Lid
BIAB = Balls In A Bowl
 BFB = Baby's First Blocks
 B&B = Box & Blocks

Table 1 lists the rankings given by each of the three judges and the Spearman Rank-Order correlation between each judge's "intuitive" ranking and the empirically obtained ranking. Correlations ranged from .64 to .97, and overall averaged .85. A $t$ test shows the least of these correlations to be significant at p<.025. Thus, there is substantial agreement between the relative rankings made intuitively and through quantifying mastery attempts. The ability to quantify a phenomenon, of course, is of special benefit, less in determining relative orderings than in deriving precise identification of age-related means and learning curves. That topic will be returned to shortly.

Predictive Validity—Pattern of Mastery Attempts Within Subjects: Predictive validation of the mastery attempt measure requires evidence that the measure helps order the seemingly unpredictable pattern of play of individual subjects. If the ranked order of behavioral mastery which was derived from AAMA's is accurate, then a subject's play should not include mastery attempts at behaviors at opposite ends of the continuum, "Removes Objects Singly—B&B" (#1) and "Posts Through the Lid—B&B" (#11). In other words, the pattern of mastery attempts should not be random; mastery attempts should be observed only for those behaviors ranked similarly according to AAMA's in the play of a given subject. Kendall's Tau coefficient allows a test of the prediction that subjects should not show mastery attempts for two behaviors ranked as developmentally distant and should show mastery attempts for behaviors ranked as developmentally close.

For this study, the inversion term in the Kendall's Tau equation becomes "all adjacent rankings which do not conform to the prediction that behaviors adjacent on the ordering should both either be or not be in a phase of mastery." Thus, the data was examined to determine the behaviors for which each subject showed mastery attempts. Then the inversions in the pattern of mastery attempts was counted for each subject, and Kendall's Tau was calculated. Table 2 presents the coefficients of relationship for each age group and the probability that this coefficient is a random event. Overall, the coefficient was .32 (p<.07). Four of the age groups showed a highly non-random pattern of mastery attempts (.40, .50, .47, and .47). The play of subjects in two age groups (16 to 18 months and 24 to 28 months) showed almost no relationship to AAMA predictions.

## MASTERY OF PHYSICAL SKILLS

Given that the measure of mastery attempts is valid and reliable, it is interesting to look at the course of mastery for the behaviors under study.

*Table 2. Predictive validity: Kendall's Tau coefficient.*

| Age Groups (Months) | Number of Inversions | Possible Total | $\tau$ | Z | p |
|---|---|---|---|---|---|
| 10–34 | 122 | 360 | .32 | 1.45 | .926 |
| 10–12 | 18 | 60 | .40 | 1.82 | .966 |
| 13–15 | 15 | 60 | .50 | 2.27 | .988 |
| 16–18 | 28 | 60 | .07 | .32 | NS |
| 19–23 | 16 | 60 | .47 | 2.14 | .984 |
| 24–28 | 29 | 60 | .03 | .14 | NS |
| 29–34 | 16 | 60 | .47 | 2.14 | .984 |

The behaviors will be discussed in order of AAMA, starting with the behavior mastered earliest.

Removes Objects Singly—BFB: AAMA=15 months. Mastery attempts occurred almost exclusively during the period between 13 and 15 months of age. A full 64 percent of the mastery attempts occurred for this age group, suggesting both that mastery is consistently attempted at this time and that the behavior is quickly learned.

Removes Objects Singly—BIAB: AAMA=16.67 months. The period of mastery for this behavior was longer than that for BFB, extending from 10 months through 18 months. Mastery attempts fell off by 60 percent for subjects 19 through 28 months of age and 90 percent for subjects 29 through 34 months. Removing the balls from BIAB was more difficult than removing blocks from BFB probably because the lip around the bowl's opening presented more difficulty than the straight-edged opening on BFB's container.

Removes Objects Singly—B&B: AAMA=18.11 months. The period during which this behavior was mastered is of similar length but occurs later than the period for the previous behavior-object combination. Extending from 14 through 23 months, efforts at mastering removal of blocks from B&B was complicated by the nesting arrangement of the B&B pieces.

Lid Fitting—BFB: AAMA=18.40 months. Mastery of this behavior occurred between 14 and 24 months of age. Note that lid fitting behaviors were far more common with BFB than with B&B, probably because the BFB lid provided many more rewards. It's circular lid did not require the effort needed to line up the edges of B&B's square lid with the square container. Thus, the lid was successfully snapped on more frequently. Also, the square lid fit on snugly but did not quite "snap" on.

Puts Objects in Container—BIAB: AAMA=19.79 months. The period of mastery for this behavior seemed to extend from 10 through 18 months of age, at which point mastery attempts dropped off by 50 percent. As mastery attempts at putting the balls in the bowl were frequently found at all ages, where to rank this behavior is unclear. The frequency curve for this behavior-object combination is virtually flat. It's AAMA ranking reasonably places it as the easiest of the filling behaviors.

Puts Objects in Container—BFB: AAMA=20.81 months. The curve for filling this toy was very similar to the curve for emptying it. The period of mastery was very definite. Mastery attempts increased by 62 percent at 15 through 18 months of age, and then immediately declined by 200 percent for subjects 19 through 23 months of age. Filling BFB may have been perceived by subjects as more difficult than filling BIAB because of the many more objects to fill and the larger container.

Lid Fitting—B&B: AAMA=20.93 months. The period for mastering this behavior seemed to occur between 15 and 18 months of age. This was the only period during which a substantial number of mastery attempts (16) occurred. Eight attempts were scored for subjects between 29 and 34 months.

Puts Objects in Container—B&B: AAMA=21.62 months. The period of mastery for this behavior-object combination was longer than the mastery period for any behavior-object combination yet discussed. Frequency of mastery attempts appeared to peak at two different times, first between 13 and 15 months of age and later between 24 and 28 months. The lengthy mastery period reflects the suitability of B&B for what was earlier referred to as "simple" fill and dump play and its additional possibilities as a nesting toy in which a piece is fit inside a larger piece, which is fit inside a larger piece, which is then fit into the container. B&B continued to offer "filling" challenges at ages at which BIAB and BFB did not.

Dumps Objects—BIAB: AAMA=23.28 months. Attempts at mastering dumping come relatively late, at 19 through 23 months, and persist through 34 months. Note the relationship between dumping and removing singly for this toy. With ascending age, the frequency of mastery attempts at removing objects singly declined to the same extent that the frequency of mastery attempts at dumping increased.

Posts Through Lid—BFB: AAMA=24.78 months. Although mastery attempts were not uncommonly observed as early as 13 through 15 months, mastery clearly began at 24 through 28 months. At that age occurred a 380 percent increase in the number of mastery attempts. Despite a drop of 30 percent, mastery attempts remained frequent (33) between 29 and 34 months of age. Mastery attempts for this behavior-object combination were more frequent at 24 through 28 months (47) than for any other behavior-object combination at any age level.

Posting Through Lid—B&B: AAMA=25.21 months. The curve for mastery attempts of this behavior is a flattened replica of that for BFB. Although not eliciting mastery attempts at anywhere near the frequency of BFB, mastery attempts at posting with B&B also point to 24 through 34 months as the critical age for mastering this behavior. The superiority of BFB in eliciting mastery attempts at posting reflects the fact that BFB permitted 15 blocks to be posted before it became necessary to once again remove the lid, dump the blocks, and then fit the lid back on again. B&B allowed only two blocks to be posted. Also, the fits between shapes of holes and pieces were not exclusive for B&B; the cylinders fit into both the round and square holes.


## MASTERY OF OBJECT PERMANENCE

It was earlier hypothesized that if, in fill and dump play, we are seeing infants in the process of mastering object permanence, then the age-group mastery attempt scores obtained during fill and dump play should closely correspond to those ages at which it is believed that object permanence is mastered. Of the five predictions made earlier, the range of ages tested only permits conclusions to be drawn concerning the last four: (2) mastery attempts will be uncommonly observed in fill and dump play between 10 and 12 months of age; (3) mastery attempts will be commonly observed in fill and dump play between 13 and 18 months; (4) mastery attempts will remain common in fill and dump play between 19 and 24 months of age; and (5) beyond 24 months, a substantial drop will occur in the frequency of mastery attempts seen in fill and dump play.

In determining the frequency of fill and dump mastery attempts for each age group, only "simple" fill and dump behaviors were included. Lid fitting and posting through the lid with BFB and B&B were excluded since they were secondary to the fill and dump routine. BIAB allowed for only the simple fill and dump play behaviors. As hypothesized, the curve for fill and dump play conforms to all four of the above predictions.

Although a more quantifiable link between object permanence and fill and dump play is highly desirable, in studying the process of mastery, it seems meaningless to inquire as to summative achievement measures. In mastery, we are concerned with the repetitious practice (with or without variation) of a behavior at a point in time after subjects have become capable of a single correct performance in a testing situation. For example, infants have been found capable of removing a block from a cup at six months of age, yet this bears little on the finding that between 13 and 15 months of age, they are most likely to spontaneously and repetitively remove objects from containers. Thus, the best that can be managed is the assertion that fill and dump play occurred during the same ages at which mastery of object permanence is theorized to occur. The likelihood that this similarity is coincidental in nature will be discussed in the following section.

## MEASURING MASTERY

Perhaps the most important finding of this study is that a measure of mastery motivation based on density of behavioral enactment in play is both valid and reliable. Prior research in the area of mastery, as noted earlier, is rare. Prior failure to test measures of mastery against the simplest psychometric criteria have left even the few findings we have inconclusive.

The reliability and validity coefficients obtained in this study lend support to density as an effective means of measuring mastery. The correlations between frequency of behavior occurrence and frequency of behavioral mastery attempts yielded evidence of discriminant validity. Evidence of concurrent validity was obtained by correlating the ranked order of behaviors by AAMA's against rankings produced by judges of the difficulty of the behaviors. Lastly, evidence of predictive validity was obtained by determining the extent to which the ranked ordering of behaviors, according to AAMA, predicted the pattern of mastery attempts in the play of individual subjects.

## MASTERY OF HANDLING SKILLS

What exactly is signified by a high frequency of mastery attempts? In defining learning as a progressive series of improved performances, do mastery attempts signify learning? A time-series analysis was run, looking for a change over time in the behaviors at which mastery was attempted. No such change occurred. What was found instead was that a given subject attempted mastery at the same cluster of behaviors about equally often across the entire play session. Within a single play session, subjects did not progress from attempting mastery at simple to more difficult behaviors.

The implication is that mastery occurs over much time and after hundreds of repetitions. At least for the development of effective handling and grasping skills, true competence is very gradually but very steadily achieved. Although letting go of an object is reflexive by school age, the coordination of eyes and hands, plus the necessary knowledge of objects, quite taxes the abilities of infants. Only after intensive repetition on many objects do handling skills become reflexive, even when they are only mastered to a certain extent; for example, the average adult does not possess the fine motor skills of an expert seamstress.

What can be inferred from the frequency of mastery attempts is the age at which children will spontaneously challenge themselves with different tasks. It allows us to identify those behaviors of developmental concern to a given child. Across subjects, it allows us to say that a given behavior is mastered between ages $x$ and $y$. The findings of this study suggest that through fill and dump play, 10- through 24-month-old children practice the grasping, dropping, dumping, and posting of objects, as well as lid fitting. It seems reasonable to conclude that this practice is part of the process eventually leading to the development of effective handling skills.

The periods of mastery for each of the 11 behaviors under study were described in the previous section. The AAMA was outside of the period of mastery for three of the behaviors, which requires a word of explanation. For all three behavior-object combinations where the AAMA was outside of the period of mastery (Puts object in container—BIAB, Puts objects in container—BFB, and Lid fitting—B&B), dense enactment was commonly seen in the course of make-believe play for subjects between 29 and 34 months of age. For example, one 31-month-old girl went "shopping" and repetitively put the "groceries" (blocks) in the "grocery bag" (container). The AAMA would be more accurate as an index of when mastery occurs if the age range of subjects was more evenly limited around the period of mastery. In this study, the AAMA, to a varying extent, overestimates the average age of mastery for all the earlier developing behaviors.

## MASTERY OF COGNITIVE SKILLS

The evidence that fill and dump play involves the infant's perfection of his object-concept was a resemblance in the curve for mastery attempts at the three simple fill and dump behaviors and expectations based on studies of object permanence. Mastery of both seems to begin at 10 months, become common at 13 months, and conclude at 24 months. Although possible that this resemblance is coincidental, there seems no reason to suppose it so. There is general agreement with Piaget's (1967) claim that at 10 months, a decrease occurs in interest in the actions that can be performed on objects and a heightening of interest in the characteristic of the objects themselves. Primary among those characteristics is the permanence of objects. It takes no leap of the imagination to suspect that the compulsive, repetitious behavior in fill and dump play, occurring parallel in time to mastery of object permanence, is more than coincidentally related.

Consider the physical skills mastered in fill and dump. The skills of grasping and letting go are precisely those which make objects appear, disappear, and then reappear. Imagine the new sense of assurance and security felt by the infant as he gradually convinces himself that objects have a reality all their own, that objects do not cease to exist when out of sensory contact. Imagine yourself in a world where this was not the case. The invocation of this sense of reassurance both motivates and is strengthened by fill and dump play. Over and over again, the infant takes pleasure in finding that objects which are put into containers can also be taken out. After repeating his experiment hundreds of times, the infant's suspicion that reality has a realness outside his own experience turns to belief and then to certainty.

Again, a more quantifiable relationship between fill and dump play and object permanence would be desirable but difficult to obtain, given the purpose of identifying periods of mastery. For example, relating spontaneous mastery attempts at fill and dump play to measures of object permanence obtained through a testing procedure would say little about the practice of object permanence in fill and dump play. The capacity of an infant to respond correctly under test conditions reveals little regarding the infant's readiness to make that response in his daily life. The gap between having the capacity and the desire to make a response is a subject which is in itself of interest and worthy of future study.

## MASTERY AND EXPLORATORY PLAY WITH SMALL OBJECTS

To the extent that "effectance motivation" is, as White (1959) suggested, captured by quantifying multiple repetitions of a behavior within a limited amount of time, the evidence presented here provides strong support for White's belief that exploratory play with small objects is, in large part, motivated by a desire to effectively interact with the environment. Fill and dump play has been shown to be related to mastery of the physical and intellectual requirements of grasping and letting go of objects.

Impressively, 35 out of the 36 subjects participating in this study attempted mastery at putting objects in containers with at least one of the three toys; the only subject not to attempt mastery at filling was in the youngest age group. Thirty subjects attempted mastery at filling with at least two of the toys. Twenty-five subjects attempted mastery at removing objects from the containers of at least one toy. Considering the near universality, especially of filling behaviors, it is tempting to consider the possibility that fill and dump play is an innate behavior. Of course, further research is needed to bring that possibility out of the realm of speculation.

Exploration of these three fill and dump toys was far from limited to filling the containers with the appropriate objects. Late in the play sessions, after intensive simple fill and dump play, many infants explored the fitting relationships between the container and parts of their own bodies. Infants between 10 and 15 months of age were often observed putting their hands into the container or through the lid holes. Infants between 16 and 18 months continued to show interest in fitting their hands into the container and through the lid, but occasionally improvised further by sticking a foot in the container or wearing the container as a hat. The period between 19 and 23 months included all of the above behaviors at a higher frequency and added sitting on the bowl to the list. Further additions come between 24 and 34 months (leg, knee, and arm in container; use of lid as mask), but the major change is the incorporation of fill and dump activities into make-believe episodes. Blocks are now skillfully poured out of the containers. The bowl is lifted to the mouth as if for a drink. The container serves as a shopping bag and is filled with block groceries, and the block laundry is taken out of the box washing machine.

Although traditional fill and dump play seems to lose a substantial portion of its appeal by 24 months, it persists in several elaborated forms and over time becomes less concerned with filling than with fitting. Nesting blocks within blocks and posting blocks through lid holes are two elaborated forms of fill and dump play. Both involve filling, but require awareness of size relationships between objects (nesting) and shape relationships (posting).

Although speculative, nesting and posting seem to branch out into the many types of fitting play observed in children three years of age. Common types of fitting play which popular commercial toys capitalize on include seriated rings on a post, pegboards, sewing cards, nuts and bolt type construction toys, seriation puzzles, and shape puzzles. Fitting of shapes easily branches into the matching of shapes, then colors, and then more abstract symbols beginning with graphic pictures. By four years of age, lotto and dominoe games are popular with most children. Empirical investigation of the many types of play with objects across a longer age range than that studied here would be very useful in tracing the evolution of the child's relationship to objects. Of particular interest would be tracing the evolution of object play within different subjects across age. What consistencies will emerge?

## IMPLICATIONS FOR PLAY THERAPY

Traditional psychoanalytic wisdom ascribes to play an "as if" quality that permits a relaxation of censoring activity and thus, makes of play a relatively uncensored medium for expressing unconscious, instinctual impulses. White's theory of effectance motivation suggests that the "as if" quality to play also permits the free expression of conscious, ego-directed impulses and adds competence to Freud's rather short list of instinctual impulses (i.e., sex). Both theories, however, are in agreement that, in play behavior, we are witnessing an externalization of internal conflicts or puzzlements. In fill and dump play, we see the child repeating those adult behaviors which seemingly made objects appear and disappear. Make-believe play, which is common to most play therapies, similarly involves re-enactment of puzzling (or disturbing) adult behaviors. Unfortunately, the more emotionally disturbing the event being re-enacted, the more symbolic, removed, or exaggerated becomes the representation in play. And once the disturbing behavior becomes identified, it often remains difficult to determine why and in what context those behaviors were disturbing to the child.

Just as object play involves mastery in the realm of fine motor skills and concepts of objects and space, make-believe play involves mastery in the realm of socio-emotional development. As such, make-believe play is a most suitable medium for therapy, even with verbally competent children. Therapists, however, would do well to note the slow process by which mastery is obtained. The behavior (event) must be looked at from different perspectives, tried out under different conditions, repeated endlessly, and experienced over a long period of time before it becomes firmly assimilated. Mastery is achieved one small step at a time. Play permits children to decide both the size of those steps and provides an "as if" context allowing trial and error experimentation. Though the road may be long, it leads to competent, well-adjusted, and satisfying interactions with the environment and justifies patience and faith in play therapy as the proper mode of treatment.

## REFERENCES

Acredelo, L. P., "The development of spatial orientation in infancy," *Child Development* (1977).

Arnold, A. *Your Child's Play: How to Help your Child Reap the Full Benefits of Creative Play.* New York: Simon & Schuster (1968).

Bower, T. G. R., "Repetition in human development," *Merrill-Palmer Quarterly, 20,* 303–318 (1974).

Braga, J. and Braga, L. *Children and Adults: Activities for Growing Together.* Englewood Cliffs, NJ: Prentice-Hall (1976).

Bremner, J. G. and Briant, P. E., "Place versus response as the basis of spatial errors made by young infants," *Journal of Experimental Child Psychology, 23,* 162–171 (1977).

Cox, R. N. and Campbell, D., "Young children in a new situation with and without their mothers," *Child Development, 39*, 123–131 (1968).

Dodwell, P. D., Muir, D., and DiFranco, D., "Responses of infants to visually presented objects," *Science, 194*, 209–211 (1976).

Gesell, A. and Ilg, F. I. *The Infant and Child in the Culture of Today.* New York: Harper & Row Pub. (1943).

Gibson, J. J. *The Senses Considered as Perceptual Systems.* Boston: Houghton-Mifflin (1966).

Goldberg, S., "Visual tracking and existence constancy in five-month-old infants," *Journal of Experimental Child Psychology, 22*, 478–491 (1976).

Goodenough, F. L., "Measuring behavioral traits by means of repeated short samples," *Journal of Juvenile Research, 12*, 230–235 (1928).

Hinde, R. A., Rowell, T. E., and Spencer-Booth, Y., "Behavior of socially living rhesus monkeys in their first six months," *Journal of Zoology, 143* (1964).

Hughes, M. M., "Exploration and play revisited. A hierarchical analysis," *International Journal of Behavioral Development, 2*, 215–224 (1979).

Hutt, C., "Exploration and play in children," *Symposium of Zoological Society, 18*, 61–81 (1966).

Kummer, H. *Primate Societies: Group Techniques of Ecological Adaptation.* Chicago: Aldine-Atherton (1971).

LeCompte, G. K. and Gratch, G., "Violation of a rule as a method of diagnosing infants level of object concept," *Child Development, 43*, 385–396 (1972).

McCall, R. B., "Exploratory manipulation and play in the human infant," *Monographs of the Society for Research in Child Development, 39*, (2, Whole No. 155) (1974).

Mann, B. L. *Comparison Testing Project: Final Report.* Environmental Programs, Inc. (1981).

Piaget, J. *Six Psychological Studies.* New York: Vintage Books (1967).

Rubenstein, J., "Maternal attentiveness and subsequent exploratory behavior in the infant," *Child Development, 38*, 1089–1100 (1967).

Saal, D. *A Study of the Development of Object Concept in Infancy Varying the Degree of Discrepancy between the Disappearing and Reappearing Object.* Unpublished Ph.D. Dissertation, University of Houston (1975).

Smith, P. K. and Connally, K., "Patterns of play and social interaction in preschool children," in *Ethological Studies of Child Behavior*, N. Blurton-Jones, ed. London: Cambridge University Press (1972).

Weisler, A. and McCall, R. B., "Exploration and play," *American Psychologist, 6*, 492–508 (July 1976).

White, B. *The First Three Years of Life.* New York: Avon (1978).

White, R., "Motivation reconsidered: The concept of competence," *Psychological Review, 66*, 297–333 (1959).

Wright, H. F., "Observational child study," in *Handbook of Research Methods in Child Development*, P. H. Musser, ed. New York: J. Wiley & Sons, 71–139 (1960).

Yarrow, L. J., "Beyond cognition: The development of mastery motivation," *Zero to Three: Bulletin of the National Center for Clinical Infant Programs, 1*, 1–5 (1981).

Part 2

CHILD'S PLAY AS THERAPY

# CHILD'S PLAY AS THERAPY

Joseph M. Diantoniis and Thomas D. Yawkey

Miller's chapter, "Therapist-child relations in play therapy," focuses primarily on three play therapy approaches and their theoretical and practical origins. These play therapy approaches are (a) psychoanalytic, (b) relationship, and (c) client-centered. Psychoanalytic play therapy is based on the assumption that play mirrors the child's ego or psyche. Children's games are seen as elaborations of experiences; if these experiences are traumatic, the ego is unable to protect the individual from self-criticisms in a healthy manner.

Relationship therapy uses both present and past situations in helping the youngster adapt to current realities. The focus of the therapist is developing adult-child relationships and assessing the feelings that the youngster has about himself. Play function, rather than content, is stressed. Finally, client-centered therapy sees the role of the therapist as passive; that is, the child has within him the ability to solve his own problems satisfactorily. The therapist accepts the children's comments and reflects their actions and feelings.

Each of the therapies have their basis in child development theories. They are derived from maturationist, cognitive-interactionist, and behaviorist mainstreams. Although the maturationist approach has contributed the majority of theoretical assumptions underlying play-therapist actions, Miller notes that cognitive-interactionist and behaviorist orientations contribute the view that play actions are cognitive-based and internal and that play can be shaped by external variables.

In addition, Miller provides guidelines for toy use and future research in play therapy. One guideline is purchasing competitive toys for children ages 10 to 12 and making sure that they are manipulative in nature. Also, the therapist should encourage the feelings of children as they use the toys. Future research should focus on, for example, relationships between chronological and mental ages and the types of statements made by the children.

In summary, this chapter makes several contributions to the understanding of play therapy. They include (a) identifying significant play therapy approaches used with children, (b) explicating their maturationist foundations, (c) describing the relations between play therapy and cognitive-interactionist and behaviorist theories, (d) detailing the toy materials and their uses by the therapist for ego development, and (e) noting possible future research studies in therapist-child relations.

In the chapter, "Alleviating aggressive behaviors using therapy and play objects in the psychoanalytic mainstream," written by Confer, special emphasis is given to varying types of aggressive behaviors and the methods used to alleviate them in settings including hospitals. Confer explains psychoanalytic theories of personality growth developed by S. Freud, E. H. Erikson, and A. Freud. Basic to S. Freud's elements of personality are the id, ego, and superego. S. Freud's psychosexual stages, a framework around which personality develops, are the oral, anal, phallic, oedipal, latency, and puberal stages. Each stage, according to Confer's description, contributes a certain type or kind of gratification to the individual.

E. H. Erikson's contributions to play therapy center on understanding the stages of emotional growth. These stages include (a) basic trust versus mistrust, (b) autonomy versus shame and doubt, (c) initiative versus guilt, and (d) industry versus inferiority. Confer feels that a child must pass through each one of these stages in order for a healthy personality to emerge. The positive development of each stage in the growth of the ego and superego proves the individual has ego continuity and a healthy personality. Central to A. Freud's analysis of personality development and play therapy are several stages of development that are assessed and diagnosed. For purposes of assessment and diagnosis in therapy, these levels of development are seen in the child's play and how he plays with objects and materials in his environment. Confer, using Freud's views, says that children will project feelings onto others, including people and objects. These feelings include acts of aggression and withdrawal. Using these states and methods of identification, A. Freud understood better the causes of aggression in working with children in individual and group settings.

The work of S. Freud, E. H. Erikson, and A. Freud also identifies other forms of aggressive behaviors. Compliance, hateful acts, and destruction of materials or property are also variations of aggressive behaviors; these acts of aggression can produce problems in personality development and for society if they are not treated in a consistent and positive way. In this sense, play therapy can be used as a tool to help understand and alleviate these aggressive actions of young children.

Confer feels that the basic premise in the use of play therapy is that the adult-therapist strives towards a sense of well-being and a realization of personal potential of the client. Play becomes the forum in which the adult-therapist observes the child and reflects back to him what is seen and heard. Stressing that certain behaviors are not accepted in play therapy, Confer feels that the adult-therapist must intervene at the point where the child may physically harm himself.

Play materials that are useful in promoting play therapy and alleviating aggressive behaviors include dolls, sandbox and sand-play materials, blocks, and puppets. Lastly, Confer abstracts from psychoanalytic literature and provides several useful principles for conducting play therapy in hospitals and other settings, such as homes and school classrooms. These principles include permitting the child choices in his play and using a wide variety of play materials. Through play therapy and use of materials, expressions of negativeness, resentment, and aggression are accepted. The child learns that expressing these actions are appropriate, and the adult-therapist lays the groundwork for acceptance and construction of ego continuity and a development of a healthy personality.

In summary, Confer's chapter aids understanding of play therapy in several unique ways. These ways include (a) providing an understanding of psychoanalytic theory upon which play therapy rests, (b) explaining the levels of personality development from A. Freud's, S. Freud's, and E. H. Erikson's orientations, (c) detailing the routines used by the adult-therapist in nondirective therapy, (d) identifying the types of play materials found useful in play therapy sessions, and (e) suggesting ways in which play therapy can be successfully used in hospital, classroom, and home settings to alleviate aggressive behaviors.

McCarthy's chapter is entitled "Effects of infant-parent social interaction on the development of attachment behaviors." The chapter focuses on the development of attachment and infant-parent play for personality and cognitive growth.

In describing the development of attachment, McCarthy stresses that it is a bond that is formed between the child and adults who nurture him. The infant's cognitive and social growth is nurtured by child care routines and practices in homes, centers, and hospitals. From cognitive personality and social perspectives, attachment can be viewed as an inner representative that can be assessed by observing attachment behaviors or responses. McCarthy describes four phases in attachment development. Phase one is "undiscriminating social responsiveness." In this phase, the infant (birth to two or three months) learns to orient himself to the people in his environment. Phase two is called "discriminating social responsiveness." The youngster distinguishes between familiar and unfamiliar people. The set of familiar people includes the child's mother and one or two other individuals.

Phase three is called "active initiative in seeking proximity and contact." This stage is marked by a significant increase in the behaviors of proximity and contact. The infant's responses are initiated to evoke a response from a significant adult. The age of acquisition is seven months. The last phase is called "goal-corrected partnership," and it occurs around three years of age. It represents a beginning of a relationship based on partnership. Partnership suggests an interaction between two or more people. The partnership, in turn, develops, according to McCarthy, as the child learns to differentiate self from nonself, which is aided by socialization processes between him and a significant adult. These four phases detail the growth of the bonding process—an essential element in personality development and cognitive and social growth.

In infant-parent play, object relations are crucial to ego development and processes such as trust—one of the keystones for healthy personality growth. This object relation, called play, originates initially from the interaction between an adult and infant during feeding situations. These infant-parent play routines consist of five types. They are (a) conventional play (e.g., peek-a-boo), (b) rough and tumble play, (c) toy mediated play (e.g., toy objects which mediate interaction between child and adult), (d) minor physical play (e.g., objects but excluding holding actions), and (e) idiosyncratic play (e.g., other forms of play not included in the above categorical types). These five types of play also increase opportunities to develop attachment behaviors between child and adult.

Parent-infant play, like other interpersonal events, evolves in hierarchical form—from smaller to larger units of behavior. This hierarchical structuring of parent-child play leads to a play activity goal. To achieve this goal, McCarthy says, adults need to diversify the level, nature, timing, and pattern of stimulation. This diversification keeps the infant's attention and maintains his arousal and interest. Even though adults initiate the play, the infant provides many actions and expressions to which they respond and provide feedback. Examples of these actions and expressions include smiling and cooing. As both respond, the adult and infant move toward the same goal of delighting one another. The relations between parent-infant play and attachment behaviors do not seem to be studied. Research studies exploring these relations are much needed.

In summary, McCarthy's chapter adds to the study of play-therapy in a number of areas. These are (a) showing relationships that exist between attachment and infant-adult play, (b) demonstrating that infant-adult play evolves naturally through social interaction, (c) identifying relations between the growth of personality and cognitive and social development, and (d) explaining strategies that adults can use in developing infant-parent play and for integrating the ego.

Melizzi's chapter is entitled "Play of infants and children: Examination of temperament and play." It focuses on examining adults' perceptions of infant's play and interaction, relative to temperament. Related to play, Melizzi views the child's temperament along several dimensions which include activity (i.e., amount and quality of motor play), approach (i.e., responsiveness to novel objects and friendliness to strangers), and distractibility (i.e., degree to which a child's attention can be drawn away from an on-going activity).

In surveying the results of several research studies, Melizzi notes that adult behaviors relate to the infant and child's temperament, in that the more qualitatively rich the adult's actions are during interaction, the better the child's responses and the higher the quality of his play. The evidence from studies suggests that a child's temperament is the result of the type and quality of interactions between parent and child; one of the major interactive variables in these settings is the child's play. In addition, adults tend to increase their participation relative to initial styles of the children. Here, the manner and mode of adult responding to the child's play also affects the youngster's play routines. Play that is repetitive of a particular tempo and that shows variable ranges is highly correlated with positive infant temperament actions.

Through research results, Melizzi describes a six stage developmental structure which shows the growth of adaptive personality organization which focuses on temperament and play. These six stages are (a) homeostatis, (b) attachment, (c) somatopsychological differentiation, (d) behavioral organization, initiative, and internalization, (e) representation, differentiation, and consolidation, and (f) limited and multiple representational systems. Relative to the stage of homeostatis, the youngsters are free to involve themselves in social interaction using play actions. At stage two, attachment, more mature play patterns and temperament emerge as the child develops associations through bonding between adult and child. For the stage of somatopsychological differentiation, the youngster organizes experiences through internal representation. Optimal growth proceeds by the child's ability to "take on" and internalize attributes of the adult through play in physical and social environments. In stage four, or behavioral organization, initiative, and internalization, the youngster shows increasing abilities to organize mental representations for play and adaptive actions. With stage five, the youngster forms mental representations through internal multisensory experiences. Limited and multiple representational systems, or stage six, evolve as the youngster's original representational systems grow toward more adaptive thought. Melizzi notes that play is a significant variable across the dimensions of temperament and stages of personality when the play environment, adult behaviors, and child actions are considered.

In summary, Melizzi's chapter contributes to the study of play and temperament as a personality variable by (a) establishing relationships between temperament as a personality and cognitive variable and play, (b) describing effective adult-child play interactions which relate to developing positive temperament behaviors, and (c) detailing the development of assimilative and accommodative structures fundamental to play and temperament in young children.

Porrata-Doria's chapter is entitled "Play: The father's primary way of contributing to the young child's development." Research literature on the nature and level of involvement of the mother and the father with the child is reviewed. Both parents, according to Porrata-Doria, are active playmates of the young child, yet the father makes his contribution to the child's development primarily through play. The father contributes a great deal of routine tasks of child-rearing and play activities with the child. The time spent by father with the child enhances his attractiveness in spite of his limited parental contact. Although the father spends the greater percentage of the time with the child engaged in play activities if he works outside the home and if the mother is a homemaker, the time the mother spends playing with the child exceeds that of the father. The survey of literature by Porrata-Doria shows that mothers and fathers have different styles of playing with their children. The mother gets involved in more intellectual and toy-mediated types of games, while the father tends to play socio-physical types of games. Also, fathers seem to have more ability to engage the children in play to make infants, for example, enjoy the play interaction and get them personally involved. In the absence of the mother in the play session, the father converses with the child and gets involved in toy-mediated play. Since the primary role of the father of the young child is that of a playmate, Porrata-Doria suggests that teaching the parents how to foster their child's development through play should involve the father.

However, the research data is limited to infants of two years of age in laboratory and home environments. Investigations considering different ages and sexes in the samples are needed. Although research done already has identified mothers' and fathers' differences in styles when playing with children, the picture is not completely clear. Thus, more investigations are needed in this area. Also, Porrata-Doria notes that the context of play interactions should be studied.

In summary, Porrata-Doria's chapter suggests several important variables for the development of father-child play. They are (a) understanding the father's active role in socio-physical types of games, (b) enhancing the child's enjoyment of adult-play interaction, and (c) detailing the father's use of unconventional games with young children.

In the chapter "Play therapy and the disruptive child," written by Trostle, five major techniques used by the therapist for ameliorating disruptive behaviors are explicated. They are (a) acceptance of feelings, (b) emphatic responding, (c) structuring (i.e., using real life experiences, toys, sessions), (d) personal messages, and (e) limits consequence.

First, the strategy of acceptance of feelings means that the parent emphasizes feelings with the children when they use disruptive behavior. Since there is usually a reason behind a child's disruptive behavior, Trostle feels that it may be interpreted by the parent, for ameliorating disruptive behavior is emphatic responding. In using emphatic responding, the parent permits the child to express his feelings without fear of criticism. The parent accepts these expressions and elaborates on the child's statements and actions. The third is structuring. Structuring gives a framework for play therapy settings and interactions. The therapist uses real life experiences, toys, and episodes for structuring.

Personal messages is the fourth strategy adults use to ameliorate disruptive behavior of children. In using personal messages, the parent communicates specific behaviors which he or she considers inappropriate because they can cause physical harm. The final strategy is limits/consequences. The parent informs the child that limits exist when he is misbehaving. Limits are also necessary to insure that the time for play therapy remains constant. There are two types of consequences. A "warning" consequence and "direct" consequence—both of which follow the limit. The two purposes of these consequences are (a) termination of disruptive behavior and (b) demonstration that rules are enforced—a "warning" consequence serves as a signal to the child to stop his disruptive behaviors. If the action persists, Trostle notes that direct consequences become necessary, and the adult intervenes.

Across these techniques, the child and his personality initially determine the appropriateness of his play actions. The more play sessions the child participates in, the more integrated are his actions of cooperation and understanding. When play sessions end, the concerned adult continues to use common routines as "positive reinforcement, natural conversation, and questions" to extend positive behavior learning during therapy.

In summary, Trostle's chapter contributes to therapy and play therapy techniques in several ways. They are (a) identifying and describing the five basic techniques used by adults to ameliorate disruptive behavior of their children and (b) extending play therapy routines to children's positive behaviors learned during therapy.

# Therapist—child relations in play therapy

**Thomas J. Miller**[2]
*Capital Area Intermediate Unit Number 15, Pennsylvania*

## INTRODUCTION

The purpose of the following discussion is to explain therapist-client relationships, or interaction, within a therapeutic setting utilizing the medium of play. Such approaches are generally oriented to the child from three to twelve years of age and exhibit various complexions depending on their theoretical base and/or the personal convictions of individual therapists (Guerney, 1981). In addition, the qualities that the child brings to the therapy setting also play an extremely significant role in determining the course play intervention will take. With these considerations in mind, it will be necessary to focus the investigation on therapeutic approaches that fall under the ruberic of "play therapy." Unfortunately, the term "therapy" may be interpreted by some to be appropriate only for those children considered severely out of synchrony with society and/or their immediate environment. However, such an interpretation does not appear to be an accurate image of play therapy as it is currently practiced.

According to Nickerson (1973), the trend toward the use of play therapy is increasingly being widened to all levels of society so as to optimize the adjustment of all children. As such, the thrust of play therapy approaches is being increasingly oriented toward prevention rather than the treatment of serious maladies. As a result, the use of play as a therapeutic modality assumes a much more general connotation and introduces a broader set of criteria for its application. For the purpose of providing a frame of reference, the following definition of "play therapy" is provided. Such a statement is thought to represent the general nature of the play therapy approaches to be discussed. Play therapy is here defined as

> participation by the child in a play setting, with an attendant adult, wherein the child is given the optimal opportunity to utilize what is a natural and en-

[2]Mr. Miller is currently employed as supervisor for preschool services and occupational and physical therapy through the Capital Area Intermediate Unit #15 (CAIU). The CAIU is a provider of special educational and support services to school districts surrounding Harrisburg, Pennsylvania. Previous professional experiences were in the area of Communication Disorders.

joyable medium (play) for the purpose of helping the child to resolve the problems of modern living.

Such a definition does not impose a specific therapeutic technique or assume any strict criteria for participation in a play therapy process. However, it should be recognized that the term "play therapy" does carry with it certain connotations or inferences as to its theoretical origins. In regard to children's play, S. Freud was the first major figure to view play as a possible therapeutic agent (Erikson, 1940). Other authorities, too, saw play as being beneficial for the child's emotional and cognitive growth. Erikson concluded that playing out troublesome situations was the most natural auto-therapeutic method that childhood offers. Piaget (1962) considered play as adaptive for the child—helping him to gradually assimilate and gain mastery of his world. Ludic symbolism, or the great pleasure and joy exhibited by children while engaging in make-believe play, was a source of fascination for Piaget, as well as for other therapists (Lieberman, 1977; Pulaski, 1976). It is little wonder then that play has evolved as a therapeutic tool for those concerned with the problems encountered by children in their growth and development.

In the following discussion, three schools of thought regarding play therapy will be discussed. These will include (a) the psychoanalytic approach, (b) the relationship therapy approach, and (c) the client-centered approach. The philosophical and theoretical base from which these therapeutic strategies evolved in regard to human development will also be investigated. Lastly, research will be reviewed regarding empirical efforts to account for play therapy outcomes, as well as the nature of selected variables, in regard to therapist-child interaction.

## THE MATURATIONIST POINT OF VIEW

Schools of play therapy can be said to fall largely into the maturationist theory in regard to child development. Brief mention of two other major developmental orientations will be provided for the purpose of comparison. An attempt will be made to provide a glimpse of the philosophical foundations of each developmental orientation.

As described by Seaver and Cartwright (1977) in a discussion of theoretical schools of thought, in regard to early childhood education, a philosophy is commonly regarded as a perspective on the world and the nature of man. A theory, on the other hand, is a set of related principles that explain or predict the course of man's development. Also, they go on to discuss the need for a strong relation between theory and practice in educational settings in order to maximize conceptual consistency. Such a relationship is desirable so that professional educators can maintain a high degree of consistency and be accountable in the manner in which they provide instructional programs. It is logical to assume that such an approach is desirable for other disciplines dealing with human behavior.

In regard to play therapy, the psychoanalytical, relationship, and client-centered approaches do seem to have maintained a consistent orientation in concert with the basic tenets most frequently associated with the maturationist point of view. These tenets would include that man is a product of his biology and that development is genetically predetermined and basically a function of time. Given a nurturing environment, the biological potential of the individual will unfold in a genetically prescribed manner. Gesell and his associates are generally considered to have evolved the most global and fully articulated nativist-maturatist theory (Seaver and Cartwright).

On child development, Gesell and Ilg (1949) state that beginning with conception, development proceeds stage by stage in an orderly sequence. Gesell and Ilg view behavior in terms of age and think of age in terms of behavior. For any selected age, they feel it is possible to sketch a portrait which delineates the behavior characteristics typical of the age (Gesell and Ilg, 1949).

This does not mean that their view of growth and development is static and lacking in dynamic relationships. Through their normative data on maturity, they are able to make comparisons of adjacent levels of growth and achieve what they term a sense of "developmental flow." Through comparative analysis of the various levels and stages of growth, conclusions can be drawn in regard to the developmental status of the individual child. Conclusions so reached are based on normative scales thought to apply to the normal developmental progression of all children.

In terms of play, Gesell and Ilg state that children play not from outer compulsion but from internally directed necessity. Though cultural influences may direct play impulses into approved channels, the child will always demonstrate the kind of play best suited to his stage of maturity. Often, such play involves a rehearsal of activities inherited from former generations, such as games depicting the hunt (hide and seek), caring for plants and animals, hoarding and collecting, and exploring. Such themes are seen as preparation for adult life and reveal the child's individuality and potential. Psycho-motor exercise such as running, jumping, balancing, and other fine and gross muscular activities were also seen as significant play activities for enhancing physical development.

S. Freud, the originator of the psychoanalytical theory, can also be said to fit into the maturationist's orientation. However, Freud's view of development was more concerned with the inner feelings and thoughts of man, rather than the more global view enunciated by Gesell. Freud's theories of human behavior stemmed from the medical clinic rather than the university laboratory. As such, Freud was primarily concerned with helping disturbed people live more normal lives, rather than the investigation of theoretical questions dealing with normal development. A parallel, however, was drawn by Freud between normal and pathological behavior, in that maladjusted activities were exaggerated components of normal personality (Baldwin, 1967).

In the maturationist tradition, Freud also maintained that development is marked by a series of stages universal to mankind that are genetically determined (Langer, 1969). Caldwell and Richmond (1967) refer to the psychoanalytical position as the biological theory of personality. They state that these biological drives are manifested within the social context of the family, and unless these drives are satisfied, the child moves forward from infancy with some degree of stage fixation. Such a scenario impairs the child's ability to adapt as he develops and can result in regression to unfulfilled patterns of behavior. Baldwin comments that, in general terms, Freudian theory of development can be summarized by describing two interlinked maturational processes. These processes are the maturation of the ego which represents rational cognitive functioning and the passage of the child through stages of psychosexual development where gratification shifts from the mouth to the anus and to the genitals. Each stage is considered frustrating and gratifying, and each stage can be thought of as confronting the child with a new problem in interpersonal relationships.

Freud saw play as the most expressive medium through which to gain insight into the child's world, due to the limitations of children to express themselves verbally (Walder, 1976). Children were seen to repeat in their play everything that has made a great impression on them in actual life, and through play, they abstract the strength of the impression. Mastery of events and emotions was seen to be gained through re-enactment via the play modality (Freud, 1957).

Freud felt that all child's play was influenced by the dominant wish for resolution of anxious occasions in the child's life. To resolve conflicts, disturbed feelings, or wishes that may have originated as a result of frustrations at a particular stage of psychosexual development, the child would project these feelings through play.

The theories of Freud and Gesell are both compatible with the maturationist view of man as a basically self-directed biological being (Caldwell and Richmond, 1967). The philosophical base from which such views of the world originate are in the romantic tradition. Such a tradition asserts that knowledge and truth stem from self-awareness or self-insight with consideration for emotional, as well as intellectual, components. Also of significance is the sympathetic understanding of others and the basic goodness of man (Kohlberg and Mayer, 1972).

## THE BEHAVIORIST POINT OF VIEW

In contrast to the maturationist point of view are those of the behaviorist and cognitive/interactivist orientations. The behaviorist considers external variables of the environment as the primary events that shape development. Such theories are often referred to as mechanistic and focus on behavioral reactions to environmental stimulation (Langer, 1969). A response to a stimulus in the environment is established when it is reinforced in some way. Such a response then becomes a conditioned reflex which is easily observed and measured. Development from the behaviorist point of view can be influenced in very specific ways to achieve desired outcomes with little regard for organic variables (Seaver and Cartwright, 1977). B. F. Skinner is one of the most prominent theorists associated with the behaviorist school. Philosophically, the orientation grows out of the perception of the mind as being a blank slate upon which sensory impressions leave a mark. The growth of the mind and development in general is seen as a quantitative accumulation of impressions supplied by the environment (Langer, 1969).

## THE COGNITIVE/INTERACTIONIST POINT OF VIEW

The cognitive/interactionist views development as occurring through self-directed interaction with the child's environment. Stages of increasingly sophisticated levels of internal organization enable the individual to reason and come to know his world (Seaver and Cartwright, 1977). Though biological and environmental factors influence how rapidly development takes place, the stages of organization that underlie psychological acts are the true determinants of intellectual and social growth. Piaget is a major theorist associated with the cognitive/interactionist school. Philosophically, the orientation grows out of the conceptions of various organic theories. Events in nature, such as the intake of plants which spring internally from seeds, are eaten and digested internally by man. Though man cannot exert conscious control of digestion, he does influence the process by what and how often he eats. Such internal forces were seen as influencing the individual's overall development (Langer, 1969).

## THE PSYCHOANALYTICAL ORIENTATION TO PLAY

The original use of analysis of children's play for the purpose of helping the child through emotional problems encountered in his growth and development is most frequently attributed to S. Freud. Freud used the analysis of play for the first time in the celebrated case referred to as "Little Hans" (Freud, 1955). The child was not treated directly, but through his father who recorded his behaviors and submitted them to Freud for interpretation and counseling. The child possessed a violent fear of horses, which Freud viewed in terms of his stage theory of emotional development. Freud reasoned that an overt fear of horses, even when triggered off by a real event such as seeing a horse fall down under a load in the street, would be taken to express anxiety about himself and his feelings towards members of his family. His spontaneous play at being a horse, which consisted of toy horses falling down, was taken as symptomatic of those fears with which the boy was trying to cope (Millar, 1968).

Freud's first analysis of a child under five years of age was of great importance, for it demonstrated to those interested in psychoanalytic techniques that such methods could be applied to small children. It was also interpreted as confirmation of infantile instinctual tendencies which Freud had discovered in the adult (Klein, 1932).

In a discussion of the psychoanalytic theory of play, Walder (1976) suggests that Freud and his followers were more concerned not with a theory of play as a universal phenomenon, but with play as an individual behavior that may have various interpretations. Academic psychology, for instance, studied what may be considered the official games of childhood in order to arrive at an all encompassing theory of play. The psychoanalytical view of play, on the other hand, was individually oriented and concerned with how play could be interpreted to provide insight into a particular child's psychic. Children's games were seen as an elaboration of events that had been experienced by the child. If the experiences were traumatic, the underdeveloped ego of the child would not be capable of performing a protective function that would facilitate the acceptance of the event in a nonanxious manner. Play then became a repetition compulsion by which these troubling experiences were divided into small quantities and assimilated and resolved in a piecemeal way by working them over and over through games and fantasy. The merging of reality and fantasy was seen as a strategy employed by the child to permit a more acceptable outcome of the disagreeable experience.

## THE PLAY-THERAPY OF MELANIE KLEIN

Klein, as a follower of Freud, started to utilize psychoanalysis of children in 1919 (Klein, 1955). Her method of symbolic interpretation of play activity was widely used in England and America under the name of "play-therapy" (Freud, 1946). Characteristic of Klein's approach to play analysis was very early use in the therapy sequence of deep interpretation of the child's verbal and play activities. Through such interpretations, it was hoped to reduce the child's initial anxiety concerning the therapy situation and thus, give him an indication as to the value of the analysis for him (Dorfman, 1951). Klein (1932), in a discussion of her technique, stated that it was surprising how children accept interpretation of their play with facility and marked pleasure. The process by which interpretation increased the child's pleasure in play was attributed to the elimination of repressed feelings and emotions as an outcome of the therapist's interaction. The intellectual capacity for children to understand interpretations was also considered by Klein (1955). She held the opinion that connections between the conscious and unconscious are closer in young children so that they have a capacity for insight greater than that of adults. Such insight was an important aspect of Klein's approach for she credited children with conscience and guilt feelings as early as the end of the first year of life. Traditional psychoanalytical theory did not accept the existence of conscience or guilt feelings until after the age of three (Millar, 1968).

Klein preferred to conduct play analysis outside the home and within a clinical setting. Play materials included toys small in size and nonmechanical so that their simplicity would enable the child to use them in many different situations and to express a wide range of fantasies and experiences. Running water and art supplies were also seen as important materials, as were materials that could be utilized by the child for sociodramatic play (Klein, 1955).

## CHILD PSYCHOANALYSIS: A. FREUD

A. Freud held a significantly different view of play within the therapy setting compared to that of Klein's. She felt that play was not necessarily symbolic of anything, in that, children engage in fantasy for various reasons. If a child, for example, builds a lamp post, it may simply be because he has seen one that impressed him. She felt that fantasy play must be evaluated in light of evidence concerning the child's recent experiences and his home situation. Freud stressed that the relationship established between the therapist and the child was the most salient issue in the psychoanalysis of the child. Play was seen as a technique to build a positive emotional attachment to the therapist, which would then make possible the actual therapy (Freud, 1946).

The issue of the therapist's role in relation to the child in the play therapy setting is the primary concern of the present discussion. It was, as well, a major point of contention between Freud and Klein. At the heart of the issue is the psychoanalytical concept of transference. This concept, as described by Klein (1976), referred to the transference of early experiences and current feelings and thoughts to the therapist. Through analysis of such transferences, the past, as well as the unconscious part of the mind, could be explored.

Freud (1946) felt that it was not necessarily the child therapist's role to encourage the production of a transference that could be well interpreted. In discussing adult analysis and the issue of transference, she likened the therapist's role to that of an impersonal and shadowy screen upon which the patient casts his transference fantasies. Her contention was that the children's analyst must be anything but a shadow and should be a person of interest to the child with a variety of interesting and attractive qualities and emotions. The necessity of transference was not seen as essential by Freud for she perceived the therapist's role in educational terms. The child should learn to know what the therapist deems desirable or undesirable. Such a well-defined personality served as a poor transference-object, or to use the screen analogy again, the more brightly colored the reflective surface, the more the projected image is distorted (Freud, 1946).

The introduction of the concept of child psychoanalysis as having educational components as proposed by A. Freud indicates her broad interpretation of the therapist's role. Her conviction was that child psychoanalysis should contribute to pedagogies and to the practices of child rearing and education. Concern should be demonstrated as to whether the processes in a child's analysis have a degree of concordance with the expectations of parents and society. Modifications in relations with parents or guardians and revision of demands made on the child by the outside world were seen by Freud as worthy therapeutic goals.

To summarize then, A. Freud stressed the relationship to the therapist as the most important therapeutic agent allowing the child to come to terms with conflicts and re-educating him with concern for social and parental expectations. She saw play as a means of establishing such a therapist-child relationship. Klein focused more on the symbolic aspects of the child's play and the early and unrestrained use of play interpretation within established psychoanalytical parameters.

## RELATIONSHIP THERAPY

In a discussion of therapeutic work with children, Allen (1976) compared two basic schools of thought. One school utilizes the therapeutic relation to reconstruct the past in order to help the individual re-experience events that have created anxiety, fear, and turmoil in the present. The therapist is often required to assume the role of the person or persons who have been central figures in these past events. The aim is to assist the child to grow up again in a better way through therapist interpretation which is intended to create insight or intellectual awareness into emotionally charged psychological experiences.

The other school of thought that was described by Allen utilizes the play setting to provide the child with the opportunity to experience himself in terms of the present and not in the past. In such a situation, the therapist is interested in helping the child to understand the client-therapist relationship as the child struggles with feelings for which he has difficulty in assuming responsibility. The child must have the freedom to develop the relationship in his own way, subject to limitations which involve the therapist's own rights. Such freedom diminishes the child's fear and anxiety of the therapeutic situation through mutual respect. The therapist respects the child's right to tell him what he wants, which enables the child to express and live with feelings and emotions that are problematical.

The conception of the therapeutic relationship as being curative in its own right became known as "relationship therapy." As mentioned, the psychoanalytic approach of recovering the past was not seen as being helpful. Troubled children were considered to be excessively bound to the past, and to be little able to live in the here and now. Therefore, therapeutic intervention was seen to be most valuable in helping the child to adapt to current realities (Dorfman, 1951).

The value of play was stressed in the "relationship therapy" approach.

Through play, the child was seen as bringing reactions and feelings common to the outside into the therapy setting. Play was the principle medium used by the child to relate himself to the therapist and the feelings he has about him. The actual content of the play was seen as less important than the use to which the child put it. In the therapeutic relationship, the therapist was not considered a passive participant. He was expected to assume a leadership role in helping the child to become increasingly active in dealing with problems with which he has some concern (Allen, 1976). Taft (1937), in a discussion of "relationship therapy," stated that often the therapist has no specific goal other than being willing to permit the child to exercise his own will on the way to resolving his problems. The patient is there to use the therapist, and the therapist must be willing to accept this role. In regard to A. Freud's concept of the therapist as a teacher, Taft felt that such a relationship would only place an additional obligation on the child to conform to someone else's idea of acceptable behavior. Many children that come for therapy are already overburdened with pressure from more powerful others to conform to certain behavioral codes, and it is not logical to think that they will respond favorably to additional structures.

In these situations, according to Taft, the therapist must always consider the priorities from the child's point of view and must yield to these priorities. Such a therapeutic orientation is one reason why "relationship therapy" is non-scientific in nature and resists structured, preconceived research designs. One factor considered to be quantitative in nature by Taft is the sense of fear in therapy situations (however he does suggest a manner in which fear can be measured). Fear is described as the anxiety associated with not being capable of achieving mastery over troubling issues or achieving mastery and not being able to maintain it.

The consideration of fear as a critical aspect of problem-solving comes from the conceptualizations of Rank (1945), as does much of the thinking translated into "relationship therapy" terms. Rank considered wanting to do something and not wanting the same thing at the same time as being the fundamental dualism of life in which fear is manifested. The fear of becoming a separate self-directed individual, on one hand, and the fear of dying without having lived, on the other, was paramount. The purpose of "relationship therapy" was seen as a process through which the child could learn to resolve these fear-related issues and know it is acceptable for the individual to have a creative will, and at the same time, relate the self to others (Taft 1937).

In regard to fear-producing events in a child's life, Levy (1976) proposed a form of treatment he called release therapy. The fear factor was seen as being produced by traumatic events in the child's life, such as night terrors that ensue following the viewing of a horror movie or other fear-inducing incidents. Release therapy was not seen as being helpful in cases such as maternal rejection or overprotection since the mother in such situations would be the object of therapy and not the child. Release therapy was described as play sessions devoted entirely to overcoming anxieties through destructive behavior, messy play, and general "naughtiness." The therapist may select the material and depict the plot which the child is permitted to repeat until he tires of the activity. Imposition of play themes and materials by the therapist relegates release therapy to a much more directive orientation to problem resolution. Here the therapist "sets the stage," and the child acts and reacts within a preconceived format (Guerney, 1982). Regardless of its directive nature, release therapy carries with it some overtones of "relationship therapy" and was cited for comparative purposes. There are many other aspects to the approach, such as resorting to interpretations in the fashion of psychoanalysis in particularly hard cases. The point is that approaches to play therapy borrow from and build upon one another and are not always pure in their implementations.

## CLIENT-CENTERED THERAPY

According to Dorfman (1951), client-centered therapy owes much of its evolution to older therapies. Contributions from the Freudians include (a) the concept of play as being the natural language of the child, (b) the value of permissiveness in the play setting, and (c) play as being cathartic for the child. From the relationship therapists have come (a) the emphasis of the present rather than the past, (b) the lessening of the authoritative role of the therapist, (c) the de-emphasis of play content and the emphasis of therapist response to expressed feelings, and (d) the use of the therapy hour by the child as he chooses.

To determine in what ways client-centered therapy is unique, there is the need to consider its theoretical base, which is attributed to the client-centered counseling approach of Rogers. According to Rogers (1951), client-centered, or non-directive therapy as it is often called, is built upon specific observations of man's behavior in relationships with others that transcend the influences of culture. It is also considered by Rogers to be a fluid and dynamic approach to human relationships that is constantly changing as a result of clinical evidence and research findings. Rogers goes on to comment that to some counselors, the non-directive approach has been interpreted as passive listening. Playing a passive, or listening only role, could be helpful to some clients desperately in need of catharsis, but many more clients will feel they have been rejected by the counselor. Another interpretation of the counselor's role has been described as an effort to clarify or objectify the client's feelings, but this description also has proved misleading. In an effort to operationalize a definition of client-centered therapy, Roger's interpretation is as follows:

> The client experiences a feeling of safety in the warmth of the relationship with the therapist. He is then able to explore certain aspects of his behavior and why it has been necessary to deny awareness of his behavior. As he voices his new perceptions of himself the therapist accepts them. The client then too finds that he can accept himself without guilt. He has been enabled to do this because another person has been able to adopt his frame of reference, to perceive with him, yet to perceive with acceptance and respect (p. 41).

Rogers states that the therapist's attitude and function so described reduces the problem found in other therapies. That problem is to prevent the therapist's biases and life orientations from interfering with the therapeutic process in the client.

Axline (1969) described the client-centered approach as it applied to children. She explained non-directive play therapy as being based on the assumption that the individual has within himself the ability to solve his own problems satisfactorily aided by a growth impulse that makes mature behavior more satisfying than immature behavior. Play therapy was described as the most favorable opportunity available to the child to experience growth since play is his natural medium for self-expression.

In order to clarify the nature of therapist-child interaction within the client-centered play therapy approach, Axline provides eight basic principles to guide the therapist in non-directive therapeutic contacts. Briefly these principles are (a) development of rapport early in the therapeutic relationship, (b) unqualified acceptance of the child, (c) permissiveness, (d) recognition and reflection of feelings expressed by the child, (e) respect for the child's ability to solve personal problems, (f) the therapist's interaction with the child as non-directive, (g) recognition of the therapeutic process as a gradual one, and (h) establishment of behavioral limitations to assist the child in accepting responsibility for the establishment and maintenance of the therapeutic relationship.

The principles provided by Axline imply there must be sensitive communication between the therapist and child. Communication emanating from the child is on the non-verbal, as well as verbal, level, and it is important for the therapist not to interject his frame of reference through actions or verbal comments. Probing questions or statements are to be avoided, and communication should be limited to reflections of feelings and descriptive reiterations of activity that takes place in the play therapy setting (Axline, 1976). The client-centered therapist is required to be cautious in regard to reinforcing particular behaviors. Reward or approval may tend to encourage the child to limit actions and expressions to those which are perceived to be favored by the therapist. In the same light, acceptance is threatened if the therapist criticizes or indicates disapproval of child behaviors that are within the limits of the therapy session (Moustakas, 1953). In responding to questions originating from the child, the therapist is expected to redirect the inquiry in such a way so as to facilitate the child's play. Here again, the child is encouraged to follow personal inclinations rather than placing the therapist in a directive decision-making role. Inquiry is responded to by indicating that within the play session, things can be any way the child wants them to be. The child then, provided with complete freedom of expression in the enactment of fantasy play, is allowed to generate genuine affect and is encouraged to achieve meaningful self-realization (Axline, 1976).

Guerney (1981), in a discussion of client-centered play therapy, states that the non-directive child therapist does not differ significantly from other therapists in developing a warm, friendly, and empathic relationship with the child. The client-centered therapist participates in the child's play and strives not to be distant or cool in interacting with the child. Most of the therapist's behaviors are designed, however, to facilitate self-direction, self-exploration, and self-growth. She goes on to state that such an approach does not mean the child is permitted to have license or to be abusive. The issue of limits within the client-centered therapy setting is therefore significant. Ginott (1976) comments that children both in therapy and real life require a clear definition of acceptable and unacceptable behavior.

However, there are differences between limits in the play setting and those in the outside world. The playroom limits are far fewer, and the child is accepted for his need to break them (Dorfman, 1951). Willful destruction of play equipment and attacks on the therapist are typical of such limitations. Limits can be introduced when the child first enters the playroom or introduced as need for limitations arises. Axline (1969) prefers the latter so that the child will not view limitations as a challenge. She also feels that limitations should be tailored to the therapist's personal requirements, though care should be taken not to allow prohibitions to interfere with the child's freedom of expression. Such an approach is seen as providing a secure environment for therapist-child interaction and prevents the manipulation of guilt feelings in the child due to poorly defined behavioral boundaries.

## PLAY MATERIALS

An important consideration in client-centered therapy is the selection of play materials. Lebo (1976) suggests that a basis for selecting toys to be used in therapy is essential. He comments that most therapists set the age of 12 as the upper limit for successful play therapy, with the lower limit being three or four. Therefore, a range of toys and materials should reflect age considerations. Guerney (1981) states that since children from ages 10 through 12 have entered a period of competition and realistic game playing, board games, target games, and games simulating competitive sports are desirable. Toys and equipment that promote fantasy play for this older age group are also desirable. These would include tape recorders, science equipment, and materials that stimulate role-playing, such as medical equipment. In her discussion of playroom materials, Guerney offers a general criteria for their selection. Such criteria would be toys that (a) can be used in various ways, such as constructional toys and toys that can be adapted for more than one purpose, (b) encourage the expression of feelings most difficult to deal with in real life, such as aggression and dependence, and (c) can be played with by more than one person so that the therapist can be included in play activities. Axline (1969) suggests that all toys should be simple in construction and easy to manipulate so as not to frustrate the child. She included dolls, playhouses and materials, toy guns, soldiers, nursing bottles, kitchen and dining equipment, pounding sets, sandboxes, art supplies, toy telephones, cars and airplanes, etc. She also felt all toys and materials should be easily accessible to the children.

## SUMMARY AND REMARKS

It seems appropriate to make some remarks regarding play therapy approaches in order to provide perspective to the discussion. It has been the intent to limit this investigation to the most significant play therapy strategies that have evolved out of the psychoanalytical tradition. The selections of the pychoanalytical play therapy of Klein and Freud, relationship therapy, and client-centered therapy are meant to be representative, rather than inclusive. There are, of course, many variations of these approaches, as well as techniques growing out of the behaviorist and cognitive/interactionist theories of human growth and development. However, the play theory orientations outlined do seem to have generated the most interest and are most frequently cited when consideration is directed toward the use of play for therapeutic purposes.

In this discussion, differentiating between relationship therapy and the client-centered approach is significant. Indeed, the two are often thrown together as being basically one and the same. Such is the case in the organization of *The Therapeutic Use of Child's Play* (Schaefer, 1976). Both the relationship and client-centered views share the conviction that the child should be self-directing in resolving issues that are problematical for him. They also share the belief that people in general are self-curative, if they are given the opportunity to be so, through acceptance of their concerns by the therapist as they arise in the therapeutic setting. Both are also rooted in the here and now as compared to the historical orientation of the psychoanalyst. However, of the two, the client-centered approach, adhering to the Rogerian tradition as interpreted for children by Axline (1969), appears to be much less directive in its therapist-child interactions. Representative transcriptions of these interactions are profuse in Taft (1933) and Axline (1969) and bear reviewing by anyone interested in a comparative analysis. In addition, the descriptions of human psychological functioning in regard to the resolution of problems surrounding self-identity as represented by Rank (1945) and Rogers (1951) are of interest. In regard to the former and relationship therapy, the altering of a specific psychologial construct (i.e., the aspects of fear and the fundamental dualism of life) was provided as one of the goals of therapeutic intervention. Rogers (1951), on the other hand, expresses a much more generalized view of the attainment of self-identity and is reluctant to presume any one causative psychological factor.

Such a distinction may well be academic but rapidly assumes significance in the sorting out and evaluation of trends in regard to rationales for the application of play therapy strategies.


## PLAY THERAPY RESEARCH

The investigation thus far has consisted primarily of a descriptive outline rather than an evaluative effort aimed at determining the effectiveness of the play therapy approaches discussed. Such a task would indeed be difficult since play therapy approaches do not lend themselves well to experimental design. The inference is not that research is non-existent in regard to play therapy. Most experimental effort has been directed to client-centered approaches. Guerney (1981) states that compared to many therapeutic approaches, a considerable amount of research in regard to the outcomes of client-centered play therapy has been done. In referring to play therapy research, Ginott (1964) comments it is difficult indeed to determine whether beneficial outcomes are related to practical procedures and theoretical rationales or to incidental variables such as a generalized increase in adult attention.

The intent here will be to provide some representative samples of play therapy studies in order to illustrate the nature and outcomes of experimental efforts. Some additional research will also be discussed in regard to therapist-child interactions and its influence on aggression and fantasy play behavior.

One of the first studies that tried to analyze what actually takes place in client-centered therapy sessions was initiated by Landisberg and Snyder (1946). Four cases were observed and evaluated according to response categories of the therapist in regard to content and of the children in regard to content, emotion expressed, and activity levels. The ages of the children ranged from five to six years. The result indicated an increase in the children's activity levels during the last three-fifths of the therapy sessions. Three-fifths of the total responses were attributed to the child, while two-fifths were attributed to the therapist. The percentage of child responses devoted to emotional release rose from 50 percent to 70 percent during the last three-fifths of the therapy sessions. The expression of negative feelings related to others, as opposed to themselves or the therapist, also increased over time. The inferences made as a result of this information were that behavior exhibited by the child conformed to the claims made by client-centered therapy advocates and that therapist responses were reflective and followed the direction set by the child.

Finke (1947) observed six play therapists and six children ranging in age from five to eleven years. She derived categories based on expressions of feeling in the belief that such expressions would indicate changing emotional reactions. It was found that the children demonstrated trends which tended to divide the play therapy into three stages: (a) child is either reticent or talkative and tends to exhibit aggression; (b) imaginative play is with less aggression and testing limits in the playroom; and (c) child draws therapist into his play in effort to establish a relationship. The conclusion drawn was that play therapy had its own characteristic pattern which was consistent over the cases observed.

Lebo (1952) devised a study to test the possible relationships between chronological age and the types of statements made by children in play therapy. Finke's categories were used with 20 children over three play therapy sessions. An attempt was made to control for intellectual and social variables. The children were grouped in age categories of four, six, eight, ten, and twelve years of age. It was found that age did seem to account for definite trends in the types of statements made by the children. The older the child, the less likely he was to share his decisions with the therapist. Less time was spent testing limitations, and they were less likely to draw the therapist into their play. Also, the older the child, the more likely he was to express likes and dislikes.

Dorfman (1958) conducted a study with children rated as maladjusted by their teachers. Control groups were used and matched with treatment children. A follow-up survey of the children was conducted one year and a half following the completion of treatment. Following an average of 19 treatment sessions in the school setting, the treatment children rated as maladjusted showed significantly greater gains on personality measures. These gains persisted and increased as indicated by the follow-up survey.

Seeman, Barry, and Ellinwood (1964) also conducted a study within the school setting with children as young as seven and eight years of age and designated as lowest in adjustment based on teacher ratings and personality tests. All of these children were higher in aggression than their better-adjusted peers. These children were randomly assigned to play therapy treatment groups and control groups. A one year follow-up survey was conducted. All children who received treatment had lower aggression scores as compared to pre-treatment ratings. Control group children who were initially rated as high in aggression remained so. These results carried over into the follow-up survey.

Reif and Stollack (1972) conducted a study directed to training undergraduate students to serve as play therapists. The goal was to demonstrate that para-professionals trained and supervised in the provision of non-directive therapy could effect positive changes in children considered to be normal. The experimental group consisted of nine undergraduate students, five males and four females, who underwent training in client-oriented therapy techniques. A control group was randomly selected and received no play therapy training. Both groups were required to find one child with whom they would interact within a play setting. Four sessions were videotaped for analysis through statistical methods. Results indicated that the student trainees demonstrated greater frequencies of the following behaviors: (a) reflection of verbal content; (b) reflection of motor behavior; (c) interpretation of feelings; and (d) reciprocal participation in fantasy behavior. Control students demonstrated greater frequencies of asking questions, rejection, direction, criticism, and nonattention. Children who were part of the experimental group demonstrated greater statement of personal and interpersonal awareness, fantasy aggression, fantasy behavior, and nonrecognition. Control children demonstrated greater frequencies of excitement behavior and, with the exception of nonrecognition, emitted lower frequencies in all of the other behavior areas. The implications of this study as expressed by the authors is the feasibility of increasing the quality of human interaction in large segments of the population by such an educational approach.

From the studies just reviewed, it is evident that research efforts in the area of play therapy have become increasingly more sophisticated in their design and level of objectivity. Such sophistication is evidenced in the increased use of research strategies associated with scientific experimental studies (e.g., control of social, intellectual, and age variables, use of control groups, pre- and post-testing, and utilization of statistical methodology). Efforts to quantify and qualify psychological phenomenon seldom reach a level of acceptance for those who demand strict objectivity and absolute control of all variables through highly sophisticated research design. Indeed, any effort to evaluate human behavior carries with it some pitfalls in regard to validity. In total, it does appear that play therapist advocates are persistent in their convictions and are beginning to bend to the demands for accountability by the professional and lay segments of society. In sum, it appears that research efforts have demonstrated the ability of client-centered play therapists to predict behavioral trends in children participating in play therapy. In addition, a student segment of the general population was able to acquire and effectively use interactional strategies with children that typify the client-centered approach. The positive outcomes evidenced by positive student and child behaviors strongly support the continued generalization of principles espoused by client-centered advocates to other professional and non-professional segments of society (Guerney, Guerney, and Stollack, 1972).

## SELECTED VARIABLES IN THERAPIST-CHILD INTERACTIONS

In the preceding discussion, certain themes having a strong influence on therapist-child interactions in play therapy settings have surfaced rather persistently. The themes referred to are (a) the degree of permissiveness and/or restrictiveness imposed by the therapist, (b) the level of interaction by the therapist with the child, and (c) the impact of these factors on the expression of fantasy and aggression. The purpose here is to cite some representative studies directed to these interaction dynamics in order to acquaint the reader with their significance within the play therapy format.

A particularly interesting study was conducted by Moustakos and Schalock (1955). Their purpose was to examine the nature of interaction between the therapist and child in non-directive play therapy settings. Of particular interest was the influence of the child on the therapist's responses. Such an orientation suggests the perception of therapist-child interaction as being circular, or one having an effect on the other, rather than a linear model which suggests a singular directional flow of behavioral influences within the play therapy setting. Two groups of children were chosen for study, one with serious emotional problems and the other without emotional problems. A category system for measuring adult-child interaction was used as well as anxiety hostility ratings. In all, 9,084 therapist behavioral responses were recorded over 18 play sessions. The children were from similar socio-economic backgrounds of middle class professional families and were four years of age.

The results of the study were stated in reference to particular questions. It was hoped that it would be answered by the experiment. These questions and their resolutions follow. Are there differences in the way in which the therapist interacts with the two groups of children? In response to question number one, Moustakos and Schalock stated that, in comparison, the therapist's responses to the children's behaviors were essentially the same for both groups. A majority, or 85 percent, of these therapist responses were (a) attentive observation, (b) recognition of stimulation, (c) giving information, and (d) reflection of feelings. Punishment or criticism were not used at all, and expressions of affection and rewards were strikingly absent. Small amounts of forbidding, structuring, restricting, and directing were observed. Basically, the child was left to operate on his own terms in a nonjudgmental atmosphere.

The second question concerning the results of the study was: What was the nature of the child's interaction with the therapist in both groups? In response to question number two, Moustakos and Schalock stated that child behaviors, representing 95 percent of those observed, consisted of nonattention, attentive observation, statement of condition or action, seeking information, giving information, recognition of stimulation, and nonrecognition of stimulation. The most frequent behavior for the group with behavior problems consisted of nonattention which comprised 45 percent of all responses. The group without emotional problems demonstrated nonattention responses in 33 percent of all responses. One third of the time was spent by both groups in behaviors that did not directly involve the therapist. This was interpreted as indicative of the high value the child places on being self-directed. The emotionally disturbed group demonstrated a marked absence of overt anxiety and any mention of overt fears. They were also more prone to attack and threats and expressed more dependency through a higher frequency of question asking. Neither group sought rewards or affection from the therapist.

The third question framing the results of the study was: Do certain kinds of therapist behaviors consistently produce certain reactions in the children within the therapy setting? In response to question number three, Moustakos and Schalock stated that approximately 80 percent of therapist responses led to some kind of recognition or further exploration on the children's part. Both groups almost always accepted the therapist's decisions regarding limits. Therapist comments oriented to time, indicating sessions were drawing to a close, were rejected by both groups 50 percent of the time. Child responses as a result of therapist reflection were nearly twice as frequent in the non-emotionally disturbed group.

The fourth, and last, question was: Do certain types of child behavior consistently produce certain reactions from the therapist? In response to question number four, Moustakos and Schalock stated that the therapists' responses to children seeking information was to give the information 75 percent of the time. In the remaining 25 percent, the children were left to cope and seek their own solutions. The therapists were careful not to create dependency relationships. Directions suggested and directions commanded by the children were almost always cooperated with by the therapist.

When the command involved an issue, however, the child was left to resolve it on his own. Therapist responses to such commands consisted of (a) delaying a direct response to his command, (b) seeking information from the child, (c) making an interpretation, (d) observing attentively, (e) recognizing command, and (f) refusing to cooperate.

In summary, Moustakos and Schalock stated that the non-emotionally disturbed children emitted more verbal interactions, shared their experiences, gave more clues to understanding, and exhibited more assertive behaviors than did the emotionally disturbed group. In general, the therapists responded to simple commands by acceptance and cooperation when the child's request did not tend to create a dependency relationship or to dominate or control the therapist. From the results, it was concluded that the non-directive play therapists were remarkably consistent in their responses to these diverse groups of children. They strived for and maintained a child-directed atmosphere and were not diverted from this goal by behavioral characteristics of the children. This is not to say that the therapists were not required to adapt, but that they did so within the criteria established for non-directive child-centered therapy procedures.

The aspect of permissiveness, which pervades child therapy approaches, and its relation to aggression was investigated by Siegel and Kohn (1959). They considered adult permissiveness as a way of reducing fear of punishment in the child. The hypothesis was that children's aggression would decrease as a result of the absence of a permissive adult in the play setting and increase in the presence of a permissive adult. Pairs of young boys were observed in two sessions separated by two days. Half of the sessions were conducted in the presence of an adult and half in the absence of an adult. Only the aggressive behavior of the oldest boys in the pairs was scored. The findings confirmed the hypothesis, as more aggression was observed in the presence of a permissive adult. Siegel (1957), in explaining the increase of observed aggression in the presence of an adult, suggested that the realization by the child that he will not be punished is not adequate. Instead, it seemed to be that the young child abdicates behavioral control (i.e., superego and ego controls) to the adult, whereas in adult absence, the child's own internalized behavioral controls are maintained. Such an interpretation is reminiscent of the psychoanalytical views of behavior, indicating that persistent linkages with Freudian personality theory exist when considering issues related to play therapy.

The quality and quantity of adult interaction in a play setting and its relation to aggression was investigated by Pintler (1945). Adult interaction was categorized under the descriptors of high-interaction and low-interaction. High-interaction consisted of frequent attention to and interest in the child's play, while low-interaction consisted of a minimal amount of interest in the child's play. Her results demonstrated that the amount of fantasy aggression was greater under conditions of high-interaction on the part of the adult.

Though levels of interaction and permissiveness are not synonymous, they are related. Ginott's (1965) definition of permissiveness as "the acceptance of imaginary and symbolic behavior" (p. 62) illustrates this relationship. It is reasonable to assume that a high level of positive interaction with the child would enhance his perception of adult acceptance and increase the expression of fantasy play. Klinger (1969) concluded that fantasy play behavior serves an important role in achieving ego mastery and coping with internal conflicts in the child. Singer (1966) defines fantasy as a shift of attention away from sensory rooted physical or mental tasks to thoughts and actions that emanate from within the individual and reinforce the concept of fantasy as functional for the child in bringing forth salient personal issues. Therefore, the enhancement of fantasy in play therapy sessions, through the use of high levels of interaction in a permissive atmosphere, relates in a significant way to the implementation of therapeutic play.

## CONCLUDING REMARKS

Throughout this investigation of play therapy, an attempt has been made to discuss characteristics of each approach that best illustrates the essence of therapist-child relationships or interactions. The emphasis has been placed on techniques utilized for intervention with the individual child. Group therapy applications, however, are also possible utilizing these same basic principles and would be most appropriate for relationship and client-centered approaches. In group settings, the therapist would encourage self-direction and acceptance in a broader social milieu. In addition, and as stated earlier, play therapy as implemented is seldom pure and is subject to the therapist's personal convictions and methodological interpretations. The basic perception of the child as being innately motivated and driven to seek his own solutions to personal adjustment problems, given a facilitating environment, does seem to prevail. Such an attitude is consistent with the maturationist view and appears to be applied in a consistent manner by play therapists, as demonstrated through various evaluative studies. The outcomes of play therapy and their persistence over time is an issue which will require additional study through longitudinal empirical investigation. Though such efforts have been undertaken on a limited scale, more quantitative, as well as qualitative, research is needed. In truth, such a statement could be made in regard to many disciplines engaged in the treatment and measurement of human behavior.

## REFERENCES

Allen, F. H., "Therapeutic work with children," in *The Therapeutic Use of Child's Play*, C. Schaefer, ed. New York: Jason Aronson, Inc. (1976).

Axline, V. M. *Play Therapy* (revised ed.). New York: Ballantine Books (1969).

Axline, V. M., "Play therapy procedures and results," in *The Therapeutic Use of Child's Play*, C. Schaefer, ed. New York: Jason Aronson, Inc. (1976).

Baldwin, A. L. *Theories of Child Development.* New York: John Wiley & Sons (1968).

Caldwell, B. M. and Richmond, J. B., "The impact of theories of child development," in *Reading in Human Development*, H. W. Bernard & W. C. Huckins, eds. Boston: Allyn & Bacon (1967).

Dorfman, E., "Personality outcomes of client-centered skill therapy," *Psychological Monographs, 73*, (3) (whole #456) (1978).

Dorfman, E., "Play therapy," in *Client Centered Therapy*, C. R. Rogers. Boston: Houghton Mifflin (1951).

Erikson, E. H., "Studies in the interpretation of play," *Genetic Psychology Monographs, 22*, 559–671 (1940).

Finke, H., "Changes in the expression of emotionalized attitudes in six cases of play therapy," Unpublished masters thesis, Univ. of Chicago (1947).

Freud, A. *The Psycho-analytical Treatment of Children.* London: Imago Pub. Co. (1946).

Freud, S., "Beyond the pleasure principle," in *A General Selection from the Works of Sigmund Freud,* J. Rickman, ed. New York: Liveright Pub. Corp. (1957).

Freud, S., "The cases of 'Little Hans' and the Rat Man'," *Complete Works.* Vol. 10. Lanelon: Hogarth Press (1955).

Gesell, A. and Ilg, F. L. *Child Development.* New York: Harper & Brothers (1949).

Ginott, H. G. *Between Parent and Child.* New York: Macmillan (1965).

Ginott, H. G., "Research in play therapy," in *Child Psychotherapy,* M. R. Haworth, ed. New York: Basic Books, Inc. (1964).

Ginott, H. G., "Therapeutic intervention in child treatment," in *The Therapeutic Use of Child's Play,* C. Schaefer, ed. New York: Jason Aronson, Inc. (1976).

Guerney, B., Guerney, L. F., and Stollack, G., "The potential advantages of changing from a medical to an educational model in practicing psychology," *Interpersonal Development, 2,* (4), 238–245 (1972).

Guerney, L. F., "Client-centered (nondirective) play therapy," in *Handbook of Play Therapy,* C. Schaefer & K. O'Conner, eds. New York: John Wiley & Sons, Inc., in press.

Guerney, L. F., "Play therapy in counseling settings," Unpublished paper, The Pennsylvania State University (1982).

Klein, M. *The Psychoanalysis of Children.* London: Hogarth Press (1932).

Klein, M., "The psychoanalytic play technique," *American Journal of Orthopsychiatry, 25,* 223–227 (1955).

Klein, M., "The psychoanalytic play technique," in *The Therapeutic Use of Child's Play,* C. Schaefer, ed. New York: Jason Aronson, Inc. (1976).

Klinger, E., "Development of imaginative behavior: Implications of play for a theory of fantasy," *Psychological Bulletin, 72,* 277–298 (1969).

Kohlberg, L. and Mayer, R., "Development as the aim of education," *Harvard Educational Review, 42,* (4), 449–496 (1972).

Landisberg, S. and Snyder, W., "Nondirective play therapy," *Journal of Clinical Psychology, 2,* 203–213 (1946).

Langer, J. *Theories of development.* New York: Holt, Rhinehart & Winston, Inc. (1969).

Lebo, D., "The relationship of response categories in play therapy to chronological age," *Child Psychiatry, 2,* 330–336 (1952).

Levy, D. M., "Release therapy," in *The Therapeutic Use of Child's Play,* C. Schaefer, ed. New York: Jason Aronson, Inc. (1976).

Lieberman, J. N. *Playfulness: Its Relation to Imagination and Creativity.* New York: Academic Press (1977).

Millar, S. *The Psychology of Play.* Baltimore: Penguin Books (1968).

Moustakos, C. E. *Children in Play Therapy.* New York: McGraw Hill (1953).

Moustakos, C. E. and Schalock, H. D., "An analysis of therapist-child interaction in play therapy," *Child Development, 26,* 143–157 (1955).

Nickerson, E. T., "Recent trends and innovations in play therapy," *International Journal of Child Psychotherapy, 2* (1), 53–70 (1973).

Piaget, J. *Play, Dreams, and Imitation in Childhood.* New York: Norton (1962).

Pintler, M., "Doll play as a function of the experimenter-child interaction and initial organization of materials, *Child Development, 16,* 145–166 (1945).

Pulaski, M. A., "Play symbolism in cognitive development," in *The Therapeutic Use of Child's Play,* C. Schaefer, ed. New York: Jason Aronson, Inc. (1976).

Rank, O. *Will Therapy; and Truth and Reality.* New York: Knopf (1945).

Reif, T. F. and Stollak, G. E. *Sensitivity to Young Children: Training and its Effects.* East Lansing: Michigan State Univ. Press (1972).

Rogers, C. *Client Centered Therapy.* Boston: Houghton Mifflin (1951).

Schaefer, C., ed. *The Therapeutic Use of Child's Play.* New York: Jason Aronson, Inc. (1976).

Seaver, J. W. and Cartwright, C. A., "A pluralistic foundation for training early childhood professionals," *Curriculum Inquiry, 7* (4), 305–329 (1977).

Seeman, J., Barry, E., and Ellinwood, C., "Interpersonal assessment of play therapy outcome," *Psychotherapy: Theory, Research and Practice, 1* (2), 64–66 (1964).

Siegel, A. E., "Aggressive behavior of young children in the absence of an adult," *Child Development, 28,* 371–378 (1957).

Siegel, A. E. and Kohn, L. G., "Permissiveness, permission, and aggression: The effect of adult presence or absence on aggression in child's play," *Child Development, 30,* 313–141 (1959).

Singer, J. F. *Daydreaming: An Introduction to the Experimental Study of Inner Experience.* New York: Random House (1966).

Taft, J. *The Dynamics of Therapy in a Controlled Relationship.* New York: Macmillan Co. (1937).

Walder, R., "Psychoanalytic theory of play," in *The Therapeutic Use of Child's Play,* C. Schaefer, ed. New York: Jason Aronson, Inc. (1976).

# Alleviating aggressive behaviors using therapy and play objects in the psychoanalytic mainstream

**Cheryl Confer**
*Sweetwater County School District (Wyoming)*
*Early Childhood Development Area*

## INTRODUCTION

Anyone working with children for any length of time notices that they hit and kick each other as a sign of anger and aggression. The adult might talk to them about walking away from an argument or telling each other how they feel, but their automatic reaction is usually "name calling" or hitting and kicking.

For example, Sam is such a child. Through conferences with his mother, it was inferred that the home environment met his needs. When he became angry, Sam would strike out by hurting other people. When he became angry with the teacher, he would kick, throw things, or rip up papers he was expected to complete. The teacher tried various types of behavior modification, and at times he would choose to control himself until, one day, he stabbed a boy with a pencil.

Now, what does the adult do in this situation? Where does the teacher go? To whom does the adult turn to for that answer?

The adult who is close to the problem will be the one who will need to develop that answer. The adult can turn to herself when this type of behavior is exhibited. It is the adult who will have to know what to do. Maier (1965) feels that understanding the developmental patterns of children provides answers to aggressive behaviors. In turn, the adult abstracts from this developmental literature the content he considers the most usable knowledge. In order for adults to be better equipped to help these children, they must strive for a wider understanding of human development.

It is also important for those in contact with aggressive children (i.e., parents, counselors, doctors) to expand their knowledge of human development, in order that they too might have a reservoir of knowledge in dealing with children. For these people to be helpful to the aggressive child, they must also broaden their knowledge and understanding of how youngsters grow and learn.

The psychoanalytic approach as a background in the development of a child's personality provides some answers in working with aggressive actions of children. The purpose of this chapter is to discuss how the use of play and play objects as therapy can ameliorate aggressive actions in young children.

## PERSONALITY DEVELOPMENT

An examination of the psychoanalytic theory of personality development aids in an understanding of the aggressive behavior exhibited by some children. The stages to be examined start with the child at birth and continue to the onset of puberty.

There are many whose names can be associated with the psychoanalytic school of thought, but for the purpose of discussion, this chapter examines S. Freud, the father of psychoanalytic theory, A. Freud, who is S. Freud's daughter, and E. H. Erikson, a contemporary follower of the Freuds.

## S. FREUD AND E. H. ERIKSON

Freud proposed psychosexual stages of development, each of which uses a certain zone of the body for gratification of the id, the unconscious source of motives, strivings, desires, and energy. The ego mediates between the demands of the id and the outside world. The superego represents what may be called reason and common sense, in contrast to the id which contains the passions (Smart, 1973). Another term is libido, which is a force of energy originating in the id.

Freud's study dealt with the id, the unconscious self which he studied through dreams. Erikson believed that the study of an individual's ego development should be based not only on the study of the individual but also on groups of individuals and whole cultures. Erikson believed that studying a child's play would also show the ego's development.

Erikson implies that the ego provides the individual with specific direction, and the superego is assumed to be composed of personal experience with the ideas and attitudes of significant adults and peers (Maier, 1965). The ego processes are developed through play, speech, thought, and actions. The use and adaptation of the ego processes are the way of human life (Maier, 1965). Maier notes that Erikson's emphasis on personality development is more social than classical Freudian theory.

## STAGES OF A CHILD'S PERSONALITY DEVELOPMENT

The personality traits being developed during each stage are the ego and the superego. Through each stage, Freud refers to sexual gratification as action accepted by society and caused by a positive reaction from the child. Behaviors which are classified as aggressive behaviors are those behaviors which are not accepted by society and get a negative reaction from society. Smart and Smart (1973) identified Freud's psychosexual stages as oral, anal, phallic, oedipal, latency, and puberal. The oral stage occurs during the first year of life and focuses on pleasure derived from the mouth. The anal stage arises in the second and third years and centers on pleasure coming from anal and urethral sensations. The phallic stage means pleasure derived from genital stimulation and exists between the ages of three and four. The oedipal stage occurs between the ages of four and five, and the child in this phase regards the parent of the opposite sex as a love object and the same sex parent as a rival. From ages six to seven, the latency stage occurs. In this stage, sexual desires become unconscious, and the child identifies with the parent and peers of his own sex. In the puberal stage, sexuality begins and arises after age eight and nine. Erikson's views of personality focus essentially on Freud's five stages and are basically restatements of Freud's ideas (Maier, 1965). Yet for Erikson, these stages

are phases of constant motion. The person does not possess personality—
he is always developing one.

Reflecting salient social institutions, Erikson viewed the ego within an
evolving time table that is psychological, biological, and social. Maier
(1965) saw the personality developing as a function of three main variables.
There are inner laws of growth which are invariant and biologically irrever-
sible. The second variable is cultural which identifies a rate of growth
relative to specific laws of inner development. For Erikson's orientation to
personality, Maier identifies the third as ideopathic responses of individuals to the demands of society. In addition, the developmental processes in personality can be repressed. In turn, the repression of personality ceases under the power of the ego. This synthesis and integration and
repression provide challenges for the ego. As solutions to these challenges
occur, personality matures.

Smart and Smart (1973) note that each of Erikson's stages nurtures the
growth of specific attitudes, abilities, and convictions. After challenges are
met, the personality becomes more integrated and unified. Each of
Erikson's stages are described in the following section.


ERIKSON'S STAGES OF DEVELOPMENT

The following stages describe Erikson's ideas of development. The first
four stages are discussed; the other four stages occur after age 11, the
onset of puberty, and are therefore not detailed in this chapter.

*Stage 1—Basic Trust Versus Mistrust:* This stage takes place from birth
through the child's first year. It is similar to Freud's oral stage. The main
characteristic of this stage is the development of trust. Trust is important
to personality development because it promotes success. Growing initially
from the process of feeding between mother and infant, the trait of trust
continues to be nourished. In similar fashion, mistrust can develop when
the baby is required to wait prior to feeding and other forms of gratification. In addition, if the infant is physically and emotionally mistreated—
mistrust can occur. For a healthy personality to develop, greater amounts
of trust than mistrust must be learned.

During this stage, the libidonal energy is generated through the id processes and also through ego functions. The libidonal energy is shown by
the infant through crying, sucking, visonal reflexes, and motor
movements. When these functions are controlled by the infant, they
become processes of the ego. The ego during this stage must have the
positive trust of objects and the care-giver. In this stage, Erikson believes
the infant's sense of hope is also established.

*Stage 2—Autonomy versus Shame and Doubt:* This stage is apparent
between 18 months to three years. It is similar to Freud's anal stage, in
which the child is capable of controlling his own eliminatory functions.

During this stage, the child wants to do everything for himself. His new
motor powers are walking, climbing, and manipulating objects. The child
also has developed his mental powers of choosing and deciding. It is important during this stage for the child to discover that his behavior is his own
and he is an independent unit.

Erikson focuses on the ego which permits an awareness of self as an
autonomous unit. For a healthy ego development, the child must regard
frustration, in any one area, as a total feature in all areas.

As an aid to a healthy ego development, the child's parents or care-giver should give him plenty of suitable choices. These opportunities become times to decide when his judgement is adequate for successful outcomes. With these experiences, he grows in autonomy. He gets the feeling that he can control his body, himself, and his environment. Shame as a negative feeling develops when adults force the child to perform complex tasks above his developmental level (Smart and Smart, 1975).

Not only do care-givers play an important role in providing experiences for the child to develop his autonomy, but also there is the importance of play in which a child can set his own rules and boundaries. Play develops as doubt and shame decrease in frequency (Maier, 1965). It is important throughout this stage that the child develops his own self and also a realization of his "will."

*Stage 3—Initiative versus Guilt:* This stage is apparent during a child's fourth and fifth years of development. It is similar to the oedipal part of the genital stage of Freud's theory. To Erikson, it is during these years that a child develops his sense of initiative. The child takes an active part in mastering specific skills. Maier (1965) notes that the youngster should be given more opportunity for responsibility in his world of body, toys, pets, and younger sibs. With increasing maturation, the youngster can assume these responsibilities because of his continued improvement of language and motor skills—both gross and fine motor movements. Within this stage, the id requires new channels or modes of expression. In similar fashion, the superego has evolved to a point where it can handle id-oriented crisis situations. The child now faces the fact that he is his own "parent," a carrier of tradition.

The child's first step to "becoming a parent" is supervising himself. That is, the child's personality mechanisms must begin to take on the functions of parents and other significant adults. As the youngster takes on these functions, the child understands more and more the role of the parent.

During this stage, the id, ego, and superego start to find a mutual balance in the individual's personality development. Maier (1965) feels that at this point of development, internalizing relations of parents, peers, and significant others take on more authority. In addition, Maier (1965) feels that at this level of personality growth, the youngster learns that sexual differences exist between individuals in his environment.

The child during this time needs adult models to aid in his determining a sense of "right" and "wrong" in the development of his conscience. Also during this time, the parents and care-givers should express "love relationship" to the child. The child needs to realize that he has a sense of purpose in the framework of his society.

*Stage 4—Industry versus Inferiority:* This phase is apparent during the years six to the onset of puberty, between the ages of six to eleven. It is similar to Freud's latency period. It is during this stage that the child evolves as a worker and a producer. The child wants to do jobs well and takes the time to explore the possibilities of the job.

During this time, the child's efforts are devoted toward improving his ego processes. Maier (1965) stresses that more and more time and energy is spent by the child in communicating with his peers. Strength, cleverness, and wittiness become assets to the growing child; these traits are nurtured and practiced among his own peer group. And, the id and superego become more integrated as these characteristics are developed.

It is important for the child to have a feeling of well-being, and feelings of inferiority and inadequacy result when he feels he cannot measure up to the standards held for him by his family or society. Although play is a significant element for the child's growth at this stage, girls and boys divide along gender lines with separate play routines, behaviors, and games. Even though gender-related differences occur, practicing sex roles in play activities become primary. However, by the end of this stage, play begins to decrease in quality and quantity, and activities related to developing adolescent values emerge. Maier (1965) suggests that at this stage, play passes into work. However, Maier (1965) asserts that adolescents tend to pursue a middle-of-the-road position between working and playing; that is, they use play and work in equal amounts of time.

This phase shows the child working towards being an industrious person. His ego is strengthened by peer acceptance and adult approval of his meeting the standards held for him by his family or society. Group play in real-life situations merges into an industrious adolescent.

The child must pass through each stage and complete each stage before moving on to the next one. The positive development of each stage in the development of the ego and the superego provides the person with "healthy" personality development.

## A. FREUD AND THE AGGRESSIVE CHILD

A. Freud and Erikson worked extensively in the area of child psychology. A. Freud worked with the child's ego or consciousness and tried to understand its functions in averting painful, ego-alien ideas, impulses, and feelings.

A. Freud, in diagnosing children's psychology problems, determined a needed for specific assessment along with developmental stages. Pumpian-Midlin (1966) outlines these stages as (a) maturation, (b) adaptation, and (c) organization. The maturation stage continues ego functioning and internally-based instinct. The adaptation stage focuses on building object relations within an environmental setting. The final stage is organization and stresses the capacity of the individual for cognitive integration and resolution of conflicts. In using these stages of development, A. Freud looked for harmony or disharmony in relation to the ego and the id. In using this developmental play, there is flexibility in which the individual can progress and regress within the limits of normality.

In her book the *Ego and the Mechanisms of Defense*, A. Freud expands on the various defense mechanisms that certain anxiety situations call into action. The principal human defense she describes is repression, an unconscious process that is used when the child learns that certain actions could prove dangerous to himself. Other mechanisms are projection of one's own feeling onto another, directing aggressive impulses against the self, and identifying with an overpowering aggressor.

In her work with children, she concluded that at times, children would identify not with the aggressive person, but with the child's own aggression. Other acts of aggression were displayed by the child. According to A. Freud (1946), these include impersonating the aggressor and assuming the role of the aggressor in response to the threat.

The aggressive child may reverse roles and demonstrate aggressive acts he feels may befall him after he has misbehaved. Thus, the child is only internalizing the other people's criticisms of his behavior.

A. Freud also discusses a stage in the development of the superego referred to as "identification with the aggressor." In addition, it is supplemented by the projection of guilt. It is through this defense mechanism that the ego incorporates these criticisms into the superego. Through this defense mechanism, the child protects himself from personal and unpleasant self-criticism.

Using these methods of identification and understanding causes of aggressive behavior, A. Freud would use play therapy as a method in working with children who demonstrated aggressive behavior.

## PRINCIPLES OF PLAY THERAPY

Underlying all of play therapy is the notion of instinctual drives. They change form throughout life and continue to determine personality because they alter their form (Josselyn, 1955). The instinctual drives include aggression and love. The urge to strike-out aggressively is first exercised to obtain relief from distressful situations. At the next level, aggression is exercised in the immediate environment; it arises from presently-occurring distress. Lastly, it is exercised against abstract discomforts that transcend the immediate environment.

There are many variations and breakdowns in defining the aggressive child. The aggressive child may act out his aggression verbally—by yelling or screaming or physically hitting or kicking. In addition, Redl (1957) notes that aggression may be hidden in a compliant child. Other variations of the aggressive child do not appear destructive (e.g., withdrawal). The child who hates another is also destructive, but it is difficult to identify. All of these variations can produce problems in personality development and for society—if these variations are consistent and taken in extreme form.

Play therapy can be used as a tool to help understand and alleviate the aggessive actions of young children. Generally, play therapy theory regards play and playful actions as natural and common mediums to express feelings (Axline, 1947).

In the use of play therapy, the basic premise is that everyone strives towards a sense of well-being and a realization of personal potential. When listening to young children at play, emotions are observed and heard. Through play therapy, the child is the center of attention.

Most work in play therapy is done in a situation of a therapist working directly with a child. During these sessions, play is used as a time for the counselor to observe the child and reflect back to the child what he saw him doing. During the first session, a basic trust is established so the child would not feel threatened by the situation or the emotions that may be expressed during each therapy session. Also, the child knows that certain behaviors are not permitted during the play sessions, such as destruction of playroom property, harm to the counselor, or harm to the child or other children in the session. During non-directed play therapy, the child is treated with respect and dignity. The child has the sense that he is controlling the play sessions.

## TYPES OF PLAY THERAPY AND MATERIALS

The following are some basic types of play therapy that can be used with children in hospitals or in classroom settings. Axline (1947), in her work with aggressive children, stresses the point that a special room is not necessary for play therapy to be used. The medium a child will play with could be brought into a room, or a teacher may set an area aside for play centers. Axline feels that there are certain play materials that can be used successfully across play therapy theories and sessions. These materials include doll family and furniture, toy soldiers and army equipment, playhouse with furniture, animal toys, clay, rag dolls and puppets, telephones, crayons, sand box, and tools used in sand play. These materials are not all necessary for a play session. The adult working with the child may let him choose the materials he wishes to play with during the session. Mussen (1960) notes that doll play is effective because it elicits both verbal fantasy and fantasy behavior. The children actively make the dolls come alive and assume imaginary roles. Mussen (1960) states that doll play has a very high degree of validity in its own right because of the extreme degree of fantasy evoked by this medium. For example, Mussen (1960) reports on the findings of Hollenberg and Sperry (1951) to support the notion that doll play materials have a high degree of construct validity. These data show that children receiving little to no punishment at home showed the lowest frequency of doll play aggression, whereas, children receiving much punishment yielded the greatest amount of doll play aggression. Mussen (1960) reports similar results for studies conducted by Searset (1953) and Levin and Sears (1956). Doll play materials have contributed to the study of aggression in children not only as a determining factor but also as a method of therapy for children who demonstrate aggressive actions.

In the *Writings of Anna Freud,* A. Freud reports the study of chronically ill children spanning 20 years. Through play therapy principles and proper use of play materials, A. Freud reports that these children can ameliorate their fears and aggressions in hospitals and clinical settings. Children in hospitals undergoing some type of surgery were observed acting out aggressively towards nurses whom they blamed for their surgery. The ego has to rationalize and put into perspective the inner and outer worlds. It is through the use of dolls that anxiety or conflict can be played out and help the child to deal with emotions. Earle (1979) reports findings that show that doll play over a three week period helped two children work through their fears of surgical amputations of their legs.

With the child being made to feel that he can control the consequences, the child understands that he is not being punished. As the child plays with the doll, the observer could communicate feelings with the child by not directing the conversation but by reflecting back the child's verbalizations.

Play therapy can also be used in hospital settings to demonstrate the care the child needs, not only to his physical but also to his mental self. Play therapy is a technique in working with maladjusted behavior that could be used in a variety of settings, with a variety of materials. Another type of play therapy is a puppet therapy.

Using puppet therapy, Axline (1947) shows that this type and use of materials provides opportunities for children to play out their feelings. Antisocial behaviors and self-blame can be changed into constructive personality-building behaviors. Puppets can be easily and very simply made. Through their use, children can reenact events in which anxiety was felt.

Blocks are a very effective tool used in many play settings. Hartley, Frank, and Goldenson (1952) say that blocks are ideal for expression of emotion. The children can use blocks explosively in block therapy; they can knock them over and rebuild them. They can express possessiveness and pleasure, and blocks can be used subtly and in attack situations. Hartley, et al. (1952) call blocks the least threatening of all materials that can be used in therapy in preschool and hospital settings.

Another effective and inexpensive play material shown to be useful in therapy is clay. Hartley, et al. (1952), like A. Freud, feel that clay is also an ideal projective medium. Children can create real and invisible worlds in tangible form. They create a visible world of social reality that is used in emotive releases. Blocks also adapt very well to providing opportunities for social mastery. Gaining mastery over their world, children pound and stamp and integrate their actions and emotions. Hartley, et al. (1952) emphasize that through clay therapy, children integrate their personality and come to understand their feelings and social reality.

Through the case studies of different children involved in play therapy, definite proof is demonstrated that play therapy can ameliorate aggressive behaviors in children. Weigle and McNally (1980) explain that play therapy and these relevant open-ended play materials provide children with freedom and responsibility which are central to the counseling relationship. Through play therapy and proper use of materials, children come to understand and respect their own feelings, while at the same time, they learn to respect the feelings of others.

## HOSPITAL PLAY THERAPY

From the psychoanalytic research literature in general, implications and procedures can be drawn for adults working with children in individual or group settings that can be useful for aiding, coping, and ameliorating aggressive behaviors. In particular, Catalda, Bessman, Parker, Pearson, and Rogers (1979) note that implications and procedures drawn from psychoanalytic theories can be successfully used by medical staff in hospital settings. They also suggest that these same procedures can be employed by non-medical staff. Regardless of setting, the purpose is to benefit the child's growth and personality enhancement.

Farnum (1963) identifies several ways that these procedures can especially benefit children in hospital settings. First, play therapy techniques provide a medium which can be used by the child to express his feelings. These procedures can vent the hospitalized child's anxieties and stressful experiences. Second, as play therapy is used with hospitalized children, their self-concepts increase because they are learning new skills. Third, the child is in command in play therapy. This procedure permits the hospitalized child to pursue choices in these institutions where almost all of the goals, choices, and decisions are made for him. Fourth, using a wide variety of play permits variety. In addition, this principle allows the youngster to make definite choices based on his own desires and wishes. Fifth, the play activities should be simple and relatively short in duration. This will reduce frustration and enhance constructive learning. Finally, children in hospital settings should be encouraged to play in groups of two or more children. This principle contributes to healthy personality growth because children realize that others have problems and fears. These procedures identified by Farnum (1963) have several implications for alleviating aggressive behaviors.

## IMPLICATIONS FOR ADULTS WORKING WITH CHILDREN

Axline (1947) notes that in using the basic principles of non-directive therapy, free expression is important. The child must feel free to share feelings and make emotional statements. However, medical and non-medical personnel must be alert to reflect the children's feelings back to them. Reflecting in this manner provides the adult with insight into the youngsters' behaviors. Reflection can be practiced by any adult if the therapeutic relationship between client and child is established. Reflection of emotive statements can also prevent problems in personality growth. The youngsters, through reflection, gain insight into their own situations before maladjustments occur.

Expressions of negativeness, resentment, and aggression are usually not accepted in normal societal functioning. Yet, they are the same expressions that provide insight into children's behaviors and at the same time provide them with outlets for hostility. Regardless of setting, if the youngster cannot express his feelings, he soon finds other ways of showing them. In this situation, feelings are driven underground, and more evasive ways are found as channels to express fears. In hospital and other settings, play activities reveal the child's inner uncertainties. By their own personal actions, Hartley, et al. (1952) feel that adults can let children know that it is quite appropriate to express negative and hurtful feelings. By letting the child know, for example, that it is "all right to cry" or that "some things are frightening," adults lay the groundwork for acceptance. Wolfgang (1977) feels that adults should not be threatened by children's expressions of hostility or rejection. Expressing impulsive, aggressive, and rejecting behaviors permits the youngster to test the limits of the world around him.

In using play materials in various settings, corners or centers of the room can be designated as areas where certain play behavior can be elicited. The adult should provide ample space, materials, and permissiveness. During play times, the therapist should move throughout the room, observing the children's behaviors and admiring their handiwork. A warning should be given as clean-up time approaches so that they have ample time to finish their needed play activities.

The block corner may serve the therapist in demonstrating behavioral cues. These behavioral cues are used in evaluating the child's growth and his own role in the client-child relationship. To understand what the child is saying, the therapist must be alert while the play is going on. Listening, looking, and relating to what the youngster does in other behaviors are also much needed "keys" to unlocking aggressive actions.

Dramatic play is another play activity that the therapist can use in hospital and other settings to gain insight to a child. In dramatic play, the therapist should be aware of the developmental norms of the youngsters with whom he is working. Hartley, et al. (1952) note especially that dramatic play gives the opportunity to act out pressing needs in real life-like settings. In acting out problems, dramatic play becomes a vehicle for developing alternatives and solutions. Through dramatic play, the therapist can help an individual to integrate into a group, to act out feelings and accept those feelings, and to demonstrate to others how people feel.

These procedures and routines derived from psychoanalytic literature are useful in hospital or other settings. They can be used effectively and efficiently with all children and to alleviate aggressive behaviors. Above all, the therapist is a careful observer and listener to what children say and do—individually and in group settings.

In summary, case studies indicate that aggressive behavior demonstrated by young children can be ameliorated through the use of play therapy. Play therapy is not a technique limited just to a therapist but has been shown to be effective in other settings as well (e.g., hospitals). Professionals involved with young children who demonstrate inappropriate aggressive behavior would benefit by further study of psychoanalytic theories for play therapy and their application in their own fields of practice.

## REFERENCES

Axline, V. M. *Play Therapy*. New York: Houghton Mifflin (1947).

Bronfenbrenner, V. and Rucciuti, H. N., "The appraisal of personality characteristics in children," in *Handbook of Research Methods in Child Development*, P. H. Mussen, ed. New York: John Wiley & Sons (1960).

Cataldo, F. M., Bessman, C. A., Parker, L. H., Pearson, J. E. R., and Rogers, M. C., "Behavioral assessment for pediatric intensive care units," *Journal of Applied Behavior Analysis, 12* (1), 83–97 (1979).

Dodge, K. A., "Social cognitions and children's aggressive behavior," *Child Development, 51* (1), 162–170 (1980).

Earle, E. M., "Psychological effects of mutilating surgery," *The Psychoanalytic Study of the Child. Vol. 34*. New Haven: Yale University Press (1979).

Farnum, S., "Play for the convalescent child," in *Play: Children's Business*, P. M. Markun, ed. Washington DC: Association for Childhood Education International (1963).

Freud, A. *The Ego and the Mechanisms of Defense*. New York: International Universities Press (1946).

Freud, A. *Research at the Hempstead Child-therapy Clinic and other Papers, 1956-1965*. New York: International Universities Press (1969).

Grieger, T., Kauffman, J. M., and Grieger, R. M., "Effects of peer reporting on cooperative play and aggression of kindergarten children," *Journal of School Psychology, 14* (4), 307–313 (1966).

Harley, R. E., Frank, L. K., and Goldenson, R. M. *Understanding Children's Play*. New York: Columbia University Press (1952).

Huston-Stein, A., Friedrich-Cofer, L., and Susman, E. J., "The relation of classroom structure to social behavior imaginative play, and self-regulation of economically disadvantaged children," *Child Development, 48* (3), 908–915 (1977).

Johnson, W. R., "Therapeutic play for beginners," *Journal of Physical Education and Recreation, 51* (2), 30–31 (1980).

Josselyn, I. M. *The Happy Child*. New York: Random House (1955).

Klein, M. *The Psycho-analysis of Children*. London: Hogarth Press (1932).

Levin, H. and Turgeon, V. F., "The influence of the mother's presence on children's doll play aggression," *The Journal of Abnormal and Social Psychology, 55* (3), 301–308 (1957).

Maier, H. W. *Three Theories of Child Development*. New York: Harper & Row (1965).

Mash, E. J. and Mercer, B. J., "A comparison of the behavior of deviant and non-deviant boys while playing alone and interacting with a sibling," *Journal of Child Psychology and Psychiatry, 20* (3), 197–207 (1979).

McCandless, B. R. and Evans, E. D. *Child and Youth: Psychosocial Development.* Homeworth, IL: Dryden Press (1973).

Patterson, G. R., Littman, R. G., and Bricker, R. G., "Assertive behavior in children: A step toward a theory of aggression," *Monographs of the Society for Research in Child Development, 32,* 113 (1967).

Pumpian-Midlin, E., Freud, A., and Erikson, E. H., "Contributions to the theory and practice of psychoanalysis and psychotherapy," in *Psychoanalytic Pioneers,* F. Alexander, S. Eisenstein, and M. Grotjahn, eds. New York: Basic Books (1966).

Redl, F. and Wineman, D. *The Aggressive Child.* Glencoe: Free Press (1957).

Seibert, S. M. and Ramanaiah, N. V., "On the convergent and discrimination validity of selected measures of aggression in children," *Child Development, 49* (4), 1274–1276 (1978).

Smart, M. S. and Smart, R. C. *Preschool Children: Development and Relationships.* New York: MacMillan (1973).

Walters, R. H. and Willows, D. C., "Imitative behavior of disturbed and non-disturbed children following exposure to aggressive and nonaggressive models," *Child Development, 39* (1), 99–110 (1968).

Weigle, H. and McNally, H., "When a child needs counseling how two children were helped through the use of non-directive play therapy," *Early Years Parent, 11* (4), 12–13 (1980).

Wolfgang, C. H. *Helping Aggressive and Passive Preschoolers Through Play.* Columbus OH: Charles E. Merrill (1977).

# Effects of infant–parent social interaction on the development of attachment behaviors

**Jessiann Dortch-McCarthy**
*Assistant Professor of Early Childhood Education*
*Juniata College*
*Department of Early Childhood Education*

## INTRODUCTION

In the past, extensive research has been conducted on attachment behaviors of infants. Psychologists, child development specialists, and others have traditionally focused on the impact of the mother's role in the emotional and social attachment behaviors of infants. In most instances, the development of mother-infant attachment behaviors was linked to child care practices. The direct link between infant-parent play and the development of attachment has not been as extensively studied.

This chapter will discuss what occurs during infant-parent play interactions and how the components of that play hold the same characteristics that are involved in the development of attachment behaviors. There were two major problems in studying the effects of infant-parent social interactions on the development of attachment behaviors—(1) the lack of information on infant-parent play interaction, specifically the relationship it has to attachment behaviors and (2) the components of the father's role in the development of attachment having not been widely studied. The father-infant play interactions have been almost ignored. Therefore, even though this chapter is addressing parent-infant play and its contribution to the development of attachment behaviors, most of the research considered only the mother-infant interaction.

## THE DEVELOPMENT OF ATTACHMENT

Attachment is a result of the bond that a child forms with those who nurture him. This becomes the core of socialization. The infant's social development is influenced by different infant care practices. There are sensitive periods during which the young infant is especially vulnerable or responsive to the influence of environmental contingencies. It is generally acknowledged that the patterns of interaction which are established between infant and mother or other figures have a strong influence on the quality of the infant's social relationship (Ainsworth, 1973).

The infant's behavior comes about through the interaction of those aspects of his environment that his natural temperament is able to cultivate. Attachment is viewed as an inner representation that can be measured only by behaviors referred to as attachment behaviors. Attachment is an innate, social need, occurring as a result of imitation, identification, and the use of symbols. These characteristics bind child to mother and vice versa (Ainsworth, 1969; Bowlby, 1958; Schaffer and Emerson, 1964).

An attachment is an affectional tie that one person forms to another specific person. Attachment implies affect, and although these affects may be complex and may vary from time to time, positive affects dominate. Usually, attachment implies affection or love (Ainsworth, 1973). This attachment binds individuals together and endures over time. It is discriminating and specific; once formed, it can withstand separation (Ainsworth, 1973).

At least four major phases in the development of attachment may be distinguished (Ainsworth, 1973).

1. Phase of Undiscriminating Social Responsiveness.
2. Phase of Discriminating Social Responsiveness.
3. Phase of Active Initiative in Seeking Proximity and Contact.
4. Phase of Goal-Corrected Partnership.

The Phase of Undiscriminating Social Responsiveness occurs during the first two or three months when the infant has the ability to orient himself to prominent traits of the environment, especially to people. The infant can differentiate and respond differently to various stimuli and, hence, discriminate. The infant does not discriminate between the persons presenting the stimuli, but the range of stimuli to which he is responsive originates from those adults.

During the Phase of Discriminating Social Responsiveness, the infant continues to orient and to signal but clearly discriminates between those who are familiar and those who are relatively unfamiliar. The people most familiar to the infant are his/her mother and one or two others.

During the third phase, the Phase of Active Initiative in Seeking Proximity and Contact, all the earlier attachment behaviors still exist and differentiate, but there is a considerable increase in promotion of proximity and contact that is initiated by the infant. No longer are his signals merely expressive or reactive; they are often deliberate to evoke a response from the attachment figure. The median age for this phase is seven months.

The fourth phase, the Phase of Goal-corrected Partnership usually occurs around three years of age. Although quite primitive at first, it represents the beginning of a relationship based on partnership.

Socialization implies the interaction of one being with another/others (Walters and Wilhoit, 1976). Baby's first attachment is to the parent, but this must develop over time. At birth, there are no object relationships, no ego; hence, no attachment or superego exists for the infant (Ainsworth, 1973; Walters and Wilhoit, 1976). The infant is viewed as existing in an undifferentiated state or as Spitz (1965) prefers, a nondifferentiated state. At this time, the infant does not distinguish between mind and body, between outside and inside, between "I" and "non I," or even between various parts of the body (Spitz, 1965).

From a stage of oneness, the infant gradually learns that things exist outside of himself. Through touch, proprioception, kinesthesis, and vision, the infant begins to see himself as a unique individual. All of the above mentioned ways of distinguishing self from nonself are aided by the association with his mother (Walter and Wilhoit, 1976).

In the process of gradually learning that objects both animate and inanimate exist outside of himself, the infant also learns to become attached to someone (Walters and Wilhoit, 1976).

The bonding concept refers to the emotional quality of the child-adult relationship, as differentiated from a custodial-care or dependency relationship (Brody, 1978). Children mature through a process of bonding or attachment with parents or other specific adults. Bonding is a two-way, two-person process. The child requires at least one specific adult willing and capable of becoming so attached (Brody, 1978). Brofenbrenner (1977) stated that to mature, a child needs at least one specific adult who is "irrationally crazy" about the child in a positive, emotionally involved way. Through this bonding process, the child learns about himself/herself and the world.

In Ainsworth's Uganda study, she found that in the fourth phase of attachment development, seeking proximity and contact did not seem wholly reactive but, rather, was often initiated entirely by the baby in the absence of any anxiety or threat. She hypothesized that the baby did not first become attached and then show it by proximity promoting behaviors, but, rather, that these are the patterns of behavior through which attachment grows—that it develops through transaction with the environment (Ainsworth, 1973). Hence, the importance of mother-infant play.

The newborn is not the passive creature most people have assumed. Recent studies show that the newborn comes well-endowed with charm and a full potential of social graces. His eyes are bright, and vision is good (Hersh and Levin, 1978). Reingold (1971) took the position that the infant is a social being from birth and that the mother-infant interaction is essential in the process of building an interpersonal relationship. The sight of social objects evokes responses from the infant almost from birth. Infants have an inherent partiality toward looking at certain patterns and at things that move, which predisposes them to pay special attention to the human face (Bowlby, 1958; Ainsworth, 1969). Shortly after birth, the infant likes to watch the human face (Hersh and Levin, 1978). Dr. T. Berry Brazelton (Hersh and Levin, 1978) studied videotapes of infant-maternal interactions. Frame by frame microanalysis of the pictures shows that the baby moves in smooth, circular, "ballet-like" patterns as he looks up at the mother. The baby concentrates his attention on her while body and limbs move in rhythm. The infant then withdraws briefly but returns his attention, averaging several cycles a minute. The mother falls in step with the baby's cycles by talking and smiling in a kind of dance (Hersh and Levin, 1978).

Wolff (1963) found evidence that eye-to-eye contact was the most efficient stimulus in eliciting a smile from the infant. Eye to eye contact elicits maternal social behavior. In this study, it was discovered that some of the mothers began spending more time playing with their infants a few days after their babies established eye-to-eye contact with them.

The baby looks at his/her mother, has contact with her, and soon recognizes and prefers her (Hersh and Levin, 1978). However, Lamb (1977) states that in stress-free circumstances, infants showed no preference for either parent in the display of attachment behaviors. It is through the parent that the infants come to recognize and to learn about their world and about themselves (Walters and Wilhoit, 1976).

## INFANT-PARENT PLAY

In the first weeks of life, the foundation for an infant-parent play relationship is formed. According to Call (1968), there is a consistent sequence of anchorage systems determined by interrelated sensory motor functions that orients the parent and infant to each other. Holding rooting behavior, hand-mouth system, and vision play a role in object orientation. Object relations that gratify both infant and mother mediate ego development, the quality of later object relation and basic early orientations such as trust (Escalon, 1968). These orienting behaviors that develop during the daily care practices and involve interrelated sensory motor functions result in an anchorage to an object. This object relationship is called play (Stern, 1974). Play often originates from the interaction that occurs as the mother accommodates the infant's hand-mouth relations during feeding (Call, 1968). In Lamb's (1977) study on the father's role in attachment behavior, he classified play into five general types: the conventional play between parent and infant such as peek-a-boo, pat-a-cake, and so-big; the physical activities of rough and tumble that usually involve touching and holding; minor physical play activities that usually do not involve holding; toy mediated play, where the toy object was used to mediate the interaction; and idiosyncratic, all activities not classified in the previous types. Lamb (1977) defined play as the occasions when the adult engaged in interaction with the infant or attempted to stimulate the infant other than by simply vocalizing, smiling, or engaging in caretaking activities. Smiling, looking, and laughing were defined as affiliative behaviors, while proximity, touching, approaching, seeking to be held, fussing, and reaching were considered to be attachment behaviors (Lamb, 1977). Call (1968) considers these sounds, movements, and oral functions as being the earliest games. There is not a concise definition for infant games, but there are some guidelines that mark game boundaries: the addition or deletion of tough speech stimuli; any major shift in the qualitative or quantitative use of the stimuli; or any major change in the timing rhythm or sequencing of these behaviors (Stern, 1974). There is a distinction between play and games. Games proceed according to rules. This causes a sequence of interrelated events that have an end-point. This gives games the quality of being more decisive than play (Call, 1968). In all games played by infants, the rules of the games are constantly being invented and changed. When the context of the game is familiar and the mood is right, repetition occurs (Call 1968).

Like most interpersonal events, mother-infant play can be perceived in terms of a hierarchical structure, where larger structural units are formed from smaller units of behavior. These units lead to a play activity goal (Stern, 1974). The mother can achieve the goal by diversifying the level, nature, timing, and pattern of stimulation (Stern, 1974). Most games occur with the infant being held by the parent. The infant feels secure, comfortable, and supported while sitting on the parent's lap (Call, 1968). In order for social play in infancy to take place, another person must be present to interact with the infant (Call, 1968). The infant's ability to play is dependent on being played with. Another factor necessary in order for play to take place is the state of the infant's motor development (Call, 1968).

The mother will often change her behavior to accommodate the child's stimulation needs, to hold, or to regain the infant's attention (Stern, 1974). She, in fact, is often the play stimulus (Call, 1968). The parent will pitch her voice to a high range, speak in a falsetto, alter the rate of pitch, and change the sound intensity. These alterations give a sing-song quality to the speech that is generally termed, "baby talk" (Stern, 1974; Ferguson, 1964). Like the voice, the mother's movements are exaggerated. The rate of movement changes drastically as the mother moves in and out of the infant's intimate range (Stern, 1974). Facial expressions, too, are exaggerated. They are often held for a long time to obtain an infant response. These facial expressions, as the voice and movement behavior, would seem quite bizarre if acted to another adult, but when interacting with an infant, these exaggerations of tempo and range may assist the infant in processing the information (Stern, 1974).

The "free play" that takes place between mother and infant is probably the purest social activity that occurs between the two individuals (Stern, 1974). Most games that are played will occur after feeding (Call, 1968) although a play period can begin at almost any time the infant is awake (Stern, 1974). The mother must seize the appropriate opportunity to play and be sociable, but not all mothers are attuned to these opportunities (Stern, 1974; Call, 1968). The mother initiates the activity, but the baby controls the play by deciding if the play activity will take place. The baby will stop and be attuned to the mother's action. If there is interest, the baby will respond. If not, the baby will continue with the preceding activity, and the "game" will not continue. In order that social behaviors may be formed, the mother must keep the infant's attention and maintain arousal so that these behaviors may occur (Stern, 1974). Even though the mother initiates the play, the infant provides a multitude of acts, smiles, coos, etc., for the mother to respond to and provide feedback (Stern, 1974). The baby can have an indirect influence on his own state of arousal by influencing the mother's behavior through his own expressive behaviors, thus, having control over the stimulus events to which he is exposed. The infant's optimal range of arousal is in a periodical state of change. The mother and infant must readjust the game that will enhance behavioral changes, thus bringing the infant's state back into an optimal range. If the optimal range of arousal cannot be obtained, the play period stops. When the baby does respond, the parent and infant are then tending toward the same goal to interest and delight each other (Stern, 1974).

DISCUSSION

In studying the characteristics of infant-parent play, it is possible to observe the use of imitation, identification, symbolism, affection, physical contact with another human being, and a direct interaction with the immediate environment. If it is correct that these are the major social needs necessary for attachment behavior to develop (Ainsworth, 1969; Bowlby, 1958; Schaffer and Emerson, 1964) and that these same characteristics appear in the play interaction that occurs between parent and child, then this would imply that parent-infant play can contribute to the development of attachment.

The direct relationship between parent-infant play and the attachment behaviors does not seem to have been highly studied. If attachment behaviors grow as the infant interacts with the environment, and since much of the parent-infant play is based on a mutual exploration of the environment, then this seems to be an area where more executed research is needed.

In most of the past research, the attachment bond between mother and infant was almost exclusively discussed with very little study completed on the father's role in development of attachment behaviors. The father's role in play interaction has been almost completely ignored. More research is greatly needed in this area.

If infant-parent play does contribute to the development of attachment behaviors, then parents should become more aware of the importance of infant play. It is necessary that infant play be more understood and valued.

## REFERENCES

Ainsworth, M. D., "The development of mother-infant attachment," in *Review of Child Development Research*, B. A. Caldwell and H. N. Ticciuti, eds. Chicago: University of Chicago Press (1973).

Ainsworth, M. D., "Object relations, dependency, and attachment: a theoretical review of infant-mother relationship," *Child Development, 40,* 969–1025 (1969).

Ainsworth, M. D., "Patterns of attachment between behavior shown by the infant in interaction with his mother's," *Merrill-Palmer Quarterly, 10,* 51–58 (1964).

Ban, P. L. and Lewis, M., "Mothers and fathers, girls and boys: attachment behavior in the one-year-old," *Merrill-Palmer Quarterly, 20,* 195–204 (1974).

Beckwith, L., "Relationships between infants' social behavior and their mothers' behavior," *Child Development, 43,* 397–411 (1972).

Bowlby, J., "The nature of the child's tie to his mother," *International Journal of Psychoanalysis, 39,* 350–373 (1958).

Bowlby, J., "The theory of the parent-child relationship," *International Journal of Psychoanalysis, 39,* 1–34 (1958).

Brackbill, Y., ed. *Infancy and Early Childhood.* New York: Free Press (1967).

Brody, S. *Patterns of Mothering.* New York: International Universities Press (1956).

Brody, Viola A., "Developmental play: a relationship-focused program for children," *Child Welfare,* 591–600 (November 1978).

Brofenbrenner, U., "The family man," *Psychology Today* (May 1977).

Cairns, R. B., "Attachment and dependency: a psychobiological and social-learning synthesis," in *Attachment and Dependency*, J. L. Gewirtz, ed. Washington DC: V. H. Winston (1972).

Call, J. D., "Lap and finger play in infancy, implications for ego development," *International Journal of Psychoanalysis, 49,* 375–378 (1968).

Escalona, S. K., "Patterns of infantile experience and the developmental process," *The Psychoanalytic Study of the Child, 18,* 197–244 (1963).

Ferguson, C. A., "Baby talk in six languages," in *The Ethnography of Communication, 66* (2), J. Gumperz and D. Hymes, eds., 103–114 (1964).

Ferguson, L., "Origins of social development in infancy," *Merrill-Palmer Quarterly, 17,* 119–137 (1971).

Hersh, S. D. and Levin, K., "How love begins between parent and child," *Children Today,* 2–6 (March, April 1978).

Lamb, M. E., "Father and mother-infant interaction in the first year of life," *Child Development, 48* (March 1977).

Robson, K. S. and Moss, H., "Patterns and determinants of maternal attachment," *Journal of Pediatrics, 77,* 976–985 (1970).

Schaffer, H. R. and Emerson, P. *Society for Research in Child Development Monographs, 29* (3) (1964).

Schur, M., "The theory of the parent-infant relationship," *International Journal of Psychoanalysis, 41,* 243–245 (1960).

Spitz, P. R. *The First Year of Life.* New York: International University Press (1965).

Stern, D. N., "The goal and structure of mother-infant play," *Journal of American Academy Child Pediatrics, 13,* 402 (1974).

Wahler, R. G., "Infant social development: Some experimental analysis of an infant-mother interaction during the first year of life," *Journal of Experimental Child Psychology, 7,* 101–113 (1969).

Walters, C. E. and Wilhoit, P., "Social development," in *Mother-infant Interaction,* C. E. Walter, ed. New York: Human Sciences Press (1976).

Wolff, P. H., "Observations on the early development of smiling," in *Determinants of Infant Behavior,* Vol. 2, B. M. Foss, ed. New York: Wiley (1963).

# Play of infants and children: Examination of temperament and play

**Mary Ann Melizzi**
*Harriet Stowe College (Missouri)*

## INTRODUCTION

Since publication of the results of the New York Longitudinal Study (NYLS) by Thomas, Chess, Birch, and Hertzig (1963), there has been interest in the development of temperament. Some of the questions asked include what role the child plays in the development of temperament, how great an effect parents' responses and the parent-child interaction have on early temperament, whether consistency exists between early and later patterns of temperament, if early temperament problems predict later social behavior problems, and in assessing temperament, whether all instruments measure the same thing. The identification of individual patterns of reactivity by Thomas, Chess, and Birch (1970) indicated that social dyadic communication patterns were dependent not only on interpersonal factors but also on intrapersonal factors, adaptability, and temperament style (Honig, 1982). Piaget's (1952) conceptualization of the infant as an organizer of the environment and Erikson's (1980) characterization of early infant-mother communication in terms of mutual synchrony and adjustment of interactions provided theoretical support for an interaction model.

Selected research regarding the use of parent perceptions in the assessment and development of temperament in the young child and research which examined behaviors which influenced mother-infant interactions will be presented. The research results will be looked at in terms of their implications for using play and play therapy to facilitate "goodness-of-fit" (Thomas and Chess, 1968).

## DEFINITION OF TEMPERAMENT

One of the major problems in studying the development of temperament or attempting to assess it is that the definition of temperament varies from researcher to researcher, but there is agreement that a child's temperament may either block or facilitate parental interactions. Allport (1961) defined temperament as those aspects of personality which were "largely hereditary in origin." Buss and Plomin (1975) espoused a temperament theory of personality development. The Buss and Plomin theory was based on the Allport (1961) definition which put forth four general personality traits with components of each as possible temperaments: emotionality;

activity; sociability; and impulsivity. The New York Longitudinal Study (NYLS) (Thomas, et al., 1963) focused on early stylistic differences in behavior without regard to etiology (Thomas and Chess, 1977). McDevitt and Carey (1978) defined temperament as the child's style of behavior when interacting with the environment.

Bates (1980), in a review of the literature, found little empirical support for the definitional criteria used most often to describe temperament. Lyon and Plomin (1981) felt temperament was most often defined according to the traits identified by the various assessment instruments. Although theories about the nature and etiology of temperament existed, Hubert, Wachs, Peter-Martin, and Gandour (1982) found no indications that operational definitions would soon be replaced by theoretical definitions.

## INFLUENCE OF NYLS

The NYLS (Thomas and Chess, 1977, 1980; Thomas, Chess, Birch, Hertzig and Korn, 1963, 1968) has had a major influence on the assessment and classification of early temperament. Thomas, et al. (1963) followed children from infancy to age ten in an attempt to identify temperament characteristics which interfered with or contributed to interaction with parents. Parent interviews began when the child was about three-months-old. Nine dimensions of temperament were delineated, and three major clusters emerged which defined distinguishable infant temperaments. The construct of "goodness" of fit was identified as the main etiological factor underlying behavioral adjustment.

*Nine dimensions of temperament.* Based upon parent responses, nine dimensions of temperament were identified. The nine dimensions were (a) activity-amount and rigor of motor activity, (b) rhythmicity-regularity of patterns (eating, sleeping, toileting), (c) adaptability-adjustment to new routines and places, (d) approach-responsivity to novel objects and friendliness to strangers, (e) threshold-responses to intense stimulation and changes in stimulation, (f) intensity-degree of response to stimulation, (g) mood-affective reactions to people and daily routines, (h) distractibility-degree to which a child's attention can be drawn away from ongoing activity, and (i) persistence-degree to which activities are sustained.

*Three infant temperament clusters.* Thomas and Chess (1968) found that an infant's temperament generally fell into one of three major clusters of dimensions. The temperaments described by the clusters were labeled the difficult child, the slow to warm-up child, and the easy child (Thomas, et al., 1968). A difficult child was described as irregular, nonadaptive, low in initial approach, and having an intense reaction of negative mood. The "easy" child was identified as regular, positive adaptive, approaching, and having a low intensity of response.

In the NYLS, 40 percent of the children were identified as "easy," 15 percent as "slow to warm up," and 10 percent as "difficult." The remaining children did not fit into any of these groups. Seventy percent of the children identified as difficult developed psychologial disorders. In comparison, 19 percent of the rest of the sample showed behavior problems later (Thomas, et al., 1968). Thomas, et al. (1968) felt that the early identification of a difficult temperament would be important in detecting later behavior problems. As a result, individuals interested in the early identification of children at-risk began to look at the development of temperament.

*"Goodness of fit."* Thomas and Chess (1968) proposed that those

children identified as difficult who did not develop psychological disorders had parents who were able to adjust their behaviors to meet the needs of their children. When the expectations and demands of the child's environment were in accord with the child's temperament and capabilities, "goodness of fit" was thought to exist (Thomas and Chess, 1968). "Poorness of fit" resulted when dissonance existed between the child's characteristics and environmental demands. The notion of "goodness-of-fit" led to interest in the effects of parent characteristics on parent-child relationships and the ability of the environment to meet the child's needs.

## CURRENT RESEARCH

Current research (Buss and Plomin, 1975; Thomas and Chess, 1977, 1980) has focused upon individual differences in "style" of behavior, the "how" and not the "what" of behavior. NYLS results provided some of the structure for describing early temperament (Buss and Plomin, 1975; Thomas, et al., 1963, 1968, 1977, 1980). The infant-caretaker relationship has been focused on in an attempt to identify characteristics or patterns of behavior which may be problematic. Environmental or constitutional factors which contributed to or maintained problematic patterns of behavior have been examined. The influence of the caretaker's perceptions of the infant has also been focused upon. This chapter will review current research which (1) discussed problems of assessment and (2) studied the use of parent perception and global ratings of temperament ratings of specific behaviors.

The studies presented here are both descriptive and empirical in nature. The descriptive studies examined the components of temperament (Bates, 1980), the concept of difficult temperament (Bates, 1980), and the adequacy of instruments used to measure infant temperament (Hubert, Wachs, Peters-Martin, and Gandour, 1982). The reliability of parent ratings were examined in the empirical studies.

## DESCRIPTIVE STUDIES

*Components of temperament.* Bates (1980) identified three components of temperament and reviewed the literature regarding each component. The identified components were (a) a constitutional base, (b) continuity from infancy, and (c) objectively definable characteristics of an individual. Genetic research was found in two major areas. They are (a) parent-reported data for temperament variables for identical and fraternal twins and (b) observer-reported data from direct observation for personality ratings. Although genetic effects may exist, the degree of heritability reflected in behaviors was not identifiable.

Continuity appeared to exist for early individual differences, but methodological difficulty interfered with measuring traits across stages of development. Evidence suggested stability existed for short periods of time with major biobehavior shifts occurring; there was little success in recording continuity, and "psychologically-sophisticated" observers appeared to be necessary if continuity was to be recorded. Bates (1980) found that continuity of temperament was evident when multivariate studies were performed. Several studies cited by Bates (1980) suggested that multivariate studies best allowed the observation of the infant's relationship with environmental factors which are important in the development of competence.

The third component referred to the validity of using care-giver reports as individual measures of infant temperament. Bates (1980) suggested that moderate validity between parents may result from communication between parents or the sharing of perceptions about the infant. Less agreement was found between parents and observers. Reasons for the low parent-observer agreement included (a) observer inability to match caretaker intensive experience with the infant, (b) generality of questions presented on the questionnaires, and (c) parent ratings of what the child does being influenced by parent perceptions. Bates (1980) summarized by stating that parent perceptions appeared to be the most valid method of measuring a temperament construct.

*Difficult temperament.* Bates (1980) found that difficult temperament was most frequently associated with fussing and crying. Being difficult was also found to be influenced by parents' perceptions and to represent qualities of the child, the parent, and the relationship between them. Although Bates (1980) found inconclusive evidence relating parent perceptions of an infant as difficult to later childhood behavior problems, he noted that parent perceptions may interact with environmental variables and affect a child's social development. Bates (1980) concluded by stating that temperament may be more accurately considered as "individual differences in social behavior" rather than a characteristic of a child. Parents' perceptions were felt to play a more important role than objective factors since one's perceptions of another seem to play a role in how the other behaves.

*Measurement of temperament.* Hubert, et al. (1982) reviewed 26 instruments used to measure temperament, 16 of which measure temperament during infancy. The instruments were reviewed for reliability and validity, and the results indicated that (a) one must rely on an operational definition of temperament which is determined by the assessment instrument, (b) most instruments were based on dimensions derived from NYLS, (c) only moderate levels of test-retest reliability existed, even during short-time intervals, (d) a low level of correlations existed for both inter-parent and parent-observer reliability, and (e) little information regarding validity was present, and that which was present indicated low convergent validity and moderate levels of predictive validity.

Results from the studies of Hubert, et al. (1982) and Bates (1980) pointed to a weakness in current approaches to the measurement of temperament. One major problem was that approaches to measurement are based on an operational definition and NYLS dimensions rather than a theoretical definition. Both studies found that difficulty existed when one tried to find indications of continuity, with Bates' (1980) findings indicating that multivariant studies were most successful in showing continuity. A low level of correlation was found to exist for both inter-parent and parent-observer correlations. Bates (1980), in examining various types of parent information, found that parent perceptions were more accurate than parent ratings of current behaviors, but the evidence was inconclusive that current perceptions could be used to predict later temperament when looking at the child identified as "difficult."

## EMPIRICAL STUDIES

*Identification of neonatal temperament.* Sostek and Anders (1977) examined the relationship between early temperament and performance on the Brazelton Neonatal Assessment Scale (Brazelton, 1973) and the Bayley Scales of Infant Development. The study included 18 normal, full-term infants and three shifts of round-the-clock caretakers in a foundling home. The Brazelton Neonatal Assessment was administered to assess four dimensions: (a) social interactive; (b) motoric interactive; (c) state control; and (d) physiological responses to stress. The Bayley Scales of Infant Development were administered at a mean age of 68.8 days (range 51–94 days) to assess mental and motor development. Caretakers completed the Carey Infant Temperament Questionnaire (Carey, 1970) to provide information concerning activity, rhythmicity, adaptibility, intensity, mood, and distractibility.

The social and motoric interactive dimensions of the Brazelton were correlated, and all dimensions contributed significantly to the total. A correlation was found between the Bayley mental scale and the Brazelton state control dimension and total score. Based on their Brazelton totals, the infants fell into two discrete groups which differed in performance on the Bayley mental scales. The seven infants identified as worrisome (mean Brazelton total 12.2; range 11–13) had a mean 10-week Bayley mental quotient of 109.29 (SD 12.8). For the 11 more optimal infants (Brazelton total 7.0; range 5–9), the mean mental score was 125 (SD 13.2). No relationship was noted between Brazelton dimensions and performance on the Bayley motor scales.

Temperamental intensity was significantly correlated with performance on the Bayley Scales of Infant Development, and it was related to the Brazelton motoric interactive process and the Bayley motor scale. A correlation was identified between distractibility and the motoric interactive processes and the total Brazelton score. Distractibility was related to the Brazelton social interactive processes and state control and the Bayley motor scale. Sostek and Anders (1977) warned that generalization of the results was restricted since the sample was small in number and included only normal, full-term infants.

Based upon the results of this sample, it appeared that the Brazelton total and state control dimension scores were predictive of Bayley mental quotients obtained at 10 weeks. A correlation was found between caretaker judgments of temperamental intensity and distractibility at two weeks and the Bayley scales and Brazelton dimensions. The data supported the usefulness of information obtained from a priori Brazelton dimensions to help conceptualize new-born behavior and the prediction of later developmental quotients based upon neonatal assessments.

Caretaker perceptions were found to correlate with the observer ratings from the Brazelton and Bayley. Perceptions of intensity and distractibility were found to correlate highest with results from the other forms of neonatal assessment.

Relationships between newborn characteristics and early mother-infant interaction were observed in two situations to study infant and material responsiveness (Osofsky, 1976). Consistencies and inconsistencies of newborn behavior were studied across situations and in relationship to measures of newborn behavior. Maternal consistency and inconsistency were evaluated in the two situations.

The subjects were 134 infants and their mothers randomly sampled from the population born at Temple University Hospital in Philadelphia, PA. The program almost exclusively served non-white, lower socioeconomic individuals, and the sample represented the population. Infants were 2–4 days old and included 73 boys and 61 girls. The mothers ranged in age from 13–37 years, with a mean of 19.9 years.

Mothers were approached in the hospital and asked if they would be willing to participate in a study about mothers and infants. They were told they would be observed two times, once during feeding and then at a time convenient for them and the baby. Questions about their family and child rearing attitudes would be asked, and their baby would receive a developmental evaluation after the observations. Convenient times were arranged during the hospital stay for those who were willing to participate.

The first mother-infant observation took place during 15 minutes of a scheduled feeding. The feeding period observation was scheduled first because it required the least amount of observer-mother interaction. All of the mothers were bottle feeding. During the feeding, maternal behaviors which were rated included attentiveness and general sensitivity, frequency and quality of auditory, visual, and tactile stimulation, and facial movement. The infant behaviors which were rated were state and state change, eye contact with mother, and responsiveness to auditory, visual, and tactile stimulation.

The second behavioral observation, "stimulation" situation, occurred during a 15-minute period 1½ to 2 hours after the feeding time. The second observation period was chosen because it appeared to be an optimal response period for a newborn in an alert, awake state rather than a crying or sleepy state (Brazelton, 1973). Mothers were directed in how to present various stimuli to their infants and then observed as they interacted. The tasks used were similar to those on the Brazelton Neonatal Assessment Scale (Brazelton, 1973). During each task of the stimulation situation, maternal behaviors and infant responses were rated separately. Individual measures of maternal behavior were rated for each situation, and an overall assessment was made of general sensitivity combining the mother's technique and persistence over all situations. At the beginning of each task, infant state was noted, and infant behavioral responses were rated separately for each task situation.

The infant developmental evaluation occurred between two and four days of age using the Brazelton Neonatal Assessment Scale (Brazelton, 1973). The infant was evaluated 1½–2 hours after feeding. Variables measuring habitation, social responsiveness, activity, alertness, irritability, and general responsiveness were of interest for the study (Osofsky, 1976).

Infant eye contact with the mother during the interaction situation related positively to infant orientation to the ball, rattle, face, and alertness. Auditory responsivity during the interaction situation related to responsiveness to the rattle. Tactile responsivity related to cuddliness, peak of excitement, startle, and rapidity of build up. Analysis of infant and maternal behaviors during feeding indicated that maternal attentiveness and general sensitivity toward the infant related to eye contact and auditory and tactile responsivity. The quality of the mother's stimulation was related to the infant's responsivity. A strong relationship was found between a mother's stimulation in a given domain and the newborn's responsivity in that domain. The auditory domain was the area with the greatest specificity in maternal and infant behavior.

Infants with mothers who handled them more during feeding demonstrated less motor maturity, less ability to pull to sit, and less hand-to-mouth facility. Those infants demonstrating more orientation to the ball had mothers who were more attentive and provided more visual stimulation. More alert infants also received more visual stimulation during feeding. The less mature infants with poorer tone received less overall stimulation in two domains—auditory and tactile. Infants showing more irritability received less auditory stimulation.

Infant behaviors during stimulation were related to similar items on the Brazelton Neonatal Assessment Scale, and several relationships were found. The responsivity factor on the Brazelton scale related to the infant state during the stimulation situation. A relationship between infant responsivity to all other stimulus items in the stimulation situation and the orientation items during the neonatal assessment was also found to exist but with less consistency. It appeared that the highly responsive infant in the stimulation situation was also highly responsive during the assessment. Infant cuddliness in the stimulation situation related positively to infant cuddliness during the assessment and negatively to the cluster of items which form the reactive factor on the Brazelton Scale (Osofsky, 1976).

It was found that maternal behavior related to infant behavior during the stimulation situation, and that the better the mother's presentation, the better the infant's response. In general, Osofsky (1976) found that the more sensitive mothers had more responsive infants. Sensitivity was found to exist across situations with mothers who were attentive during feeding also being attentive during the stimulation situation. The same pattern of cross-situational consistency with regard to attention was found to exist for infants (Osofsky, 1976).

It was concluded that mother-child interaction patterns are established almost from birth and that both individuals, mother and child, contribute. These patterns of interaction also appear to be consistent across situations. The relationship between the results of the observations and the results of the Brazelton Neonatal Assessment Scale should be noted since they indicated a relationship between constitutional factors, labor, and Apgar scores, and the information obtained from the observations. The Osofsky (1976) study indicated that very early in the mother-child relationship, the mother's perceptions about the child may begin to develop as a result of patterns of interaction and infant responsivity. The relationship between Brazelton scores and observation results also indicated that at an early stage, formal and less formal methods of assessment are more closely related than they are in later stages of development.

## PARENT PERCEPTIONS TO IDENTIFY EARLY TEMPERAMENT

McDevitt and Carey (1981) examined the stability of individual differences from early infancy to one-to-three years and maternal general impressions based on a caretaker questionnaire using NYLS temperament characteristics. One hundred and fifteen infants were randomly selected from a private pediatric practice in suburban Philadelphia. The sample consisted primarily of middle class families although some high and low class families were also included.

The infants were rated by their caretakers (i.e., mothers) using the Revised Infant Temperament Questionnaire (Carey and McDevitt, 1978). Average age for the first rating was 5.6 months. A second rating was obtained using the same caretakers, and the average infant age was 23.4 months. In addition to measurement of NYLS temperament characteristics, a separate global rating of difficulty was obtained for each infant. The rate of return was reported about 95 percent for each rating.

The results of the study indicated a significant stability for the nine temperament characteristics. A change was found in mothers' impressions of degree of difficulty over time. Only 5.2 percent of the children were rated as difficult between 4–8 months, but from 1–3 years, 8.7 percent were rated as difficult. Of the children rated as difficult during infancy, half were rated as difficult at 1–3 years. Mothers' perceptions of difficulty during infancy were significantly correlated with high activity level, negative mood, and low distractibility. Difficulty at 1–3 years of age was related to low adaptability, high intensity, and negative mood.

The stability of the rating was higher than previous research had found. McDevitt and Carey (1981) stated that the increased power of prediction resulted from improved psychometric properties of the questionnaire. The stability of general impressions or perceptions was less than the stability of ratings. The difference in stability was interpreted as indicating that general impressions and ratings are not the same; therefore, their results cannot be compared. Perceptions were defined as referring to the caretaker's frame of reference and not to specifics about behavior. Ratings, in comparison, provided a measure of the frequency of a behavior in specific situations. McDevitt and Carey (1981) stated that perceptions and ratings result in the collection of different types of information and that there is a need to distinguish between the types of information collected.

Lyon and Plomin (1981) examined the usefulness of parental ratings of temperament considering (1) the extent to which parents project their own personality into ratings of their children's temperament and (2) the degree of agreement between mothers' and fathers' ratings of their children's temperaments. One hundred and thirty-seven families with twins between two and six years old (M=3.5 years) were included. Both parents rated themselves and each other on an adult version of four general personality traits believed to be components of temperament: emotionality; activity; sociability; and impulsivity (EASI) (Buss and Plomin, 1975). Then they rated both twins on the child EASI.

A comparison of parent and child ratings indicated that parents did not project their personality into ratings of their children or spouses. Less parental agreement was found on child ratings with an average correlation of .51 when corrected for reliability. Lyon and Plomin (1981) pointed out that this was more impressive than it appeared when one considered parents were rating broad dimensions of temperament. Generally, observer agreement for specific behavior was .90 and above; ratings which do not involve counting may average 0.70, and agreement for global ratings is considerably lower. The results indicated that when parents provided perceptions or global ratings of behavior, their personality was not projected into the ratings. Lyon and Plomin (1981) felt that the degree of correlation (.51) for inter-parent rating was impressive since parents were rating global dimensions rather than specific behaviors.

The relationship between difficult temperament and infant cry characteristics was the topic of a study conducted by Lounsbury and Bates (1982). More specifically, the effects of infant cry characteristics, other than duration and frequency, and individual listener characteristics on the perception of infant cries were examined. The relationship between difficult temperament and the properties of cry was looked at in three ways. First, the subjective impact of cries on mothers not related to the infants was examined. Second, the acoustic properties of cries were explored, and third, the role of individual listener characteristics in how infant cries were perceived was evaluated.

The subjects were 4- to 6-month-old male and female infants and a sample of 134 mothers. The infants were chosen so that their cries represented average and difficult levels for the difficult-fussy factor on the Infant Characteristics Questionnaire. Birth announcements were used to gather the mothers.

The Infant Characteristics Questionnaire was completed by the mothers, and based on descriptions of their infants, 45 of the original 134 mothers were chosen to participate in the study. The mothers averaged 24.7 years of age, and their infants averaged 4.6 months of age. The group was predominantely middle class. The mothers were divided into three groups: low-, medium-, and high-difficulty based on the descriptions of their own infant and response to the fussy-difficult factor on the questionnaire.

A 2–3 minute spontaneous crying episode was taped for each infant. The tape was done in the home prior to a delay of a regular feeding, and the mother was out of sight. It was assumed the cry was in response to hunger since no external stimuli was applied. At the end of the 2–3 minutes of crying, the mother entered and picked up the infant. A 30-second interval of crying was then chosen, based on amount of crying and absence of long pauses or sudden changes in volume. This segment was to represent crying most characteristic of the child, and it was used for subjective listener ratings and spectrographic analysis.

The unrelated mothers completed four questionnaires prior to listening to the taped segments of crying. The Personality Research Form Nurturance Scale (Jackson, 1974) and the Empathy Scale (Mehrabian and Epstein, 1972) were administered to assess maternal sensitivity to the needs of the infants. Maternal mood and attitude toward maternal role was assessed through the Postnatal Research Inventory (Schaefer and Manheimer, as cited by Lounsbury and Bates, 1982). The mother also completed a biographical sheet concerned with experience with and attraction to infants.

The listeners heard two sample cries to become aware of the potential loudness; one was 22 db below, and the other was 44 db above the stimulus cries. The mothers rated each cry on six hypothetical behavior intervention scales, six emotional reaction scales, and a perceived cause of crying list. The tape was stopped between cries to allow for the ratings. A Voice Identification Series 700 sound spectrograph was used to acoustically analyze the master tape. For each infant, two sets of tracings were made on the 30 second sample, one for intensity and one for fundamental frequency.

The results indicated that difficult and average infants were perceived as more spoiled than easy infants. Listeners indicated more anger and irritation towards the cries of difficult and average infants than toward easy infants' cries.

Crying due to a psychological or emotional cause was associated with the average or difficult infant 28 percent and 30 percent of the time, respectively, while easy infant cries were attributed to this cause 19 percent of the time. Minor physical discomfort was identified as the cause of crying 69 percent of the time for easy infants, 57 percent for average infants, and 54 percent for difficult infants. Crying due to major physical discomfort did not differentiate the groups.

Infants identified as most difficult cried at a higher fundamental frequency at peaks of intensity but did not maintain a higher pitch throughout the cry. With regard to pauses, difficult infants paused longer than easier infants between the end of the expiratory segment of one cry and the inspiratory segment of the next cry, and they tended to have a longer total pause time.

When listener ratings were compared to the biographical data, prior experience with infants was found to be most predictive of the listener's response to each cry. Highly experienced mothers tended to rate easy and average infants as less spoiled than did inexperienced mothers, but they rated the cries of difficult infants as more spoiled than inexperienced mothers. The cries of average and difficult infants were less irritating to experienced mothers than inexperienced mothers.

Empathy was found to be the strongest predictor of type of response to cries. Women rated as high empathic rated the easy and average infant cries as less spoiled sounding and the difficult infant cries as less irritating than did less empathic mothers. Acceptance of the maternal role followed empathy as predicting the perception of average cries as spoiled and anger-irritation for difficult cries. Lounsbury and Bates (1982) concluded that a relationship exists between a mother's perception of infant temperament, the acoustic properties of a cry, and the listener's responses to them. Individual listener differences, especially amount of experience with infants and acceptance of the maternal role, were found to affect listener reactions to infant cries.

## DISCUSSION

The studies cited in this section suggested that, except at the neonatal stage, parent perceptions of temperament and global ratings may be more useful than ratings of specific behaviors when assessing temperament. Sostek and Anders (1977) found that, early in infancy, the Brazelton Neonatal Assessment Scale was useful in conceptualizing newborn behaviors. Caretaker perceptions were found to be positively correlated with observer ratings from the Brazelton Scale and the Bailey Mental Inventory. Osofsky (1977) also found that formal and informal assessments were more related for neonatals than for children in later stages of development. McDevitt's and Carey's (1981) findings also supported the existence of differences in what was being rated. In assessing temperament, the use of ratings or perceptions produced different types of information, and therefore, ratings and perceptions could not be compared (McDevitt and Carey, 1981).

Osofsky (1976) found that at 2–4 days of age, infant and mother behavior was related. In general, she found that more sensitive mothers had more responsive infants. Sensitivity was found to exist across the experimental situations, and as a result, infants who were rated as attentive during feeding were also identified as attentive during the stimulation situation (Osofsky, 1976). Lounsbury and Bates (1982) also found that mother personality had an effect on mother response. They found that empathy was the strongest predictor of the type of mother response to infant crying. After empathy, acceptance of the material role was found to be the best predictor of mother response.

With regard to infant behaviors, McDevitt and Carey (1981) found that the factors contributing to a child's being viewed as difficult changed with the age of the child. At infancy, difficulty was a result of a child being viewed as high in activity, low in distractibility, and having a negative mood. During 1–3 years of age, low adaptability, high intensity, and negative mood were found to correlate with a child being viewed as difficult (McDevitt and Carey, 1981). Lounsbury and Bates (1982) identified acoustic properties of infant crying which influenced parent perceptions of an infant's temperament. Infants who cried at a higher fundamental frequency and who had longer pauses in their cries were rated as more difficult than other infants.

The results of the studies cited suggested that a child's temperament was a result of the types and quality of interactions between parent and child. The research pointed to the early establishment of patterns of interaction. With regard to assessment, it appeared that measures of specific behaviors, ratings and measures of perceptions, and a more global approach produced different types of information which were difficult to compare.

Ratings appeared to be effective early in development and global measures more accurate later in life. One reason ratings may lower their accuracy as a child gets older is that the child's behaviors become more complex, and as a result, specific behaviors are more difficult to isolate and evaluate. A second reason for the increased accuracy of global measures may be that parents have established their perceptions of or attitudes towards a child and respond based on these perceptions rather than to the immediate behaviors. Once a child is perceived as "difficult," parents may find it hard to identify a situation in which the child could be identified as "easy."

The results of the studies in this section pointed to the importance of the development of parent-child interactions. Patterns of interaction appeared to begin forming at birth, but the base for responding in early and later interactions may be different. If parents initially respond to specific behaviors, and later respond according to perceptions or attitudes towards the child, there is a need to review assessment instruments and see if they are consistent with these changes for responding. The early establishment of patterns of interaction also suggest that it is important to do further research to (1) identify factors which lead to "goodness-of-fit" and (2) identify intervention techniques when "poorness-of-fit" is thought to exist.

## INFANT-CARETAKER RELATIONSHIP

Different care-giver patterns may result in a variety of infant communication behaviors which vary in type and intensity (Honig, 1982). Reciprocally, Cohn (as cited by Honig, 1982) found infants may direct care-giving activities by exhibiting a variety of behaviors. Synchrony between care-giver and infant was found to begin at birth (Stern, 1971; Condon, 1975) and was identified as important for infant survival. When synchrony was not maintained, the infant attempted to re-establish synchrony. Brazelton (1975) found that infants became irritable when overloaded and developed a pattern of prolonged periods of non-attention with brief periods of attention to control the amount of stimulation received. It appears then that care-giver patterns affect infant communication, and infants develop patterns to control the amount of stimulation they receive from the care-giver.

In this section, three studies will be presented, two which look at mother-infant interaction and one which examines classification of personality organization using a developmental structuralist approach. The first study, by Arco and McCluskey (1981), examined the infant's awareness of the temporal organization of the mothers' behavior and, more specifically, the effect of changes in the mother's temporal organization. The second study, by Beebe and Gerstman (1980), examined the relationship of maternal facial-visual engagement and kinesic rhythms to infant facial-visual engagement during the face-to-face play. "Packages" of maternal stimulation were thought to exist, and the organization of the "packages" was of primary interest.

The descriptive work of Greenspan and Lourie (1981) illustrated a developmental structuralist approach to the classification of adaptive and pathological personality organization. Levels of organization, examples of adaptive and disordered behaviors for each stage, and the environments which support the behaviors were presented. The results of these studies (Arco and McCluskey, 1981; Beebe and Gerstman, 1980; Greenspan and Lourie, 1981) will be reviewed and their implications for developing "goodness-of-fit" in infant-caretaker relationships through play will be considered.

## MATERIAL ORGANIZATION OF STIMULUS

Arco and McCluskey (1981) investigated infant awareness of the temporal organization of maternal behavior. Infant reaction to the natural, usual temporal patterns of the mother was compared to reaction to manipulated temporal patterns—faster than usual. The differential response to periods of usual pace and periods of changed pace of playful stimulation was the primary interest of the study.

The subjects were 32 white middle class mother-infant pairs. Sixteen of the infants were three-months-old, and 16 were five-months-old; each age group contained eight males and eight females. The mother-infant dyads were videotaped during eight minutes of free play. The eight minute session consisted of four two-minute play sessions in the following order: natural tempo; slower than normal; return to natural tempo; and faster than usual.

During the play sessions, the infant was seated in an infant seat placed on a standard sized feeding table, and the mother was seated in a chair facing the infant. A special effects generator allowed for split-screen, full-face video recordings of the dyads. The onset, duration, and off-set of specific behavior variables were recorded using an Esterline-Angus event recorder. A 1977 revised version of the Ainsworth Maternal Sensitivity Scale by DeMeis (as cited by Arco and McCluskey, 1981) was used to measure levels of maternal sensitivity. The Ainsworth Scale considered six dimensions of maternal sensitivity: accessibility; threshold of responsiveness; freedom from distortion; over- and understimulation; resolution of response; and promptness.

Prior to the videotaping, mother and infant were given time to relax in the new surroundings. The mother was told that the purpose of the study was to investigate "infants' abilities to detect changes in the ways their mothers play with them" (Arco and McCluskey, 1981). The infant was positioned by the mother, and directions were given to play as they would at home for two minutes (see Arco and McCluskey, 1981, for more detail). After each play session, the experimenter returned and gave the directions for the next two-minute session, ". . . play with your baby as you have been. . . slow down the overall pace of play participation. . . , . . . return to your usual style of interacting. . . as you typically do at home," and ". . . continue playing. . . speed up the overall pace of your play" (Arco and McCluskey, 1981). The experimenter rejoined the dyad after the final play session and explained to the mother why she had been asked to alter her tempo.

Two categories of dependent variables were identified—variables coded directly from videotapes and variables from continuous records of directly scored behaviors. Three observers worked in pairs to code the variables. Observers were trained using tapes of mother-infant interactions as well as learning the definitions and procedures.

Arco and McCluskey (1981) based measures of initial maternal temporal style on the structural unit of play behavior called a *bout*. A modified definition of bouting behavior was adapted from the cited 1978 work of Crawley, Rogers, Friedman, Iaccabbo Criticos, Richardson, and Thompson. The Arco and McCluskey (1981) definition of bouting behavior defines a bout as "a rhythmic coordination of maternal vocal and/or motor activity which is preceded and followed by a pause."

Based on two temporal variables, median split for the mean number of bouts per minute and mean duration of bouts (in seconds), the sample yielded four groups of varying initial pacing of stimulation: initially faster-paced mothers with interactions characterized by several short bouts; initially slower-paced mothers with interactions characterized by few long bouts; mothers whose interactions were characterized by several long bouts; and mothers whose interactions were characterized by few short bouts. A repeated measures analysis of variance with initial temporal style (four groups) as the between-subjects source of variance and play phase (baseline, slow return-to-baseline, fast) as the within-subjects source of variance determined the effectiveness of experimental instruction on alteration of maternal temporal style across play phases. The results indicated an absence of a group x phase interaction for temporal variables. Mothers, although efficient in complementing phase changes in temporal patterning of play, were found to increase their participation relative to initial, individual temporal styles.

Arco and McCluskey (1981) found that changes in the temporal organization of maternal play had an effect on infant and maternal social interactive variables. Across the play phases, mothers maintained similar activities (games, songs, and riddles), but changes occurred in maternal facial expressiveness and vocal participation. The slowing of play appeared to result in less facial responsivity. The reduction of facial responsivity was thought to result from the awkwardness of prolonging facial expressions during slower bouts and fewer bouts requiring less facial responses to punctuate the beginning and end of a bout. An increase in vocal activity was observed during the faster play phase. Mothers appeared to use the vocal behaviors to regulate their motor behaviors to the quick staccato effect of this phase.

High levels of infant social behaviors and infant interaction were present during the initial natural play phase. The fast temporal style phase was the next highest in terms of level of infant, maternal, and interactive behaviors. High levels of infant positive facial expressiveness, infant visual regard of mother, mutual visual regard, and mother-infant synchrony were similar to those of the initial play phase.

Comparisons of infant positive facial expressiveness, positive facial coaction, and mother-infant synchrony were significantly higher during the fast play phase when compared to the slow play phase. Arco and Mc-Cluskey (1981) stated that the high level of the positive infant interactive variable indicated infant preference for fast-paced, rather than slow-paced, maternal play. Comparison between phases one and three, both phases of natural temporal style, indicated that some of the infants had difficulty in re-establishing the baseline level of interaction. The inability to obtain a baseline level of interaction was thought to represent an infant's need to receive moderately discrepant stimulation (i.e., increased temporal patterning) to return to the initial high level and the need to consider sequencing effects (Arco and McCluskey, 1981). In addition to providing information concerning the effects of temporal changes upon infant, maternal, and interactive behaviors, the study revealed no significant differences between 3- and 5-month-olds' abilities to discriminate differential temporal patterns and that 3-month-olds preferred faster-paced rather than slower-paced stimulation.

Beebe and Gerstman (1980) considered the relationship of maternal facial-visual engagement and kinesic rhythms to an infant's facial-visual engagement during face-to-face play. It was argued that "packages" of maternal kinesic-rhythmic-facial behaviors systematically covaried with levels of infant facial-visual engagement. A purpose of the study was to provide documentation of the functional significance of maternal "packages" for facial-visual engagement during social play. Primary interest was in the organization of maternal stimulation which resulted in a positive visually attentive face-to-face encounter with the infant.

The study examined the social interactions between a four-month-old male infant and his 27-year-old mother. The mother was an upper middle class woman who volunteered for the study. The infant's delivery was uneventful, and development up to the time of the study had been reported as normal. The purpose of the study was explained to the mother as being concerned with the social development of normal babies, and the mother was instructed to play with the infant as she would at home.

Mother and infant were filmed seated opposite of each other. Two cameras were used, one on the mother's face and torso and the other on the infant's face and torso. Cameras were built into the walls, and the room was bare to minimize interference from outside stimuli. Mother and infant were alone to interact for approximately 30 minutes. A one minute and fifty-five second portion of the videotaped portion was selected for analysis. The portion for analysis was chosen based on the rhythmic nature of the maternal stimulation and the change in the affective tenor of the interaction as a result of the rhythmicity.

A frame-by-frame analysis which allowed for the examination of subtle timings of beginning and ending behaviors was conducted. Face-to-face interaction behaviors were coded for mother and infant. Once behaviors were individually coded, the complete sample was recoded into two univariate engagement scales, one for mother and one for infant. The levels of engagement were ordered with a higher number representing a more engaged state than a lower number. It was stated that the levels of engagement not only implied "magnitudes" of relatedness but also formulated complex "modes" of interpersonal relatedness across a continuum from high positive engagement to the inhibition of responsivity (Beebe and Gerstman, 1980).

Five modes of maternal hand movement were labeled, and three distinct kinesic patterns of excursion in space were identified. Together, the modes of hand movement and kinesic patterns defined kinesic-rhythmic bundles. The bundles were labeled full-out games, half-out games, short-out games, transitions, and hand pauses (see Beebe and Gerstman, 1980, for further detail).

Initiation of maternal hand games had a noticeable effect on the infant's engagement level. As the mother grasped the infant's hands and began to swing them rhythmically, the infant oriented, looked at the mother, and moved from sober-faced to positive expressiveness. During the 20 minutes prior to the mother's movement, the infant had been avoiding the mother.

Median levels of maternal facial-visual engagement covaried in heirarchy with the five maternal kinesic-rhythm conditions. Except for the conditions of half-out games and transitions, the covariations resulted in coherent maternal kinesic-rhythmic "packages." Infant median level of facial-visual engagement systematically varied with the maternal packages.

Although covaring relationships were found to exist between maternal packages and infant facial-visual engagement, a change of maternal package did not always result in a difference in infant social engagement. The mother's facial engagement and kinesic-rhythm were identified as important distinctions for the infant, but the relative importance of each must be considered in relation to the package being considered. The packages associated with high positive infant engagement were full-out games, half-out games, and transitions.

Full-out and half-out games were found to be "expectable, repetitive sequences of particular tempo and variance range" (Beebe and Gerstman, 1980). It was suggested that transitions were associated with positive infant engagement but at a somewhat lower median infant engagement because they served as a cue to both partners of a period of minor readjustment or re-regulation of arousal levels. Beebe and Gerstman (1980) stated that the results supported the hypothesis put forth by Brazelton, Koslowski, and Main (1974), Stern, Beebe, Jaffe, and Bennett (1977), and Stern and Gibbon (1978), which identified expectable and rhythmic sequences as important for positive infant affect.

Short-out games, although repetitive rhythmic games, were found to be associated, along with hand pauses, with the more major readjustment of infant avert gaze and head. If mother's face was considered important, the difference between short-out games and full-out and half-out games was characterized by two factors—tempo and degree of variability. The tempo for short-out games was very rapid and a lesser degree of variance around the cycle mean. Beebe and Gerstman (1980) stated their findings supported the findings cited from the 1979 work of Tronick, Als, and Adamson, which suggested slower maternal tempos appeared to achieve a higher level of affective involvement. With regard to variance, Beebe and Gerstman's (1980) findings provided support for the 1977 work cited of Stern, Beebe, Jaffe and Bennett, which stated that an optimal range of variability existed for repetition suited for gaining and holding an infant's attention. Wolff's work of 1967, which was cited by Beebe and Gerstman (1980), postulated that neonatal micro-rhythms were directed by external pacemakers, but Wolff thought it was difficult to conceive of the external pacemakers or "clocks" as having frequencies which were appropriate for infant micro-rhythms.

In summary, the study provided an illustration of the multi-model nature of communication. Specifically, maternal kinesic hand rhythms and facial display variations were found to change together, and maternal "packages" were found to be communicative since they covaried with infant facial-visual displays (Beebe and Gerstman, 1980). It was found that the elements of the maternal package could be perpetrated, and the rhythmic factor alone was important enough to covary independently with the infant's engagement (Beebe and Gerstman, 1980).

## STAGES OF EXPERIENTIAL ORGANIZATION

A developmental structuralist approach to the classification of adaptive and pathologic personality organizations and behaviors in infancy and early childhood was applied by Greenspan and Lourie (1981). The developmental structuralist approach identified levels of organization of experience, and the characteristics which define the experiential organization were viewed as a structure. Experiential organizations or structures were defined for each stage of emotional and cognitive experiences.

Greenspan and Lourie (1981) stated that the degree to which an individual was able to experience stage- and age-appropriate experiences indicated not only involvement in that stage but also readiness to progress to the next stage. Thus, the most optimally adaptive structure at a given developmental stage facilitates further development; "catch-up" learning could occur, but the developmental sequence and final configuration was thought to be different (Greenspan and Lourie, 1981).

Six levels of stage-specific capacities were presented to describe the developmental structural classification from infancy through adolescence. The sequence was reflected when the capacities became important in the organization of behavior and facilitation of development, not when the capacities first emerged. The stages and a description of capacities for each stage were provided (Greenspan and Lourie, 1981).

| | | |
|---|---|---|
| Stage I: | Homeostasis | Achievement of self-regulation. Child is free to become involved in social interactions. |
| Stage II: | Attachment | Child forms human attachment. More mature patterns of communication emerge as the child develops. Differentiation facilitates the development of the third stage. |
| Stage III: | Somatopsychological Differentiation | Infant organizes experiences through internal representation. Care-giver reads and responds to infant cues. Optimal development characterized by toddler's ability to "take on" or internalize attributes of the caretaker. |
| Stage IV: | Behavioral Organization, Initiative, and Internalization | Increased ability to organize mental representations. Ability to use mental representations plays greater role in organizing the child's behavior. |

| | | |
|---|---|---|
| Stage V: | Representation, Differenti-ation, and Consolidation | Child forms mental representa-tions or evokes internal multi-sensory experiences. Differen-tiates "self" representations from representations of the ex-ternal world. |
| Stage VI: | Limited and Multiple Representational Systems | Child develops representational systems derived from the origi-nal representational system. |

Greenspan and Lourie (1981) identified child behaviors which indicated adaptation and maladaptation and characteristics of the environment which would prevent maladaptation or act in a therapeutic way for the child exhibiting maladaptive behaviors. Child behaviors and environ-mental characteristics during infancy and early childhood were discussed. A supportive caretaker was identified as important throughout the child's development.

*Somatopsychological differentiation.* During the period of somato-psychological differentiation (3–10 months), the adaptive infant is capable of a wide range of differentiated experiences. These experiences are multi-sensory and affectively rich. Stable, reciprocal, highly personalized organ-ized patterns provide cohesion to the changing structural capacity of the infant. According to Greenspan and Lourie (1981),

> The adaptive environment supports the early stages of development. . . the infant's basic need for a calm, regulated internal state, and overall interest in the environment; maintains an appropriate, basically pleasurable, bilaterally rewarding attachment; and facilitates differentiation along multiple develop-ment lines (cognitive, affective, interpersonal, etc.)(p. 729).

In an adaptive environment, a wide range of baby signals can be read and responded to in the appropriate manner.

Problems during the stage of somatopsychological differentiation may exist at different levels. A child may experience a total lack of development of differential responses, or differentiation may be lacking in only one area. A non-adaptive environment during this stage is one in which the care-giver is either unable to read or respond differentially to the baby's signals. Difficulty in responding to signals may result from misreading of signals, accurate reading of signals but attempting to control the baby, or the fact that the baby may be a weak "sender" of signals and it's interests are dif-ficult to identify.

In an attempt to identify strategies for prevention or treatment, Greenspan and Lourie (1981) suggest that problems contributing to a deficit in somaticpsychological differentiation may exist in the environ-mental system, make-up of the baby, or both. Once the problem is iden-tified, the approach is to strengthen the missing component. Specific ap-proaches would include strengthening the component leading to differen-tiation, helping family members read signals, encouraging the infant to send stronger signals, and encouraging the use of a variety of communica-tion modalities.

*Behavioral organization, initiative, and internalization.* Greater behav-ioral organization, an ability to take initiative, and an increasing capacity to internalize describe the capacities of infants from 9 to 24 months. The toddler is viewed as an organized being who is able to initiate behaviors.

Adaptive patterns include an ability to be a part of complex interpersonal communications and to put together several related events. The child is able to respond with varying degrees of, rather than extremes of, emotions. The child is also able to respond to changes in the organization of the environment if they are not too limiting.

The adaptive environment is one which allows the initiating toddler an opportunity to interact and admires, supports, and helps organize following the child's lead. The adaptive caretaker helps the child respond with organized interpersonal responses. Periods of anger followed by relaxing experiences help the child integrate emotions. Limit setting is appropriate but should be provided within the context of a stable relationship.

Disorders at this stage may result from an inability to organize behaviors, internalize, or take initiative. Greenspan and Lourie (1981) include temper tantrums, lack of motor or emotional coordination, lack of self-control, and delayed language development as symptoms of disorders during this phase. The environment which supports disordered development at this stage is one which does not encourage the child's attempts to organize and initiate behaviors. Interactions may be short and fragmented, and attempts at autonomy may be met with fear rather than admiration.

Prevention and treatment approaches at this stage must examine (a) what the child is doing which contributes to the problem and (b) the environment the child must function in. In dealing with the child, one may find that it is necessary to go back and identify missing earlier experiences. Environmental issues may require the correction of limitations, an auxiliary support system which includes other family members, or educational and modeling approaches.

## PLAYING TO FACILITATE INFANT-CARETAKER INTERACTIONS

Bentovim (1977) identified play as a "paradoxical activity." He cited Bateson's (1954) description of play and playing as consisting of actions which are not what they look like or appear to stand for. Groffman (as cited by Bentovim, 1977) stated that the contradiction resulted from the "frame" within which the play activity occurred. The existence of this "frame" distinguished play from reality. Therapy, like play, according to Bentovim (1977), has a "frame." The "frame" allows a problem to be redefined as a psychological truth, which once faced and understood, could lead to change. He felt that play and therapy came together because play allowed therapy to occur. Play provided an opportunity to redefine what was happening, to look at reality in a different way. Therapy or development occurred because the individual was able to view a problem in a different way. In separating play from reality, the frame may provide the participants with freedom to explore different styles of interaction. The final section of this chapter will present some considerations for using a play setting to develop "goodness of fit."

*Characteristics of the environment and participants.* In examining "goodness of fit" between infant and caretaker, one must look at the interaction within the context in which it occurred. The environment which supports successful mother-infant interactions was described by Greenspan and Lourie (1981) as adaptive. Some characteristics of an adaptive environment included allowing for a wide range of signals to be read and responded to appropriately—"initiation of and participation in activities by the child" and setting of realistic limits (Greenspan and Lourie 1981).

Characteristics of the participants have also been suggested. Osofsky (1976) found that more sensitive mothers had more responsive infants; in stimulation situations, she found that mother presentation had an effect on infant response. Lounsbury and Bates (1982) and Greenspan and Lourie (1981) described the caretaker as "having empathy" and "supportive."

In real-life, three factors need to be considered in looking at "goodness-of-fit": the environment; adult behaviors; and infant behaviors. In the play situation, the environment should be considered to control for a sense of playfulness and freedom to explore new ways to interact. Infant and adult behaviors should be viewed from two perspectives. First, the sending of signals by both participants must be considered. Second, the reading or interpretation of signals must be examined. Signals must be viewed in terms of clarity of message, strength, and how accurately the message is interpreted or how well the sender's message is answered.

Both participants may send signals which are weak or signals which are unclear. When the child's behavior is such that weak messages are being sent, the parent may be provided with techniques which would help develop stronger signals while being aware of the child's needs. An example of a child sending weak signals would be one who makes feeble attempts for objects. In working with the child, parents would be given activities which would use successive approximations to get stronger, more definite reaching behavior. Desired outcomes would include parents' developing awareness of and an ability to read subtle child behaviors and parents' feeling more successful in interactions because they are able to respond more appropriately.

Parents who send weak or unclear signals may be guided in an analysis of their behavior. Parent self-analysis would include verbal and non-verbal behaviors which interfere with communication. Intervention with parents, concerning verbal responses, may include learning to use language that is appropriate for the child's developmental abilities and practice in giving statements which are specific and letting the child know exactly what is being requested or expected. In analyzing non-verbal behavior, parents would be guided in developing non-verbal behaviors which are complementary to and enhance the verbal message.

When the resources are available, interactions may be videotaped to provide an opportunity for parents to analyze non-verbal behavior. In looking at these observations, the work of Beebe and Gerstmann (1981) would suggest that caretakers be guided in analysis of clusters or "packages" of behavior. Arco and McClusky (1981) and Beebe and Gerstmann found that tempo or rhythm of the interaction was important and also needs to be considered.

In summary, it appears that there is a need for observational tools which can be used by adults to evaluate interactions. Parents need to be guided in practicing and refining behaviors which will facilitate more positive and enjoyable interactions. Once behaviors are developed in a play situation, strategies need to be implemented which will help generalize these behaviors.

## REFERENCES

Allport, G. W. *Patterns and Growth in Personality*. New York: Holt, Rinehart & Winston (1961).

Arco, C. M. B. and McClusky, K. A., "'A change of pace:' An investigation of the salience of maternal temporal style in mother-infant interaction," *Child Development, 52*, 941–949 (1982).

Bates, J., "The concept of difficult temperament," *Merrill-Palmer Quarterly, 26*, 299–318 (1980).

Beebe, B. and Gerstman, L. J., "The 'packaging' of maternal stimulation in relation to infant facial-visual engagement. A case study at four months," *Merrill-Palmer Quarterly, 26*, 321–337 (1980).

Bentovim, A., "The role of play in psychotherapeutic work with children and their families," in *Biology of Play*, B. Tizard and D. Harvey, eds. Philadelphia: J. B. Lippincott Co. (1977).

Brazelton, T. B. *Neonatal Behavior Assessment Scale*. London: Spastics International Medical Publications (1973).

Buss, A. H. and Plomin, R. *A Temperament Theory of Personality Development*. New York: Wiley-Interscience (1975).

Carey, W. B., "A simplified method for measuring infant temperament," *Journal of Pediatrics, 77*, 188–194 (1970).

Carey, W. and McDevitt, S., "Revision of the Infant Temperament Questionnaire," *Pediatrics, 61*, 735–739 (1978).

Erikson, E. H. *Identity and the Life Cycle*. New York: Norton (1980).

Garside, R. F., Birch, H. G., Scott, D. M., Chambers, S., Kolvin, I., Tweddle, E. G., and Barber, L. M., "Dimensions of temperament in infant school children," *Journal of Child Psychology and Psychiatry, 16*, 219–231 (1975).

Graham, P., Rutter, M., and George, S., "Temperament characteristics as predictors of behavior disorders of children," *American Journal of Orthopsychiatry, 43*, 328–339 (1973).

Greenspan, S. and Lourie, R. S., "Developmental structuralist approach to the classification of adaptive and pathological personality organizations: infancy and early childhood," *American Journal of Psychiatry, 138*, 725–735 (1981).

Honig, A., "Infant-mother communication," *Young Children, 37*, 52–62 (1982).

Hubert, N. C., Wachs, T. D., Peters-Martin, P., and Gandour, M. J., "The study of early temperament: Measurement and conceptual issues," *Child Development, 53* (3), 571–600 (1982).

Jackson, D. M. *Personality Research Form Manual*. Goshen, NY: Research Psychologist (1974).

Lounsbury, M. L. and Bates, J. E., "The cries of infants of differing levels of perceived temperamental difficultness: Acoustic properties and effects on listeners," *Child Development, 53* (3), 677–686 (1982).

Lyon, M. and Plomin, R., "The measurement of temperament using parent ratings," *Journal of Child Psychology and Psychiatry, 22*, 47–54 (1981).

McDevitt, S. C. and Carey, W. B., "The measurement of temperament in 3–7 year old children," *Journal of Child Psychology and Psychiatry, 19*, 245–253 (1978).

McDevitt, S. C. and Carey, W., "Stability of ratings versus perceptions of temperament from early infancy to 1–3 years," *American Journal of Orthopsychiatry, 11*, 342–345 (1981).

Mehrabian, A. and Epstein, N., "A measure of emotional empathy," *Journal of Personality, 40*, 525–543 (1972).

Osofsky, J., "Neonatal characteristics and mother-infant interaction in two observational situations," *Child Development, 47*, 1138–1147 (1976).

Piaget, J. *Origins of Intelligence in Children*. New York: Norton (1952).

Rowe, D. C. and Plomin, R., "Temperament in early childhood," *Journal of Personality Assessment, 41,* 150–156 (1977).

Sostek, A. M. and Anders, T. F., "Relationships among the Brazelton Neonatal Scale, Bayley Infant Scales and early temperament," *Child Development, 48,* 320–323 (1977).

Thomas, A. and Chess, S. *The Dynamics of Psychological Development.* New York: Brunner/Mazel (1980).

Thomas, A. and Chess, S. *Temperament and Development.* New York: Brunner/Mazel (1977).

Thomas, A., Chess, S., and Birch, H., "The origin of personality," *Scientific America, 223,* 102–109 (1970).

Thomas, A., Chess, S., and Birch, H. *Temperament and Behavior Disorders in Children.* New York: New York University Press (1968).

Thomas A., Chess, S., Birch, H. G., Hertzig, M. E., and Korn, S. *Behavior Individuality in Early Childhood.* New York: New York University Press (1963).

# Play:
# The father's primary way of contributing to the young child's development

**Zoraida Porrata-Doria**
*Division of Social Sciences*
*The University of Puerto Rico*

## INTRODUCTION

This chapter focuses on the role of the father as a playmate of the child. Research data from the 1970's on the dimensions of the paternal role are analyzed to contend that (a) mothers and fathers differ in terms of the level and nature of their involvement with the child and in the styles of influencing the child through play, (b) the father's contribution to the child development is primarily through play, and (c) home intervention programs should be aimed at teaching parents to use play as a means to foster the child's development and should involve the father.

Traditionally, theorizing and research on child development had been characterized by an imbalanced focus on the mother's influence (Parke, 1981; Lamb, 1976; Pedersen and Robson, 1969). For the most part, the absence of research on paternal behavior can be attributed to the long-standing assumption that fathers do not have interaction with their infants and small children and that, as a result, fathers have minimal influence on development until children get older (Lamb and Stevenson, 1978). However, during the 1970's, there had been an increasing interest in the role of the father in child development. Lamb (1976) gives three reasons for the current attempt to counterbalance previous research: (1) so much emphasis on mother-child relationships, especially in infancy, has made some researchers ask if it is indeed true that the father is an almost irrelevant entity in the infant's world; (2) current characteristics of contemporary belief include the disintegration of the family and the frequently disrupted father-child relations; and (3) the great deal that has been learned about the infant's psychological abilities in the early months and years of life has made researchers think that the social world of the infant is far more complex than much of the theorizing has assumed.

As a result of the research done on father-child relations, the importance of paternal influence in child development is now generally accepted, but actually, very little is known about fathers' relationships with children—particularly in the earlier years (Pedersen and Robson, 1969; Lamb, 1978).

The father establishes relationships with the child through the performance of his paternal role. Huston and McHale (1982) analyzed cross-cultural and historical literature on parental roles and identified a range of ways in which parents and children adopt their respective roles in the family. From the literature, four dimensions were considered as useful in differentiating parental roles. These components are the:

a. level of involvement each parent has with the child, that is, the proportion of the parent's daily activities that involves the child (e.g., centrality of the child in the parent activity field, frequency of contact with the child);

b. nature of the involvement, that is, the types of activities in which the parents get involved with the child (e.g., amount of care-giving activity, amount of leisure activity, amount to which involvement is instrumental vs. recreational);

c. social context of involvement, that is, which persons are involved in the interaction (e.g., amount of care-giving activity in presence vs. absence of spouse); and

d. parental style of influence, that is, the ways in which parents attempt to influence their children (e.g., frequency of response to the child's signal, proportion of different kinds of influence techniques).

The above-mentioned dimensions are useful in assessing the particular ways in which both the mother and the father fulfill their parenting roles.

On the other hand, early childhood specialists, psychologists, educators, social scientists, and others have been advocating play as an effective way of educating young children (Yawkey and Fox, 1981; Curry and Arnaud, 1974). In the book *Learning is Child's Play,* Yawkey and Trostle (1982) contend that work and play should not necessarily be considered separate activities. At times, play may seem to be work, and work may seem like play. Other researchers such as Piaget (1962), Lieberman (1965), Freyburg (1973), and Michelich (1975) believe play is a significant influence on the child's social, emotional, and cognitive development. When studying the role of play in the child's development, researchers have not only been considering the types of play in which children get involved but also the contribution that particular types of play can make. We do know that the young child is continuously involved in play, play contributes to child development, and home is the context in which the young child spends most of his/her time. The level and nature of involvement of both mother and father with the young child and the styles of influencing the child through play will be discussed to contend that intervention strategies aimed at teaching the parents how to use play as a medium in fostering child development should include the father.

This intellectual exercise is considered important for a student of early childhood. The planning of early childhood educational services transcends the school. Services with home components, especially those using play as a way to help in fostering child development, represent not only a comprehensive approach to young children's educational services but a service that increases the probability of helping the child in his/her development.

## LEVEL AND NATURE OF INVOLVEMENT OF MOTHERS AND FATHERS WITH THEIR CHILDREN

Research data suggest that mothers and fathers differ in both the level of involvement and the nature of their involvement with the child.

Milton Kotelchuck (1976) conducted four laboratory studies with the general purpose of examining the child's behavior in an unfamiliar playroom as a function of the presence or absence of his/her mother, father, or an unfamiliar female. In all four experiments, maternal and paternal home caretaking and interaction data were obtained from a joint interview with the mother and the father following the completion of the experimental session. The interview sought to determine who took care of child care routines, who played with the child, how long each parent played with the child, and so forth. The first and largest of the studies included 144 children, 12 boys and 12 girls at each of 6, 9, 12, 15, 18, and 21 months of age. The subjects were middle class, first-born children in the Boston area.

The results of all four studies indicated that infants and toddlers relate to their fathers. In relation to who did the child care routines, the data showed that mothers had principal child rearing responsibilities. More were present for more time with their children than were the fathers, 9.0 versus 3.2 hours (p<.001), and more were available essentially for the child's whole waking day. Mothers spent more time feeding than did the fathers, 1.45 hours versus 0.25 hour (p<.001), and they spent more time than fathers cleaning the child, .92 hour versus .15 hour (p<.001).

The distribution of the caretaking responsibility dramatizes the extensiveness of maternal caretaking in a middle class sample. Of the mothers, 64 percent were totally and solely responsible for the child care; 9.1 percent shared caretaking responsibility jointly with another person. Only 7.6 percent of the fathers shared infant-caretaking responsibilities equally with their wives, and only 25 percent had any regular daily caretaking responsibilities. In other words, 75 percent of middle class fathers in Boston did not physically care for their children on a regular day-to-day basis. Even more remarkably, 43 percent of all the fathers reported they never changed diapers at all!

Mothers spent more absolute time in play with their children than the fathers did, 2.3 to 1.2 hours (p<.0), a difference that is statistically significant but that showed the least mother-father difference of any home variable. These data reveal that fathers were involved only in a minimal amount of the child's care, especially those tasks of child rearing that are often viewed as routine and somewhat boring. Fathers spent, however, a greater percentage of time (37.5 percent) in enjoyable play activities with the child than mothers did (25.5 percent). Kotelchuck (1976) comments that the exact consequence of the differences in proportion of play to total time spent with the child is unclear, but it appears reasonable to suggest that the amount of play contributes to the father's attractiveness to his child, despite his restricted availability.

In summary, the parents' interview data suggest that the level of involvement of the mothers with 6- to 20-month-old, middle class children is greater than that of the father. In terms of the nature of involvement, the data suggest that the mother is the primary caretaker. Both the mothers and the fathers play with their children, but the fathers spend a greater percentage of their time with the children in play activities, while the mothers spend less time playing with their children.

Huston and McHale (1982) made a longitudinal study on the premarital and early marital experiences of 168 couples of central Pennsylvania. In the second phase of the study, data were collected about the extent and nature of involvement of mothers and fathers with children. For this purpose, a subsample of 37 couples who became parents between Phase I and Phase II of the study was selected. The children were born between 2 weeks and 12 months after their parents' marriage. The mean age of the children was 7.8 months, S.D. = 2.9 months. The data were collected by means of a telephone interview.

It was found that the activities of the mothers centered around the home and leisure more than did the activities of the fathers. Women engaged in roughly 2.7 times as many of these activities as men. Although the parenting role was found salient in the activities of both parents, it comprises a larger portion of the total activities of mothers, as compared to fathers. Mothers engaged in child-oriented activities almost four times as often as fathers, $f(1,35) = 109.2$, p<.01. Moreover, despite the fact that mothers carry out a far greater number of household tasks, a greater proportion of their home and personal activities involves the child. That is, children are more central to the lives of the mothers than the fathers, $f(1,35) = 19.9$, p<.01.

The nature of the involvement of fathers differs from that of mothers. Almost half (49 percent) of fathers' activities with their children involves leisure rather than care-giving; the corresponding proportion for the mothers is 20 percent.

In summary, in terms of the level of involvement, the data suggest that mothers have more frequent contact with their children. When the nature of the involvement is considered, the data show that the mother is the primary care-giver. Both mothers and fathers play with their children, but fathers spend the greater percentage of their time with their children playing, as compared with the mothers who spend less time playing.

Lamb (1977) makes reference to a study of English parents made by Richards, Dunn, and Antonis (1977), in which it was found that play was the most common activity for fathers of 30- and 60-week-old infants. Ninety percent of the parents played regularly with their infants, while less than half participated in caretaking.

In summary, the investigations of Kotelchuck (1976), Huston and McHale (1982), and Richards, et al. (1977) suggest that fathers are usually secondary care-givers, but they do have an important role in play matters.

However, fathers are not always the primary playmate, according to Pedersen, Cain, Zaslow, and Anderson (1980). Observing mothers and fathers with their 5-month-old infants, they found that fathers played more than mothers only if the father was employed and the mother did not hold a job outside the home. In families where both parents were employed, mothers played more than fathers. Since the observations took place in the evenings after both parents came from jobs, Pedersen, et al. (1980) suggest that the mother played more as a way of reestablishing contact with her baby after being away from home for the day. One result was that fathers in the two-earner families had less play time with their infants. Parke (1981) comments that the Pedersen, et al. (1980) study shows that family organization clearly can affect the father's status as primary playmate.

Taken together, then, most of the studies suggest that both fathers and mothers are active playmates for their young children. Mothers contribute to the child's development in a number of ways, while fathers make their contribution through play. If the mother is not working outside the home, she probably spends more time in playing with her baby. Nevertheless, fathers devote a higher proportion of their time with the baby to play than mothers.

After presenting the level and nature of involvement of the mother and the father with the young child, a third dimension of the parental role, that of the parental style of influencing the child through play, will be considered.

## PARENTAL STYLES OF PLAYING WITH CHILDREN

Studies suggest that there exist differences in the play styles used by mothers and fathers.

Lamb and Stevenson (1978) state that most of the available data concerning parent-infant interaction in infants older than six months have been gathered in "free play" situations at home and at the laboratory. Some of the investigations that have observed babies at home with their parents are Lamb (1976, 1977a, 1977b), Rendina and Dickerscheid (1976), Clarke-Steward (1977), and Parke and Sawin (1977).

Lamb (1976, 1977a, 1977b) made a longitudinal study with the purpose of gaining insight into infant attachment to their fathers. One of the objectives of the investigation was to explore the nature of the mother- and father-infant play relationships by focusing on two classes of interaction—play and physical contact (holding).

The subjects were 10 boys, 10 girls, and their parents, recruited from the birth records of the Yale-New Haven Hospital. The infants were observed in their homes when both parents were present. Each family was observed on several occasions from the time their infants were seven months old until they reached 24 months of age. Each visit lasted between one and two hours. On the average, each infant was observed for a total of 153.3 minutes.

It was found that though both parents engaged in equivalent amounts of play, mothers and fathers engaged in different types of play. Mothers initiated more conventional play activities (peek-a-boo and pat-a-cake), stimulus-toy play (jiggling the toy to stimulate the child), and reading. Fathers' play, by contrast, involved more physical stimulation and was more unpredictable. The physically stimulating and idiosyncratic play in which fathers engaged was the type of play to which babies responded most positively.

Differences between mothers and fathers were also evident when holding interactions were examined. Up to 13 months, mothers held their babies more than fathers. Further, a greater proportion of mothers' than of fathers' holding was for caretaking purposes and for the purpose of removing the baby from some forbidden activity. Fathers' holding was more likely to be in the course of play. Not surprisingly, therefore, babies responded more positively to being held by their fathers than by their mothers. These data suggest that the traditional roles assumed by mothers and fathers are translated into differences in their styles of interaction with their infants.

In summary, the data suggest that fathers of 7- to 24-month-old infants engage in more physical games and more unusual or idiosyncratic games than mothers. Mothers, in contrast, engage in more conventional play activities, stimulus-toy play, and reading than fathers.

In another observational study, Rendina and Dickersheid (1976) observed the families of 6- and 13-month-old infants at home. Although the mothers were present during the visits, only paternal behaviors were recorded. There was great variability among fathers. Some spent as little as 12 percent and others as much as 84 percent of the observation time (interacting) with their babies. The average was 36 percent. The most common activity was watching the baby (12.8 percent), with 9.2 percent of the time spent providing affective proximal attention and 3.8 percent of the time caretaking. The remaining 10.4 percent of the time was spent in social activities such as games, conversation, toy play, and rough-and-tumble play.

In summary, the data suggest that when the father plays with the 6- to

13-month-old infant, he converses and gets involved in toy play and in games such as rough-and-tumble play.

Clarke-Steward (1977) made a longitudinal investigation with the purpose of studying the father's contribution to child's development. The subjects were 14 children from 1 to 2½ years of age, who were randomly selected from hospital birth records. All families were white, but a range of socio-economic levels from working class to professional class were represented. All mothers were non-working and their children's primary care-givers. The data were gathered by means of an unstructured "natural observations" scheme of child and family at home and semi-structured situations in which (a) parents were asked to choose and do things with their child that were either social (like having a pretend tea party) or intellectual (like reading a story), (b) children's attachment to their parents was assessed by having each parent go through sequences of social interaction, separation, and reunion with the child, and (c) parents were called upon to do specific activities with the child (e.g., blowing bubbles, playing ball) under dyadic (with parent and child alone) and triadic (with all three, mother, father, and child, present) situations.

The data showed that there is a significant difference between mother and father behavior when playing with children. Fathers gave more verbal directions and positive reinforcement than mothers. Furthermore, observers gave fathers higher ratings than mothers on their ability to engage the children in play, on the babies' enjoyment of the interaction, and on their involvement in it. On the other hand, mothers spent more of the observation period interacting with the babies than did fathers. No differences were found in the responsiveness of the parents or in the amount of social-physical play in which they engaged. When the same parents were asked, as part of a laboratory task, to choose an activity to engage in with their infants, mothers tended to select intellectual activities, while the fathers chose social-physical activities.

In summary, fathers and mothers differ in the way they behave when playing with their children. The fathers gave more verbal directions and positive reinforcements and seemed to have more ability to engage the children in play, to make the babies enjoy their play interaction, and to get them involved. The mothers' level of involvement was greater. When given the opportunity, fathers tend to select socio-physical activities, while mothers choose intellectual activities.

Lamb and Stevenson (1978) summarized an observational study made by Parke and Sawin (1977). In the investigation, an observational one, parent-infant interaction in the newborn period, as well as when the infants were three weeks and three months of age, was recorded. During five minutes of toy play, fathers provided their newborns with more visual and auditory stimulation than did the mothers, while mothers spent more time caretaking than did fathers. With the older infants, however, the roles were reversed; mothers provided more stimulation, fathers more caretaking. Although the findings of this one study are inconsistent, most of the available data indicate that mothers are identified with caretaking, while fathers are more involved in play.

The differences between fathers' and mothers' styles of play are found in the home as well as the laboratory. Parke (1971) summarizes a study conducted by Power and himself (Power and Parke, in press) with the purpose of finding out whether mothers and fathers have different styles of play with infants and in situations other than face-to-face play. The types of games that fathers and mothers played with their eight-month-old infants were examined in a laboratory playroom. The situation was relatively unstructured, and toys were available for the parents and infants to use. A number of distinctive games that were played were identified. They ranged from "distal" games which involve stimulating the baby at a distance by shaking or showing a toy, to "physical" games which involve directly touching, lifting, or bouncing the baby. Other games, such as grasping and retrieving games, require the infant to hold or retrieve a nearby toy.

It was observed that fathers play many of the same games as mothers, but there are clear differences in their styles. Fathers engaged in significantly more physical games, such as bounding and lifting, than mothers. Mothers, in contrast, used a more distal, attention-getting approach and played more watching games. A favorite game of the mothers was to show the baby a toy and then shake and move it to stimulate the baby. Fathers were particularly likely to play "lifting" games with their boy infants and were less physical with their girls.

In summary, fathers and mothers play similar games, but the father engaged in more physical games and mothers in more watching games.

Another laboratory study aimed at assessing parental differences in play style was that of Yogman, Dixon, Tronik, Als, and Brazelton (1977). In the lab situation, infants were observed with three different play partners: father; mother; and a stranger. Each infant was placed in a reclining chair (or baby seat), and the face-to-face interactions that developed between the infant and the adult as they played together were filmed. There were clear differences in the ways the adults played with the infants, as revealed by talking and touching patterns. Mothers spoke softly, repeating words and phrases frequently and imitating the infant's sounds more than either fathers or strangers. A burst-pause pattern was common for the mothers—a rapidly spoken series of words and sounds, followed by a short period of silence. Fathers were less verbal and more tactile than mothers. They touched their infants with rhythmic tapping patterns more often than mothers or strangers. Father-infant play shifted rapidly from peaks of high infant attention and excitement to valleys of minimal attention, while mother-infant play demonstrated more gradual shifts.

In summary, mothers' play was characterized by soft speaking, repetition of words, and imitation of the infant sounds, while fathers' play was less verbal and more tactile.

The studies presented differed in terms of methodologies and goals. Despite this difference, all indicate that fathers are more likely than mothers to engage in physically stimulating and unconventional games.


## SUMMARY AND CONCLUSIONS

The results of all the studies surveyed, in which the level and nature of involvement of the mother and the father with the child was investigated, showed that the mother is the primary care-giver of the child. Second, all of the studies suggested that both the mother and the father are active playmates with their children. Third, the results of Kotelchuck (1976), Huston and McHale (1982), and Richards (1977) indicated that the father is the primary playmate of the young child, while the Pedersen, Cain, Zaslow, and Anderson (1980) study suggested that fathers are not always the primary playmates, for fathers played more than mothers only if the father was employed and the mother did not hold a job outside the home.

All the investigations surveyed, in which the parental styles used in playing with the child were assessed, showed that there exist differences in the play styles used by mothers and fathers. Second, the results of Lamb (1976, 1977a, 1977b), Rendina and Dickersheid (1976), Clarke-Steward (1977), and Power and Parke (in press) showed that fathers get involved in more physical play than mothers. Third, the investigations done by Lamb (1976, 1977a, 1977b) and Clarke-Steward (1977) suggested that the mother engaged in a more intellectual type of play. Fourth, the research done by Power and Parke (in press) and Lamb (1976, 1977a, 1977b) showed that the mother engaged in toy-mediated play. An observation study made by Rendina and Dickersheid (1976), in which only the father-child play was observed, showed that the father also got involved in toy play and conversed with the child. Fifth, Clarke-Steward (1977) suggested that fathers have more ability to engage the children in play, to make babies enjoy the play interaction, and to get the baby more involved.

All of the studies surveyed showed that the father spends the greater proportion of the time in which he is involved with the child playing. Accepting that play fosters the child's emotional, cognitive, and social development, it can be concluded that the father makes his major contribution to the young child's cognitive development mainly through play. However, the mother also contributes to child development through play.

Intervention programs aimed at teaching the parents how to foster the child's development through play should, without underestimating the potential contribution of the mother, involve the father. This strategy is very important because, although researchers have accepted that the father is not an accident in the child's life and that he contributes to the child's development, it is not very uncommon to find intervention programs in which this is forgotten.

## RESEARCH SUGGESTIONS

The survey of the literature, nevertheless, showed that the investigations have used children from birth to two years of age. It is therefore recommended to include infants, as well as preschoolers, in the research samples.

The data presented suggest that the father's predominant style of interacting with his child is physical. Investigations addressed at getting a deeper insight of the parental style considering the age and sex of the child are suggested. Also, the contextual component of the parental roles have not been examined empirically (Huston and McHale, 1972). Research in this area is needed, for it could show if a triad (mother-father-child) interaction affects development positively or not.

## REFERENCES

Clarke-Steward, A., "The father's impact on mother and child," Paper presented to the Society for Research in Child Development, New Orleans (March 1977).

Curry, N. E. and Arnaud, S. H., "Cognitive implications in children's spontaneous role play," *Theory into Practice, 13* (4), 273–277 (1974).

Huston, T. and McHale, S., Research on newlywed couples. College of Human Development, The Pennsylvania State University (1982).

Kotelchuck, M., "The infant's relationship to the father: Experimental evidence," in *The Role of the Father in Child Development*, M. E. Lamb, ed. New York: John Wiley and Sons (1976).

Lamb, M. and Stevenson, M., "Father-infant relationships: Their nature and importance," *Youth and Society, 9,* 297–298 (1978).

Lamb, M. E., "The development of mother-infant and father-infant attachments in the second year of life," *Developmental Psychology, 13,* 637–648 (1977).

Lamb, M. E., "Father-infant and mother-infant interaction in the first year of life," *Child Development, 48,* 167–181 (1977).

Lamb, M. E. *The Role of the Father in Child Development.* New York: John Wiley and Sons (1976).

Parke, R. D. *Fathers.* Massachusetts: Harvard University Press (1981).

Parke, R. D. and Sawin, D. B., "The family in early infancy: Social interactions and attitudinal analyses," Paper presented to the Society for Research on Child Development, New Orleans (March 1977).

Pedersen, F. A. and Robson, K. S., "Fathers' participation in infancy," *American Journal of Orthopsychiatry, 39,* 466–472 (1969).

Pedersen, F. A., Zaslow, M. T., Cain, R. L., and Anderson, B. J., "Variation in infant experience associated with alternative family organization," Paper presented at the International Conference of Infant Studies, New Haven, CT (April 1980).

Rendina, J. and Dickerscheid, J. D., "Father involvement with first-born infants," *Family Coordinator, 25,* 373–378 (1976).

Richards, Dunn, and Antonis, "Caretaking in the first year of life," in M. E. Lamb's, "Father-infant and mother-infant interaction in the first year of life," *Child Development, 48,* 167–181 (1977).'

Yawkey, T. D. and Fox, F. D., "Evaluative intervention research in child's play," *Journal of Research and Development in Education, 14* (3), 40–57 (1981).

Yawkey, T. D. and Trostle, S. L. *Learning is Child's Play.* Utah: Brigham Young University Press (1982).

# Play therapy and the disruptive child

**Susan L. Trostle**
*The Child Development Council of Centre County (Pennsylvania)*

## INTRODUCTION

The disruptive child may manifest a variety of different behaviors. Ranging from extremely aggressive at one end of the spectrum to extremely docile at the other, the child's behavior is classified as disruptive because it interferes with normal, ongoing daily routines (Axline, 1969). The teacher, caretaker, or parent may notice that the child fails to conform to the home or the school's established procedures. The child may be overly loud, temperamental, or bossy. His behaviors may be labeled as rude, selfish, uncaring, or thoughtless by one or more of the child's caregivers or by the child's playmates or siblings. When unusually active, loud, and aggressive behaviors or, conversely, unusually quiet, reserved behaviors occur, the most important consideration is the child's overall state of health (Ilg and Ames, 1955). A thorough physical examination by a medical specialist is the primary and most eminent step toward modifying the child's unacceptable behaviors. Once the existence of hyperactivity, minimal brain damage, disease, learning disability, or other health or learning abnormalities has been either overruled or determined and medically alleviated, the second step becomes systematically dealing with the child's environment and unacceptable behaviors on a day-to-day basis. Through the use of play therapy, the parent allows the child to discover his own route to attaining more integrative behaviors. Five skills are involved in dealing systematically with the child during the play therapy sessions. The parent must first learn to accept the child's feelings. Disruptive behaviors always occur for a reason. Sometimes the reason is clear to discern, such as the sudden absence of the child's parent, a new or fearful situation, or an annoying health problem. At other times, the explanation is more difficult, if not impossible, to discover. However, regardless of the explanation for the disruptive behaviors, the parent learns to accept the fact that the child feels overly shy, overly bossy, or overly aggressive. The child's unruly or withdrawn behaviors mirror the child's internal feelings of isolation, loneliness, insecurity, anger, incompetency, or rebellion. Disruptive behavior, in a sense, is the child's "cry for help" to rid himself of these unhealthy, but very universal, internal feelings and emotions (Guerney, 1976). The parent, consequently, realizes that the child behaves

157

unacceptably because of an internal need. An understanding of the child's developmental stage, the child's ongoing life circumstances, and the child's unique personality provides the parent with some of the necessary criteria for understanding and accepting the child's feelings.

Second, during play therapy sessions, the parent uses a responding technique which allows the child an unrestricted freedom of expression. The technique is called "empathic responding" for it involves the parent's responding without either criticism or support to the child's physical and verbal behaviors (Guerney, 1982). The child is given complete freedom to experiment, explore, and express; the parent shows acceptance for all behaviors through statements which paraphrase, summarize, or elaborate upon what the child has said or done. As a result, the child feels no limits to his need for free expression and emotional release.

Third, the parent uses the structuring tool in the play therapy room environment and in his/her own verbal and facial expressions. The parent structures the environment so that available toys remain consistent for each play therapy session. The play therapy room is arranged in the same manner each week, and the time and duration of the weekly sessions remain relatively the same each week. Additionally, the structuring tool involves the parent's using the same mode of empathic responding during each session and the personal messages, limits, and consequences (which will be discussed) at the appropriate times. Generally speaking, the use of structuring provides the framework for the setting and the interactions in which play therapy proceeds under consistent and optimal conditions.

The fourth skill which the parent learns is the use of personal messages. During play therapy, the child is the leader or the "person in charge." Every effort is made by the parent to allow the child complete freedom of expression and action. However, there are times in which the parent must express a personal concern or message to the child. During times of personal safety concerns, feelings of discomfort or, during other extenuous circumstances, the parent informs the child that his present behavior arouses uncomfortable feelings in the parent. The parent states the child's specific behavior which results in this specified feeling.

Limits and consequences constitute the final play therapy tool or skill. Depending upon personal preferences, available space, and surroundings, the parent needs to impose rules or limits on the child's actions or statements. The child is informed of the fact that limits exist. However, a specific limit is not stated until the child engages in an unacceptable behavioral mode. Limits are necessary in order to insure that the time which is set aside for play therapy remains consistent. Moreover, good health and safety maintenance of both the parent and the child is insured. A consequence warning accompanies a limit which must be stated more than two times during a particular incident. If the child continues to repeat the offensive behavior a third time, a direct consequence results. By using consequences, the parent accomplishes two goals. They are (a) immediately ending the unwanted behavior and (b) demonstrating to the child the existence of rule enforcement and necessary structure during the play therapy session.

Play therapy serves three important functions (Guerney, 1978). One purpose of a play session is to allow the child to recognize his own feelings. As the parent attempts to understand and accept the child's feelings, the child learns to deal with these feelings—openly and honestly.

Another purpose of play sessions is that of establishing a feeling of the child's trust in the parent. As the adult demonstrates unlimited empathic responding to even the most bizarre behaviors of the child, the child gains a sense of trust and confidence in the parent. He is not bridled by a fear of loss of parental affection or respect.

Additionally, a third benefit of play sessions results from the child's developing a trust in the adult. The child learns to have confidence in himself. He learns that he can trust the parent; he learns that the parent trusts him. Therefore, he learns that he can trust himself. He learns, moreover, to make his own decisions and gains a sense of responsibility and maturity. Self-confidence arises and develops as the child learns to see himself as a worthwhile and accepted person (Guerney, 1982).

For parents to learn the play session tools effectively, it is necessary that they attend a training program which is conducted by a trained play therapist (Abidin, 1980). Approximately ten training sessions are required in order for parents to learn the play therapy skills. During the training sessions, the parents practice the tools: recognizing feelings, empathic responding, personal messages, structuring, and limits/consequences. Other parents role-play the part of disruptive children. After about eight training sessions, most parents are prepared to apply the newly acquired skills with their children in play therapy sessions. Competent and regular supervision by a trained play therapist will help to insure correction of the misuse of any of the tools. The therapist's reinforcing of the parent's progress in new skills and discussing confusing areas assist the parent in becoming an effective, capable home therapist.

## RECOGNITION AND ACCEPTANCE OF FEELINGS

Before beginning the play sessions, the parent must first be aware of the many factors which influence a child's present feelings and subsequent behaviors. The child's chronological and mental age, his present state of health, his past experiences, and his present surroundings all interact with the child's basic personality and contribute to the child's integrated and complex set of feelings. At the very foundation of an effective program of play therapy lie parents who understand and accept the multitude of variables which interact to produce the child's state of emotions at any given time (Erikson, 1950). A parent must step out of his own role temporarily and attempt to see the world through the eyes of the child. At this point, the parent begins to empathize with the child and his world. Empathy is clearly distinguished from sympathy, the latter involving a more distant, less involved type of feeling regarding a person or a situation. Empathy, on the other hand, involves the parent's stepping into the child's world—nearly "becoming" the child momentarily. As a result, the parent obtains a clear perspective and understanding of many of the factors which affect the child and gains substantial insight into the child's reactions to these circumstances (Paul, 1970).

For example, six-year-old Jeffrey sits at the dinner table and begins to cry uncontrollably. The sympathetic parent might run to Jeffrey, hug him, and offer him a cookie so he will "feel all better." The non-empathic parent might simply assume that Jeffrey is being difficult, again. He might state, "Jeffrey, there's no reason for that type of behavior at the dinner table. Please go to your room until you have finished behaving like a baby." The empathic parent, conversely, considers Jeffrey's (a) present developmental level, (b) his state of health, (c) his ongoing life circumstances, and (d) his basic personality make-up. In so doing, Jeffrey's parent may realize that lately, Jeffrey has been undergoing a number of developmental changes which characterize the typical six-year-old child—crying more than usual, feeling tired, and a fear or dislike of school. Also, Jeffrey has been tired lately because he has been staying up and watching television with his older brother since they now share a bedroom. Additionally, Jeffrey has been quite concerned about correctly learning his spelling words; today was the day in which the cumulative word test was given. Finally, Jeffrey is, by nature, a shy, sensitive child and often suffers from the older children's ridicule and teasing on the bus ride home from school. He has been self-conscious about his short hair cut and the older boys' reactions to it. Thus, considering the overall atmosphere in which Jeffrey's world is currently revolving, the parent is better prepared to understand and honestly accept Jeffrey's feelings and emotional reactions (Axline, 1947). The following sections will discuss empathic methods of dealing with Jeffrey's behavior.

Frequently, there are instances in which the child's feelings and resultant behaviors are less clear to the parent than was the case with Jeffrey. The busy parent often lacks information and details about the child's daily interactions and encounters. Even the extremely attentive and alert parent often experiences puzzling behaviors from the child, however. Perhaps no biological, environmental, or physical explanation seems obvious for the child's withdrawn, unruly, careless, or generally incorrigible behaviors (Freud, 1955; Axline, 1947). Acceptance of the child's feelings during these times must nonetheless proceed, unaccompanied by full parental insight or understanding of the behaviors. Now the parent must simply recognize and accept the fact that the child is feeling aggressive or moody or lethargic. A conveyance of this acceptance to the child with or without a preceding causal explanation is achieved through using a skill which is called empathic responding.

## EMPATHIC RESPONDING

As the title suggests, empathic responding involves the parent's responding on an accepting and understanding level to the child's actions and verbal statements. Empathic responding also incorporates usage of the first tool, recognizing feelings. Therefore, in many instances, the perceptive parent may choose to simply *listen* empathically to the child as the child freely expresses feelings of hurt, anger, joy, rebellion, or grief. Empathic listening and responding involve the overall verbal and non-verbal messages which the parent conveys to the child. Eye contact with the child expresses parental interest, friendliness, and acceptance. The parent remains in close proximity to the child. He refrains from using nervous or distracting mannerisms and attentively faces the child in a calm and relaxed kneeling or sitting position. While empathically listening, the parent learns to smile, laugh, nod, frown, show confusion or anger, or occasionally, to simply remain neutral, yet interested and attentive. The child's own expressions—verbal and nonverbal—will always determine the parent's empathic listening behaviors (Rogers, 1951). At other times, it is evident that the child desires the parent's more verbal, overt empathic responding. Indications of these instances include a child's pausing while talking, a child's continual looking at the parent after he states each feeling or a series of overt reactions, or the child's questioning the parent during a play session. Once again, the nature of the parent's verbal response is directly determined by the child's verbal or nonverbal cues. The parent attempts to determine the child's feelings through his actions and/or words before responding empathically (Dorfman, 1951). Rephrasing, clarifying, expanding statements, and simply stating "um-hum" are examples of empathic responding. Under no circumstances does the parent use the following responses during a play session (Guerney, 1976):

(a) ask questions;
(b) give suggestions;
(c) offer criticism;
(d) praise, offer approval, encourage, or reassure;
(e) state his own feelings on the matter;
(f) give directions;
(g) disagree;
(h) share a personal experience;
(i) moralize;
(j) ridicule;
(k) threaten;
(l) lecture;
(m) offer invitations or leads, initiate an activity;
(n) interfere or interrupt; or
(o) give information (unless directly requested by the child).

The child, alone, determines the nature of the play session. All decisions which are made are those of the child. The parent merely follows the child's lead in an attentive, uncritical, supporting, and warm manner. The parent practices empathic responding by reflecting the child's actions and feelings. Stating aloud what the child is feeling. The parent uses statements such as, "You'd like to throw the lady in the water; it's funny when you make a different face in the mirror; when the ball rolls away, it makes you pretty mad." The parent may also summarize the child's actions with statements such as, "You're really scrubbing that plate," or "you're jumping higher and higher!" The child's age, mood, and verbal and nonverbal cues alert the parent to appropriate word choice and appropriate statements in response to the child's observed feelings and actions (Ilg and Ames, 1955). At all times, primary attention should focus upon how the child wants the parent to participate. The activities may range from a ring-toss game to a role-playing episode between "father" and "daughter" to "watch me draw" activity in which the child draws while the parent, showing much attention and interest, observes.

Empathic responding is used even when a child plays a game with altered rules. For example, although the parent and the child are both aware that the child is cheating, the parent plays according to the child's rules and responds to the child's need to "win" or to "earn extra points." The parent offers no criticism of the cheating behavior. Maria, for instance, steps one foot closer to the ring post each time it is her turn. The parent states warmly, "You want to be *sure* you'll get that ring on the post this time!" Empathic responding ceases only under a very limited number of conditions. When a child asks the parent to pretend to be another person or inanimate object or uses a puppet or mask, the parent momentarily departs from the role of empathic responder. Instead, the parent "becomes" Clancy Clown or Hermit the Frog and talks and acts the role until the child is ready to terminate the role-play (Hawkey, 1976). For example, Theresa states, "Mommy, I'm Mindy; you be Alonzo." Mommy answers in a deep, manly voice, "Okay, Mindy." "Mindy" states, "Alonzo, dear, how do I look?" "Alonzo," (Mommy) answers, "You look beautiful today, Mindy."

The spirit in which the parent engages in empathic responding and listening is the most important step in assuring successful play sessions. As the parent remembers to incorporate the following suggestions during play sessions, the child feels accepted and completely free to express himself in the most beneficial ways (Guerney, 1976):

(a) put yourself in the child's place—see the world through his eyes;
(b) try to understand the child's feelings—his verbalizations, facial expressions, and overt behaviors provide clues as to the child's underlying feelings;
(c) communicate to the child that you understand and accept whatever he says and does;
(d) forget about your own feelings and personal worries and communicate to the child your total involvement and undivided attention; choose a weekly time when you will be most able to devote this uninterrupted, quality time to the child; and
(e) accept even behaviors and language which you would ordinarily consider repulsive, offensive, or reprimandable. While in the play session, treat these behaviors with the same respect and warm attention which is given to the other more traditional behaviors. Naturally, when these behaviors extend beyond the reasonable safety and health limitations, the parent must temporarily step out of the empathic responder role and impose a limit.

When the parent has learned to recognize, understand, and accept the child's feelings and has acquired the empathic responding skill, the third tool—structuring—is exercised.


STRUCTURING

To envision the play sessions symbolically, it is helpful to envision the child's environment under two types of conditions. The first condition is that of the child's real world in which he spends the majority of his time, attending day care or school, eating, interacting with parents or friends, and participating in musical, artistic, or sporting events. In symbolic form, this life style or these conditions might be depicted as a 1' x 1' x 1' box, with sturdy walls, rigid corners, a firm, fitted lid, and tight boundaries. The child's rules, such as brushing teeth, bathing daily, studying, picking up clothing, and using "nice" language fit neatly into the "box." When the child's behavior varies too markedly from the conditions which are set forth by the parents (or the walls of the relatively small box), the child is reprimanded or punished. Conversely, the second condition is that of the child's non-directive play environment. Under these conditions, symbolically, the "box" expands to a new 12' x 12' x 12' size. Although walls (limits) do exist for the child in this new environment, they are considerably less restrictive. Resultantly, the child achieves a new sense of freedom and is not fearful or inhibited as he may have been under the ordinary, more restrictive walls or rules. Thus, fantasy play and emotional expression are given free rein.

For a parent to structure the environment correctly for the child's play sessions so that it approximates the latter "box-like" example, the parent needs to employ a number of structuring considerations. These considerations include the following: (a) toys; (b) times; (c) setting; (d) introduction and termination of the session; and (e) limits and consequences.

Toys for all play sessions include, generally, those items which are open-ended in function, toys with which the child is easily able to represent his own meaningful life—persons, places, and events. The toys are inexpensive, plastic, and/or unbreakable. The toys which are conducive to representative-type play and are, consequently, recommended for inclusion in the play sessions are the following (Guerney, 1975; Fein, 1975):

puppet family
doll family
house box for doll family and furniture
tinker toys, lincoln logs, or legos
crayons, paints, chalk
chalkboard
paper
paint brushes
cups and saucers
water pitcher
baby bottle
plastic cowboys, Indians, soldiers
modeling clay or Play-dough
rubber knife
dart gun, darts
ring toss game
playing cards
rope
inflated plastic hop bag (at least four feet high)

The child may neither bring toys into the session nor remove toys from the session. The toys remain in the room, unused, at all times other than during the play sessions. Other children, likewise, should not be permitted to play with the toys at all. When the toys become, to the child, a token of his "special time" in the "special room," they lead to increased feelings of freedom for the child and enhanced representative play. Therefore, it becomes paramount that these selected toys remain exclusively a part of the play session experience (Axline, 1964).

Play sessions are usually scheduled on a once-a-week basis if one parent is involved. Should both parents desire to hold play sessions with the child, they may decide upon one of two options.

(a) Schedule one play session early in the week with the mother and one session, later on in the week, with the father or

(b) alternate parents who conduct the play sessions on an every-other-week basis (e.g., mother holds session one week; father holds session the following week). If more than one child in the same family will receive play sessions, both parents or a single parent should devote an equal amount of time to each of the children (Levy, 1933). Consistency is very important. Play sessions should be held on the same day and at the same time each week, if possible. The child should be kept well-informed, in advance, of the time schedule for play sessions. In the event of necessary cancellations, the parent should immediately reschedule the play session and return, as soon as possible, to the original schedule. The child's confidence and trust in the adult will diminish otherwise. Choose a time when there will be no interruptions to the play time; ringing doorbells and telephones, visitors to the play room, or other outside noises only serve to inhibit or restrict the child; under these conditions, he is not completely free to be himself, to relax, and to express his needs fully. Additionally, the scheduled time should be one in which both the parent and the child are well-rested, free of outside obligations, and are free to devote true "quality time" to the play session. Duration of the play session is, at first, 15 minutes; after the first three sessions, the duration may extend to one-half hour. Finally, after ten or more sessions have been held and if the parent and child are both willing, the time may extend to 45 minutes for each play session (Guerney, 1964).

The choice of a playroom in the home is also an important one. Among the primary questions for which the parents should answer affirmatively are the following:

(a) Is the room sufficiently quiet and secluded from other household activities?
(b) Will I be relaxed in this room, free from concern about the safety and well-being of the child, the floors or rug, the windows, and the walls?
(c) Is the room uncluttered from other items; is there sufficient space for the special toys to be displayed and used?

Additionally, a room in which either water from an available sink or in which a pitcher may be used is desirable. A tile-floored playroom, a basement section, or the kitchen area are also possible room sites.

Structuring the play session also includes the use of an introduction and a termination message. The introduction is not involved or complicated; the parent simply states, for example, "Joan, this is our special room. You can do almost anything you want in here for this half-hour. If there's something that you shouldn't do, I'll let you know." The "almost anything" is embedded within the introductory sentence to allow the child a sense of total freedom with very few exceptions. Five minutes before the conclusion of the half-hour (or 15-minute or 45-minute) session, the parent states, "Joan, you have five more minutes to play in the special room today." When the time has drawn to a close, the parent says firmly, "It is time for our special play session to end for today, but we'll play again next week." Upon stating this message, the parent stands and beings to walk toward the door. Again, parental consistency in adhering to the few important structuring mechanisms instills a sense of continuity, trust, and security in the child (Ginnot and Lebo, 1961).

The final structuring consideration for play sessions is the designation and application of limits and consequences. The parent decides, in advance, upon three or four play session rules. They might include safety and/or health issues or property maintenance considerations, such as the following:

(a) no hitting the parent on the face or head;
(b) no pouring water on the parent;
(c) no kicking the bop bag while wearing shoes; and
(d) no destruction or massive damaging of the floor, ceiling, or walls.

While rule imposition is a personal and individual decision, the parent must remember that the greater the number of restrictions which greet the child, the more the play session resembles the small, rigid "box" of his real world. Fewer restrictions represent the looser, more flexible "box" or world, and the child will react accordingly. It is important that the parent's attitude convey total and equal acceptance for each of the child's behaviors in the play room. If the parent cannot accept, at least temporarily, a child's particular behavior, imposing a limit is a necessary and appropriate decision. However, limits should remain relatively consistent from week to week so that the child will not need to fear his being reminded or reprimanded at one session for a behavior which was acceptable at a previous session. Acceptable techniques for applying limits and consequences during a play session will be discussed.

## PERSONAL MESSAGES

There are times, during play sessions, in which the parent needs to momentarily depart from the empathic responding behaviors. These times include the previously mentioned role-play situations which the child instigates. Other instances in which empathic responding is not used include those times in which the parent begins to state a personal limit and/or impose a resultant consequence. For example, Teresa holds a pitcher full of water above her father's head. Feeling uncomfortable about becoming wet, Teresa's father states, "Teresa, you are having a good time with that water" (empathic response to Teresa's previous and present water play). "But I worry that my hair and my new suit will get wet, and I'll need to spend lots of money to have it dry cleaned" (personal message expressing feeling—worry and [optional] reason, wetness and a cleaning bill). If necessary, a limit is stated at this time, as well.

Personal messages need not always accompany empathic responses nor precede limits and consequences. The particular situation determines the nature of the sequence of parental responses. If Teresa, for example, began to approach her father very quickly with the water, her father would not spare the time involved in an empathic response. Rather, he would immediately state the personal message thus, "Teresa, when you run to me that way with the water, I get nervous. I'm afraid that you'll spot my new suit." Following the personal message, a limit may be stated if Teresa persists in her approach.

Personal messages allow the child to realize that parents, too, have some specific feelings and concerns during the play sessions. Relative time which is used for personal messages expression is minimal when it is compared with the time involved in empathic responding. Yet, personal messages provide the necessary structure to the sessions which permits freedom and spontaneity within wide boundaries which health, comfort, and safety factors necessitate.

## LIMITS AND CONSEQUENCES

Aside from session time planning and toy provisions, limits and consequences exemplify the highest degree of structure which the parents use in the play sessions. Limits themselves must be limited, however, so that the child maintains the sense of complete freedom which is necessary in order for optimum symbolic play and accompanying emotional release and problem-solving to occur (Freud, 1955; Ellis, 1973). As more and more limits are imposed upon the child, the play session begins to resemble the child's "other world" of demands, rules, and obligations. However, a few limits are necessary, nonetheless, in order to preserve the participants' safety and comfort during the sessions. Limits are stated by the parent only as the situation which necessitates them arises. When the child breaks a limit, the parent states that this behavior is not allowed. If the statement does not suffice, the parent clearly restates the limit and adds that if the behavior occurs again—a third time—the play session must end. If the offensive behavior is repeated a third time in spite of the warnings, the session immediately ends. This session termination is the direct consequence which results from the child's breaking the limit three times. If, during a subsequent session, the child breaks the same limit, the parent states the warning. If the behavior occurs a *second* time, the play session ends. The parent remains concise and firm while stating limits and, if necessary, imposing consequences. The parent does not, however, express anger or frustration.

The following limits are imposed each time the child engages in the undesirable behavior (Guerney, 1976):

(a) the child may not hit or endanger either himself or the parent (the parent may impose optional limits on the use of water or dirt on his body, as well);
(b) the child may not poke or kick the bop bag with a sharp object or with shoes; and
(c) the child may leave the play session no more than one time (for a bathroom trip only).

Optional, additional limits might include the following:

(a) the child may not shoot the darts at the parent or at the walls or ceiling;
(b) the child may not use crayons on the chalkboard;
(c) the child may use no paint, crayons, or clay on the floors or walls; and
(d) the child may not smear, tear, or destroy the nearby furniture.

A child should not be discouraged from breaking a limit. Rather, the parent reflects the child's desire to engage in the behavior and, matter-of-factly, states the limit. A personal message which precedes the limit is optional. The parent's purpose is not to prevent the questionable behavior. The child must be allowed to choose his own behaviors and, when necessary, to experience the consequences which result. An example of a limit and consequence is the following: Kate begins to write on the wall with a crayon. Her mother states, "Kate, do you remember that I said I'd let you know if there was anything that you may not do in here? Well, writing on the wall is one of those things you may not do." If Kate continues to draw in spite of two warnings, the session ends "for today."

## A SAMPLE PLAY SESSION

Parent enters playroom (kitchen) with six-year-old Joseph.

**Mother:** "Joey, it's time to use our special playroom again this week. You may do just about anything you want in here. You may say anything you'd like. If there's something that you may not do, I'll let you know" *(structuring play session).*

**Joey:** "I know, I know. In here, I'm allowed to be really *bad* or really *silly.* Yip-peeeeeee!" *(runs around the room flapping arms and leaping).*

**Mother:** *(smiling)* "You're excited that it's time to do just about *anything* you want!" *(acceptance of feelings; empathic response)*

**Joey:** *(nodding)* "Yep. Today I'm gonna be a grandpap" *(holds mask to face and looks at mother; bends down at waist; in shrill, weak voice he imitates an aged grandfather).* "Alright Elizabeth, my girl" (mother's name). "Help me take off my coat. I'm warm today. And I'm getting old and sick."

**Mother:** *(in girl-like position)* "Alright, Father" *(using young girl's voice, mother pretends to remove coat).* "Your coat is off now. You won't be so warm. It's too bad that you're so old and sick" *(role-playing).*

**Joey:** "Well, my girl, I'm 130 years old today. I guess I am pretty old" *(pretends to nod off to sleep).* "But I do like to paint!" *(drops mask and briskly walks to large paper and paint set).*

**Mother:** "You were an old, sick, and sleepy grandpa. Now you're Joey, and you want to paint!" *(empathic response to Joey's intent).*

**Joey:** "Do you like to paint, Mom?"

**Mother:** "You'd like to know if I enjoy painting" *(empathic response).*

**Joey:** "Yeah; will you paint with me?"

**Mother:** "It's nice to have company when you do things that you like" *(empathic response).*

**Joey:** "Yes, I like for you to be with me. Well, will you?"

**Mother:** "I'll paint with you. You like for us to *paint* together and *be* together" *(compliance with child's wishes; empathic response).*

Note that mother allowed Joey to ask a similar question three times before providing an affirmative answer for Joey. In refraining from supplying an immediate answer to a question, the parent allows the child to explore the feelings *underlying* the question. In Joey's case, the feelings were a need for affiliation which were not revealed until the question was repeated and empathic responding provided three successive times.

**Joey:** *(using brush on wall)* I'll paint everything I see!"

**Mother:** "Joey, I worry that the paint won't come off the walls *(personal message).* "So, one of the rules that we have in our special room is 'no painting on the walls' " *(limit).*

**Joey:** *(continues to paint the wall)* "Oh, hell; I'll paint whatever I want, stupid."

**Mother:** "You're pretty angry at me. You really want to paint those walls and everything else" *(acceptance of feelings; empathic response).* "But Joey, in this room, one rule is that you may not paint the walls *(limit).* If you do that again, our session will end for today *(consequence).*

**Joey:** *(continues to paint a small area)* "I'm only painting it a little teeny bit now, see? It's pretty."

**Mother:** "Joey, you decided to keep on painting even though you knew that the session would end if you did. So, our session is over for today. We will play again next week."

**Joey:** *(frowning)* "No way. I'm staying here. I'll quit painting; honest, Mom" *(backs further into play room).*

**Mother:** "Our session is over for today, Joey" *(consequence; leads Joey firmly to the door; shuts off lights).*

## SUMMARY AND CONCLUSION

Five major skills are employed when a parent decides to conduct play sessions with the child:

(a) acceptance of feelings;

(b)  empathic responding;
(c)  structuring (times, toys, and sessions);
(d)  personal messages; and
(e)  limits/consequences

Play sessions provide the opportunity for considerable self-awareness and growth for both the parent and the child (Hornsby, 1978). Children behave in a variety of ways during early, mid-way, and later play sessions. Some children may be shy and withdrawn during the first few play sessions; during the fifth or sixth sessions, these same children may display highly aggressive, loud, or bold behaviors. By the tenth session, these children may display well-adjusted, friendly, mature, and sharing behaviors. Other children may behave in a completely opposite fashion (Guerney, 1976). Whatever the case, the *child* and his unique personality and life circumstances always determine what is "appropriate" behavior for any of the play sessions. You will learn a great deal about your child and his feelings during the play sessions. A closer day-to-day relationship may result. By the tenth play session, many parents report that a noticeable change has occurred in the child at times other than playtimes. More integrative, mature, or cooperative behaviors often characterize the child who has completed ten or more home play sessions with well-trained, consistent, and accepting parents (Hornsby, 1978).

When play sessions have ended and the child's disruptive behavior has subsided, the conscientious parent continues to use many of the play session skills. Additionally, "positive reinforcement, natural conversation, and questions/suggestions" may be added. The parent and the child continue to meet for "Special Times." The special times are arranged in advance by both the child and the parent. The two may, for example, attend a movie together, ride a boat, walk in the park, or roller skate. No other friends or family members should be present. The parent uses, predominantly, empathic responding as the child conveys various emotions and carries on a conversation. Additionally, at times, the parent uses reinforcement or praise, questions the child, offers suggestions, and generally, conveys acceptance and recognition of the child's feelings throughout the time which is spent privately together. Special times may be held once each week or every other week for one or two hours; the scheduling is dependent upon the circumstances, the child's need for continuance of the accepting, empathic parental mode, and the parent's willingness to enthusiastically participate. As was the case with play sessions, the parent's attitude and acceptance of the child are primary conditions for successful interactions and for both parental and child growth.

The hope and promise for play therapy lies in the fact that, through using the tools of therapy, the parent comes to better know, accept, and understand "the whole child"—his expectations, feelings, emotions, fears, and life circumstances (Axline, 1947). Furthermore, as the parent exercises skill usage, he becomes adept at utilizing this new-found knowledge of the child in a highly positive manner. He allows the child to learn and follow life's blueprint in an atmosphere of freedom and acceptance and, in the most promising fashion, through self-discovery. Through play therapy, the child learns that his anxieties, fears, and guilt need not overwhelm him (Kanner, 1948). He "releases" them, and while symbolizing life's significant or troubling events, he learns to design his own path which leads toward a more well-adjusted, integrated personality.

REFERENCES

Abidin, R. *Parent Education and Intervention Handbook.* Springfield, IL: Charles C. Thomas, Inc. (1980).

Axline, V. *Play Therapy.* Cambridge, MA: Houghton Mifflin Co. (1947).

Axline, V. *Play Therapy* (Revised edition). New York: Ballantine Books (1969).

Dorfman, E., "Play therapy," in *Client-centered Therapy,* C. Rogers, ed. Boston: Houghton Mifflin Co. (1951).

Ellis, M. *Why People Play.* Englewood Cliffs, NJ: Prentice-Hall (1973).

Erikson, E. H. *Childhood and Society.* New York: Norton (1963).

Fein, G. A., "A transformational analysis of pretending," *Developmental Psychology, 11,* 291–296 (1975).

Freud, A. *The Psycho-analytical Treatment of Children.* New York: International Universities Press (1955).

Ginott, H. and Leko, D., "Play therapy limits and theoretical orientation," *Journal of Consulting Psychology, 25,* 337–340 (1961).

Guerney, B., "Filial therapy: Description and rationale," *Journal of Consulting Psychology, 28,* 303–310 (1964).

Guerney, L., "Client centered (non-directive) play therapy," in *Handbook of Play Therapy,* C. Schaefer and K. O'Connor, eds. Philadelphia, PA: John Wiley and Sons (1982).

Guerney, L., "Filial therapy program," in *Treating Relationships,* D. H. Olson, ed. Lake Mills, IA: Graphic Publishing Co., Inc. (1976).

Guerney, L. *Foster Parent Training: A Manual for Trainers.* University Park, PA: Pennsylvania State University Consultation Center (1975).

Guerney, L. *Parenting: A Skills Training Manual.* Ideals (1979).

Hawkey, L., "Puppets in child psychotherapy," in *Therapeutic Use of Child's Play,* C. Schaefer, ed. New York: Jason Aronson (1976).

Hornsby, L. and Applebaum, A., "Parents as primary therapists: Filial therapy," in *Helping Parents Help their Children,* L. Arnold, ed. New York: Brunner/Mazel (1978).

Kanner, L. *Child Psychiatry.* Springfield, IL: Charles C. Thomas Co. (1948).

Levy, D., "Hostility patterns in sibling rivalry," *American Journal of Orthopsychiatry, 3,* 266–275 (1933).

Paul, N. L., "Parental empathy," in *Parenthood: Its Psychology and Psychopathology,* E. J. Anthony and T. Benedek, eds. Boston, MA: Little, Brown, and Co. (1970).

Rogers, C. R. *Client-centered Therapy.* Boston: Houghton-Mifflin Company (paperback) (1965).

Schaefer, C. E., ed. *Therapeutic Use of Child's Play.* New York: Jason Aronson, 216–227 (1976).

# AUTHOR AND SUBJECT INDICES